95

Submitted to the IT-University of Copenhagen as
partial fulfilment of the requirements for the PhD degree

February, 2005

Candidate:

Simon Egenfeldt-Nielsen

Weysesgade 1

2100   Copenhagen

+45 40107969

sen@game-research.com

Supervisors: Anker Helms Jørgensen and Carsten Jessen

Abstract

Computer games have attracted much attention over the years, mostly attention of the less flattering kind. This has been true for computer games focused on entertainment, but also for what for years seemed a sure winner, edutainment. This dissertation aims to be a modest contribution to understanding educational use of computer games by building a framework that goes beyond edutainment. A framework that goes beyond the limitations of edutainment, not relying on a narrow perception of computer games in education.

The first part of the dissertation outlines the background for building an inclusive and solid framework for educational use of computer games. Such a foundation includes a variety of quite different perspectives for example educational media and non-electronic games. It is concluded that educational use of computer games remains strongly influenced by educational media leading to the domination of edutainment.

The second part takes up the challenges posed in part 1 looking to especially educational theory and computer games research to present alternatives. By drawing on previous research three generations of educational computer games are identified. The first generation is edutainment that perceives the use of computer games as a direct way to change behaviours through repeated action. The second generation puts the spotlight on the relation between computer game and player. Computer games become interesting because they are believed capable of offering a variety of ways to learn with varying degrees of difficulty. The third generation includes the context of computer games and how they facilitate learning environments with peer-collaboration, constructions of knowledge, new teacher role and a changed student role. These three generations all become part of the framework for educational use of computer games avoiding a narrow focus on a few popular elements.

In the third part the main empirical study is laid out with the purpose of examining the actual use of computer games in an educational setting from a 3rd generation perspective. The empirical study was conducted at a Danish high-school involving 72 students and two teachers. The study examined the use of a commercial historical strategy game (*Europa Universalis II*) in a 2½ month history course where the computer game played a significant role. The empirical study aims at examining some key findings around the barriers for educational computer game use, the scepticism towards the historical understanding of computer games, the problems related to linking of experiences with computer games to other domains and the effectiveness of learning from computer games. It is found that we can benefit from looking at teaching with computer games at three levels: Appreciation, exploration and linking with each level having its own problems. Students progressed through these levels with the appreciation as a prerequisite for exploration and linking. The appreciation caused problems for many students, as they did not have the necessary knowledge of history and computer games to identify the relevant elements in the game experience. When relevant elements were recognized students failed to explore due to distrust of the value of the game experiences. Finally the linking between the game experience and other areas rarely happened.

The last part presents the general framework for understanding educational use of computer games, where the ends from the three previous parts meet. The theory extends from an experiential learning approach, where concrete experiences are the starting point that can be transformed through reflection, instruction and active experimentation. In this process computer

3

games provide rich concrete experience that can be manipulated in the game universe providing more handles for the student compared to other media. It is concluded that in ideal educational use of computer games the student is playing and constructing knowledge through interaction with the game universe. Slowly building on top of existing knowledge from previous experiences arising from inside the game universe and other spheres of life facilitated by instruction. It is an experience-based hermeneutic exploration in a safe rich environment, potentially scaffolding the student while maintaining student autonomy and ensuring a high emotional investment in the activity.

Preface

The wicked sirens still sing their song
luring me to venture dangerous places

This dissertation has been a journey through a landscape not seen in its full by many people. My background as a psychologist slowly, but steadily determined this dissertation supplemented with clear directions from game research. Over the years game research has become as much my starting point as my psychology training. It feels strange looking back at the road travelled, seeing the twisted passages one chooses, when one could have stayed on the main road. I have however, more than once been amazed by the rich experience-base, just under my nose, which seems to have gone unnoticed by me and other researchers for many years. I hope that the work you are about to read will bring the field forward and show new paths for educational practice with computer games.

I believe this dissertation has been 3 years of hard learning and solid work. I have dissected the field of educational use of computer games, with a bit of luck paving the way for new insights. I have taken pride in being reluctant to settle with just the necessary findings and discussions, but have kept pushing on – taking chances. The empirical study could have gone wrong in so many ways and actually, it did, but still it produced valuable insights. In time, I came to see the chaotic, contradictory and preliminary nature of the empirical findings as a great strength.

I have come to believe that to the practitioner good research is what in the end seems to be unfinished, unnecessarily hard work anticipating more enquiries. What I am now handing in can to the best of my knowledge be described as 'unfinished business'. For me the dissertation has left more questions unanswered than answered even though it may not seem so from the outside. I cannot wait to continue the journey.

The dissertation was written during a 3-year period at the IT-University of Copenhagen but a large part of it was written in frenzy while visiting the University of London, Institute of Education, for 3 months. A warm thanks to the University of London for having me as a visiting PhD student and the academic discussions engaged in.

I would like to thank the following people who have played a significant role in the process. My three supervisors Anker Helms Jørgensen, Carsten Jessen and Andrew Burn who have given valuable insights, discussions and academic shelter over the years.

In connection with the main empirical study, I wish to thank Gitte Nielsen, Henrik Wegener, Anders Kloppenborg and Anne Marie Asmussen for making this possible. I also want to thank the 72 students who participated in the 2½-month long study - none named, none forgotten. I am also grateful to the distributor Pan Vision and the developer Paradox Entertainment who made it possible to conduct the study by sponsoring the game titles and by making *Europa Universalis II* such an excellent game.

For academic discussions in general thanks to everybody mentioned above but also to: Jonas H. Smith, Fin Egenfeldt-Nielsen, Susana Tosca, T.L. Taylor, Jesper Juul, Jesper Tække, Debra Lieberman, Caroline Pelletier, Siobhan Thomas, Diane Carr, Gareth Schott, David Buckingham,

Espen Aarseth, Sara de Freitas, Marie Laure-Ryan, Martin Sønderlev, Lars Konzack, John Kirriemuir, Patrick Bergman and all the anonymous reviewers of papers along the way. Thanks to Pernille Heegaard Deichmann and Ann Heegaard for the proofreading.

For the statistics in connection with the empirical work I wish to express recognition to Fiona Steele who taught intermediate statistics with great skill at University of London and to Jane Hurry who was kind enough to give me some personal pointers along the way, and to Peter Allerup who straightened it all out. Also Alex Moore was valuable in grasping the limits and possibilities of qualitative methods.

In addition, warm thanks to the listeners at conferences, public talks and seminars who raised their hands with comments, criticism and questions. Moreover, thanks to the people that went before me and to those that come after me.

Simon Egenfeldt-Nielsen, February, 2005.

Dedicated to Sidsel Hæggelin
who paints life in bright colours.

Contents

Introduction

Tell me and I will forget. Show me and I may remember.
Involve me and I will understand.

Confucius around 450 BC

Computer games are increasingly becoming the topic of serious research with more active researchers worldwide. This happens as computer games are strengthening, as a mainstream entertainment activity, with a broader player base and a rising number of sold titles (ESA, 2003). One area that has early on attracted interest is educational use of computer games. Not surprisingly, the increased general interest in computer games research is rubbing off on educational computer games research. However, many questions remain unanswered, largely due to the fragmented nature of the research into educational use of computer games. There exist only half-baked attempts at integrating research within this area. Obviously, this does not imply a lack of recent research in the field of computer games, education and learning, but researchers have mostly spoken from one perspective with a limited wish to engage in the entire research field or settling for presenting empirical results. Recent research examples include, but are not limited to, Prensky (2001b), Konzack (2003), Gee (2003) and Squire (2004).

This dissertation's primary goal is to build a framework that can bring some of the many pieces together, challenging the dominance of edutainment. Edutainment play the role of the villain in this dissertation and is defined as the current dominating titles on the market for educational computer games. Edutainment titles are characterized by using quite conventional learning theories, providing a dubious game experience, relying on simple gameplay and are mostly produced with strict reference to a curriculum (more elaborate definition in chapter 4). Thus, the framework, I intend to build, is in opposition to conventional learning theory, avoids a narrow-minded understanding of curriculum and shuns simple gameplay to facilitate strong learning experiences through computer games. The most important focal point of the framework is the ability of computer games to offer concrete experiences providing relevance and engagement leading to students' investment in the learning activity. Instruction extends from the concrete experiences from the game and the student's investment – instruction providing the necessary direction, order, exploration and linking to other areas – leading to strong abstract concepts.

We may start by asking where the infatuation with computer games for education stems from? Is it just a passing phenomenon so well known from other new media emerging or does it have more holding power? Simply put, is it worth our time? Educational researchers have embraced radio, television, computers and computer games for their ability to engage and motivate students, but the fascination often dries up relatively fast. The current focus of researchers on students' increased motivation and interest is somewhat superficial as it only addresses the manifestation of other underlying factors. It doesn't get us very far to conclude that computer games lead to increased interest and motivation, when the underlying variables continue to influence the learning process haphazardly. We need to describe these underlying variables (Buckingham & Scanlon, 2002; Calvert, 1999; Loftus & Loftus, 1983; Prensky, 2001a).

The idea of using computer games for education is not just a concept forged by hopeful educators and ambitious researchers, but is also found in leading game designers' description of the most basic incentives for playing computer games. In the words of game designer Chris Crawford (1982: Chapter 2, unpaginated), "The fundamental motivation for all game-playing is to learn". Crawford points out that learning is not necessarily a manifest motivation when playing computer games, it lies latent. He is especially pointing to the universe you can explore and learn about. I will add, that for a computer game to work you are required to learn on a very basic level – playing computer games is not just explained by an abstract idea of a basic human desire to learn new things. Learning is incorporated in the structure of computer games making learning a prerequisite for playing. You need to learn different things depending on the genre and game to advance. The elements that support learning in computer games may take very different forms. In the action game *Space Invaders* you improve your ability to react swiftly with utmost precision and shoot down those damn aliens. In adventure games like the *Leisure Suit Larry* series you are constantly forced to acquire new knowledge and solve puzzles in order to advance. If you fail to get a hold of a clue or figure something out, you are stuck. The game will come to a halt. Computer games may have different tolerance levels for 'bad' learners, rely more critically on constant learning and changing demands on the player's capacity for learning, but in the majority of games you at some level need to learn to advance further.

A very basic premise of playing the majority of computer games is to engage with an unknown universe, slowly learning more about this universe. The structure of computer games demanding learning makes them different from other media, where you can move forward without necessarily learning more to gain access to more of the representation. Computer games have a prerequisite for learning as introduced above, purporting to more than most representations, having a number of engaging game features, providing a richer experience with different modalities and having different potentials for interaction compared to other media. When computer games work they draw the user into the experience, make him lose sense of time and place and demand the user's full concentration, focus and energy – making the user invest in the learning experience. Computer games challenge the user to his limit and the user loves it. For every action the game demands a counter-action – a constant and often a high-paced ping-pong in the most popular genres. The actions are performed within a simplified game universe where the player experiences the consequences of different actions and observes the relations between actions. It is the characteristics above that make researchers and educators believe in the learning potential of games and their superiority compared to other media - potentially a valuable supplement to more traditional teaching methods by virtue of its engagement. This despite the fact that evidence of computer games providing better learning experiences compared to other learning forms remains at best ambiguous.

Against the above background it doesn't make much sense to treat learning in computer games from a narrow perspective, where learning is perceived as occurring only in computer games specifically constructed for educational purposes (i.e. with a curriculum in mind). Obviously, we must see all computer games as relying on the player's learning to ensure the progress of the computer game and the educational part is to a high degree a matter of framing. A beat'em up computer game with female avatars fighting bad guys may be considered educational in connection with a self-help class for battered women while it from a parent perspective may be considered deeply anti-social. The context of a computer game obviously has an impact on its perceived educational value.

Gee (2003) points out that computer games today are mostly coined as entertainment and that the educational framing may be alien to many. Players do learn the relevant actions in a given computer game in order to acquire the wished for game outcome. However, it is highly unlikely that we can automatically expect the computer game to also facilitate a wished for educational outcome as this is seldom part of either the game universe or the game culture. For this, we need to consider different educational interventions forming the computer game experience through the surrounding context or the design of computer games that support an educational framing. This is the role instruction needs to take upon itself: Transform the concrete experiences computer games present through building appreciation of relevant elements, exploring these elements and linking these elements to other areas external to the game experience.

The significance of the surrounding context for facilitating educational experiences could indicate that the specific computer game used is of minor importance; however, this is not the case. Some computer games are more useful for educational purposes than others exemplified with the popularity of *SimCity* and *Oregon Trail* in educational circles. One computer game may lend itself better to educational use as a consequence of the contents in the game, the skills required in the game, the challenge of established attitudes, its ability to support the learning experience or the genre being closer to the students' expectations. The hard part is to identify the strong learning features of computer games in connection with educational practice and to determine how computer games facilitate learning in alternative ways compared to traditional teaching methods. This doesn't indicate that computer games as a medium has one unique educational characteristic separating them from all other educational media if anything, the opposite is the case. It has consistently been found that focusing on a medium in itself for providing better learning experiences is not that fruitful (Mayer, 2001). We should rather examine how the new medium connects important parts of education in new ways for example teaching style and student role. One returning question in educational theory is the transfer of knowledge across contexts, which will also play an important role in this dissertation.

For some knowledge forms in computer games there seem to be better indications of a direct transfer, for example behaviours and low level skills. This is especially clear in research on health related use of computer games (Brown, 1997; Lieberman, 2001). Still, even these studies indicate that a great deal of the transfer may be dependent on peer-discussions and a general improved home climate for health related considerations. This indicates that the transfer doesn't just happen, but has to be facilitated by the context surrounding the computer game experience. The facilitation and qualification of this transfer remains a key topic in studying educational use of computer games. Transfer is in this dissertation not conceived as automatic or unproblematic, but as depending on a variety of factors, most prominent the richness of the learning experience combined with the construction of supporting structures in and around the computer game. Based on the introduction above some key areas for our further inquiry in the field of educational use of computer games emerge.

First of all the inherent learning features of computer games should be maintained when designing and thinking about educational game titles - commercial computer games should not be seen as alien to educational practice. The learning features in commercial computer games, especially the strong engagement, should be explicitly nurtured in the educational context where the computer game is used. An educational computer game should in theory be able to exhibit the same holding power on players as any other commercial computer game.

The second area concerns facilitation of learning in computer games and how we perceive this process. It is important to resist seeing the current practice for educational use of computer games as the way forward, and in general to be limited by current teaching practices, broadly in the educational system. Computer games should challenge educational practices while seeking the realisation of realistic educational scenarios. This balance is delicate, but also critical if computer games are to have a real impact and justification in educational efforts. Without the challenge of current practice computer games risk becoming of little interest to anyone; trapped in the caricature of edutainment, pointing educators back in time instead of forward.

Thirdly, we need to address how we can be certain that knowledge obtained in relation to educational use of computer games is accessible in other contexts and establish ways to support these links. This is seen as one of the main areas, where computer games through their more rich experiences can really bring something to the table. Computer games offer concrete experiences that can be elaborated on by the teacher resulting in knowledge that is not merely abstractly tied to the teaching process but is more accessible in different contexts and provide a strong experience-base for concepts.

These guidelines should be kept in mind when trying to fulfil the ultimate goal of this dissertation: To provide a counter-weight against the tidal wave of unsubstantiated and dissipated claims that computer games are a serious contender in the educational system. This ultimately entails developing an understanding of *how to use computer games in education* that goes beyond the current limited focus on edutainment.

Research focus

Building a framework for educational use of computer games requires a thorough discussion of the current contributions to the field. The main theoretical perspectives in this dissertation are: Educational psychology, learning theory and computer games research. This theoretical starting point is preferred based on my previous background, and the predominance of these perspectives in previous research.

In recent years the research area of educational computer games use has received increased attention from researchers, educators and government bodies, but only partly from the game industry probably mainly due to the tricky market conditions (see appendix online). Government interests have especially been on a content level trying to pinpoint existing computer games' educational potential. British Educational Communications and Technology Agency (Becta) has been one of the main forces in the UK saying that,

> Titles such as Caesar III and Age of Empires operate within the context of ancient history and so include factual information about that period. With the increase in processing power and memory capabilities of new computers, there is an increasing demand for technically accurate simulations involving situations that would normally be impossible for the user to experience in real life. Genres such as real time strategy (RTS) can lead to the development of game play, which demands that the user is able to test and develop strategies and reassess decisions.

Becta (2001:3)

In the US the Games-to-teach project has helped kick-start the field with collaboration efforts between MIT and Microsoft to build a number of game prototypes to explore computer games from a learning perspective. Recently, work at the Wisconsin-Madison University has taken the lead with a strong research group on educational use of computer games especially championed by James Paul Gee and Kurt Squire. The American research approaches are less interested in examining whether existing computer games push some content that may be of relevance to educational purposes and oppose a narrow focus on content, skills and attitudes (Squire, 2004). Instead they look to the structural characteristics in computer games that could be used for educational computer games and social processes surrounding the educational experience.

The research area of educational use of computer games is by no means unexplored, but it remains haunted by fragmentation and unclear boundaries. From the onset, the research has been distributed over a number of disciplines with little in common except perhaps the interest in computer games. Some of these are literature, psychology, media studies, anthropology, ethnography, sociology, history, business studies, military tactics, literary theory, educational theory, instructional technology and computer games studies. This variety gives the area vitality and nerve. However, it has also somewhat hindered the field from moving forward. This may seem counter-intuitive to some and it is in opposition to the increasing recognition of the potential of cross-disciplinary work both on an overall research agenda and within computer games research[1]. There is, however, a number of problems within the field related to its interdisciplinary nature: The two most important being scattered information and the lack of a common theoretical frame.

These two factors make scientific progress hard as we cannot locate relevant work and if we do, we have trouble discussing it, and certainly building on it. Although this is, to a certain degree

---

[1] The Ivory tower column has attested to this several times as a special trademark of computer games research (http://www.igda.org/columns/ivorytower/)

unavoidable we can benefit from a closer adherence to educational use of computer games as a specific research area. A closer adherence to a specific field implies that a shared foundation is constructed that addresses what is seen as relevant and important theory, practice and discussions. There is a 'canon' that a researcher is expected to know although not necessarily in-depth. One example might clarify the problem. In research on educational use of adventure games it seems obvious that you should draw on earlier work that examines this subject, but it is often haphazard what earlier research is acknowledged. Relevant work goes unnoticed and broader discussions in education are embarked on without reference to basic educational research. For example several research projects on computer games for teaching math has been started up without acknowledging each other existence (see chapter 4). This is avoided through the overview in chapter 2 and 4. A first step in such an overview is the awareness of the two parallel communities researching educational use of computer games, simulations and non-electronic games described in the following. The acknowledgement of these two communities is especially important for examining the educational use of computer games as the two communities approach the area quite differently.

The current state of game research

The research field of computer games is not yet well-established, although the last five years have seen strong progress. This is true on several levels. On the individual level researchers still struggle for acceptance and academic credibility. On an institutional level the field hasn't yet found its feet characterized by the lack of common language, basic theoretical discussions and scarce funding of research. Within game research there exists two parallel research communities examined below and one is often ignored in favour of the other. The split between the two communities is supported by the fact that game researchers in general have quite diverse backgrounds, and that the majority of references within the fields are still from neighbouring disciplines. This entails that a lot of the research is not published in a specific journal for game research, but rather in well-established traditional peer-reviewed journals within a researcher's own field. Furthermore, researchers already need to follow up on their background discipline and the game research discipline. This makes it very hard to keep up with the development and hence to build on top of earlier research and results in pockets of research in different hubs. The Ivory Tower column has discussed this issue of a cross-disciplinary approach as both a strength and a weakness for game research (Kirkpatrick, 2003; Pearce, 2003).

Seldom are both communities consulted when approaching computer games and it is, therefore, initially worthwhile to stress the strength of each community. A historically awareness will benefit us so we don't constantly reinvent the wheel.

The simulation research community

The simulation community is older than the computer game research community. It is today centred on the journal Simulation & Gaming and the supporting academic organisations in different countries like ABSEL, ISAGA, JASAG and NASAGA. This research tradition started in the mid-1950's, especially promoted by business gaming and the perceived potential of learning through games (Butler, Markulis, & Strang, 1988). The focus is on games in general not necessarily computer games, but a majority of the research is relevant for computer games research.

The field broadens from the early 1970's and up through the 1980's with books like *Simulation Games in Learning* by Sarane Boocock & E.O Schild (1968), *Learning with Simulations and Games* by Richard Duke & Constance Seidner (1975) and *Gaming-Simulation: Rationale Applications* by Cathy Greenblat & Richard Duke (1981). Conferences are regularly held over the years and especially the business area has gotten a good foothold, maintained up to the present times. The business area has increasingly come to dominate with a strong emphasis on simulations and less focus on games. This development is clear when looking at the older issues of the Journal of Simulation & Gaming, where fundamental discussions on games and simulations occur. The simulation and games research community has seen a decline over the years and need to reconsider its organisation and goals, which was also an explicit goal of the anniversary conference in 1994 (Dorn, 1989; Duke, 1995).

The computer games research community

The other community focuses on computer games and takes its first steps in the early 1980's with classic books like Chris Crawford's *The Art of Computer Game Design* (Crawford, 1982), Geoffrey Loftus and Elizabeth Loftus' *Mind at Play* (Loftus & Loftus, 1983) and Patricia Greenfield's *Mind and Media* (Greenfield, 1984). These books were quite broad in their treatment of computer games and clearly approached them as a new media form, although Crawford's book was an important exception.

From the 1980's and the next ten years the closest you came to seeing active academic achievements aimed primarily at computer games within this tradition were *The Journal of Computer Game Design*, some research projects mainly within math and science and quite extensive studies of the potential negative effects of computer games. The focus on small specific areas lasted until the late 1990's. From the late 1990's the research into games slowly accelerated exemplified with the appearance of resource sites like Game-culture, Ludology, Game-research and Joystick101. At the same time conferences exclusively on computer games saw the light: The IT-University of Copenhagen held *Computer Games and Digital Textualities* in March 2001 and the University of Chicago hosted *Playing by the Rules* in October 2001[2]. From this several initiatives emerged: Several conferences exclusively on game research, the peer-reviewed journal *Game Studies* dedicated to humanistic game research, and the forming of the *Digital Game Research Association*.

Extending from the fragmented nature of the research field a sub-goal of this dissertation is to establish the field's boundaries as a future reference point for researchers, educators, decision-makers, developers and lay people.

Defining computer games and simulations

The discussion on how to define computer games and simulations has a long history and it has been the primary interest of a number of theorists (Coleman, 1970; Crawford, 1982; Salen & Zimmerman, 2003; Seidner, 1975; Aarseth, 1997). Especially the differences between computer games and simulations are a returning problem, which will be discussed in some length below. The computer game versus simulation discussion is important when the dissertation later looks at the problems related to the learning experience when considering the representational nature of computer games.

I will start with the game definition by Jesper Juul (2003), which is one of the most recent, grounded in an extensive examination of previous attempts at defining games.

> A game is a rule-based system with a variable and quantifiable outcome, where different outcomes are assigned different values, the player exerts effort in order to influence the outcome, the player feels attached to the outcome and the consequences of the activity are optional and negotiable.

Juul (200330)

---

[2] There was an conference as early as 1983 but it never really caught on

It is obvious from the definition above that computer games are quite far reaching and maybe the definition does not really exclude educational software or simulations. The major difference seems to be the attachment of the player, which can also be instilled in educational software and simulations. Juul (2003) is aware of the problem as he discusses a number of borderline examples that share a lot of characteristics with games. The addition of conflict to the game definition solves some of the problems, especially in relation to differentiating games from simulations[3]. One example of an early simulation definition is by Seidner (1975):

> In the broadest sense, simulation refers to the dynamic execution or manipulation of a model of some object system. In education, simulation entails abstracting certain elements of social or physical reality in such a way that the student can interact with and become a part of that simulated reality.

Seidner (1975:15)

The definition by Seidner may seem to cover computer games, but if we look to other game definitions important properties are missing, namely artificial conflict and the player's investment (Salen & Zimmerman, 2003). These elements are far from trivial as they point to the focal point of most computer games. The construction of an artificial conflict and the balancing of this conflict to best challenge the player is one of the trademarks of a good computer game. When this element is missing, we have a simulation. Seidner (1975) also describes this when she points to the lack of goals in simulations as the difference from games. The close relationship is best captured by Coleman's (1970) term simulation games that describe how simulations become games when we apply goals to the possible activities in the simulation. Goals are tied to the conflict and necessary for the player to really invest strong feelings in the game. Even when computer games do not set up specific conflicts and goals most players will invent their own, and use the simulation to achieve these goals, making up their own game experience.

The difference between what you might call implicit and explicit goals has important consequences in how the game universe is constructed. The explicit goals are those set by the game whereas implicit goals are those the players are capable of setting and very often do (Salen & Zimmerman, 2003). Relying on implicit rules will provide a more open-ended game universe akin to a simulation, whereas explicit goals will make the game universe more game-like.

Also, in simulations, the realism of the model has high priority, whereas a computer game will often sacrifice realism if it benefits the overall game experience. The computer game is not primarily about simulating, but rather providing an interesting experience by the player fulfilling certain explicit goals. Thiagarajan (1998) suggests a useful division between low fidelity and high fidelity simulations to address the difference between game and simulation. High fidelity simulations attempt to resemble the real world as closely as possible, whereas low-fidelity simulations "focus on only a few critical elements and use a simplified model of the interactions among them." (Thiagarajan, 1998:37). Most computer games will be located closest to low-fidelity simulations on the continuum.

The closeness between computer games and low-fidelity simulations is due to computer games' priority of entertainment over realism. This is captured in relation to the design of conflicts in computer games, where you will aim at the most interesting and balanced conflict at the expense of realism. Few would say that the *Civilization* series embraces realism, but it certainly includes simulation properties with a dynamic model representing civilizations you can manipulate. Most

---

[3] Approaching early research on educational use of games, we find that researchers prefer simulation to the term game. The reason for this may be more cosmetic than a reflection of real use. Simulations invoke fewer associations with fun and making it easier to transfer simulations to a serious educational context.

computer games have degrees of simulation, but it is not necessarily a property of computer games. In an adventure game, you can have a branching structure that does not have the characteristics of a dynamic structure. It has a finite number of options contrary to a simulation, where you have a basic set of rules that the player can manipulate in almost endless ways. Action games are basically low fidelity simulations where you engage in a simulated universe with explicit rules for the potential activities.

This dissertation concentrates on computer games that fall within the simulation genre, although not explicitly stated throughout the dissertation. These are typically genres like simulation, strategy and partly action, whereas adventure falls outside (see brief vocabulary at the end of dissertation for genre descriptions).

Educational theoretical background

With a basic understanding of computer games it seems obvious to gain a better understanding of the educational aspects. Within educational theory you can choose from a very wide range of theories and have to be selective. Research into the educational potential of computer games spans the entire spectrum of theories of education, teaching and learning. For some learning is conceived as achieving skills like analysis and problem-solving, others refer to concrete facts, while some will focus primarily on the social setting around the learning experience. This dissertation purports to an inclusive understanding of learning, education and teaching.

Learning, education and teaching

The concepts learning, education and teaching are certainly broad and potentially very inclusive. We need to get a firm idea of what we really refer to, when we use these different terms. Some overall criteria for the definition of these central concepts are helpful for guiding the unravelling as a number of different paths can be taken. Our understanding of learning should not be limited to for example education of children, education in a school context or deal exclusively with edutainment titles. Our definition should be able to describe both the interaction with the computer game and the interaction around the computer game. The definition should also be able to provide a perspective for understanding and exploring different practices that lend themselves better to using computer games for educational purposes. These criteria are critical if we are to cover the existing spectrum of research done on educational use of computer games and build a viable framework.

The first important property is that learning, education and teaching is not conceived as limited to any one context or person. In some distant past it may has been easy to say what education was: Education took place at the school. This is hardly the case anymore with new broader concepts appearing: Home learning, lifelong learning and supplementary training have expanded the scope of education beyond childhood, school and teachers. Education and learning often takes place within an educational system, but cannot exclusively be limited to a certain context. On an overall level education is still an attempted controlled socialization and qualification of a given individual for the benefit of society (Ljungstrøm, 1984). However, this happens through still more subtle practices, handing over responsibility to the individual. Education is continuously becoming a task for everybody else than teachers. The increased home learning, that has strong ties with edutainment, hands over responsibility to the parents and to some degree the students, partly accelerated by information technology (Egenfeldt-Nielsen, 2001). Also life long learning and supplementary learning transfer responsibility to the student. Finally, schools are increasingly relying on the students to be masters of their own educational fate with individual teaching plans and 'career' goals formulated by the student at a still earlier stage (Buckingham & Scanlon, 2002; Egenfeldt-Nielsen, 2001). Similarly, teaching is not restricted to a teacher or school and learning can take place in all situations. It may be more appropriate to talk about instruction than teaching inspired by Vygotsky's concept zone of proximal development.

Inspired by anthropologist Gregory Bateson I use learning as an overarching term that refers to activities and contexts we engage in that result in changing or supporting our patterns of action. We can see learning as the ability to appreciate the difference that makes a difference (Bateson, 1972). More specifically, the dissertation introduces the experiential approach to learning as formulated by David Kolb extended with John Dewey. These theorists cover the development of experiential theory from the early 20th century and are situated within the constructivist learning approach founded by Jean Piaget. The experiential approach stresses the connection between concrete experience, reflection, concepts and application. This is seen as a learning cycle and as will become clearer fits well with the playing of computer games. The important characteristic of the experiential learning approach is the focus on the concrete experience, as the starting point for students' learning. Computer games offer such concrete experiences that can be reflected, conceptualised, and applied continuously.

An additional argument for drawing on the experiential learning tradition is the foothold it has within the research area of educational games (i.e. Gentry, 1990; Ruben, 1999). It lends itself well to understanding the active processes involved in using games for facilitating learning. It, therefore, makes good sense to build on this theory to understand computer games that share some basic properties with traditional games.

Overall education refers to a purposeful learning process and hence is a sub-category of learning. I define education as a mostly planned activity we engage in with the purpose of changing specific contents, skills or attitudes. This can be content, skills or attitudes in different forms: defined by curriculum (i.e. arithmetic, reading, writing), parents find worth pursuing (i.e. information on local history or family history), offered as a supplementary project in youth centre projects (i.e. build a house learning basic handy-man skills or learn how to cook) or considered important by students to set aside time for (i.e. learn programming through online tutorials or Spanish at evening courses for a holiday trip) (Good & Brophy, 1990).

When I defined education, I stated that we learn contents, skills and attitudes. These are imprecise concepts, but are inspired by the work by Bloom et al. (1956) and Kratwohl et al. (1964). The delimitation serves as a starting point and is throughout the dissertation a useful analytic tool. In this introduction, I cannot bring justice to the comprehensive work behind the taxonomy, but will outline the main idea behind the taxonomy of educational objectives. The work on the taxonomy was initiated in 1948 with the explicit goal of including the different educational theories to construct an overarching description of what outcomes were relevant in education. The aim was to describe three main areas: Cognitive domain, affective domain and psychomotor domain. However, the taxonomy was never fully developed for the last area and I will not concentrate on this last area as it seems to have limited bearing on the current educational research related to computer games[4]. In the affective domain there are five categories: Receiving, responding, valuing organization and characterization. The first two categories describe the necessary basic attitude of the students towards the learning process, whereas the next levels refer to, how values will be internalised in the students. This taxonomy has not experienced the same success among educators and researchers as the cognitive domain, but is still useful for pointing to the importance of the affective objectives in the educational process.

The taxonomy of the cognitive domain (often referred to as Bloom's taxonomy) includes the following hierarchy: knowledge, comprehension, application, analysis, synthesis and evaluation. The last levels presuppose to some degree mastery of the basic level and comprehension. It is worth noting that the first levels are what we could call facts or information, whereas the next levels are actually skills used in constructing knowledge.

---

[4] Although researchers have connected computer games with learning psychomotor skills, especially eye-hand coordination, it has a fundamentally different theoretical basis than this dissertation (Egenfeldt-Nielsen, 2003d).

Learning through or about computer games

On a very general level it is relevant to distinguish between two areas in relation to computer games and learning, which are quite different. On one hand you can use computer games for facilitating learning of different contents, skills or attitudes. From another perspective computer games can be worth learning about as a separate medium as part of what is usually referred to as media education (Buckingham, 2003). The focus of this dissertation is using computer games for facilitating learning of contents, skills or attitudes and not to learn about computer games as such. In that sense computer games are seen as a medium for education.

This split may be hard to maintain as the discrepancy between students in respect to playing computer games (game literacy) may be larger than in most other areas. In classic literacy skills like reading and writing you will have underachievers, but this is nothing compared to the difference between some children having played for 20 hours pr. week the last 7 years and other children who still have the first troll to slay or car race to win. Therefore, it may turn out that to learn efficiently *through* computer games you need to learn *about* computer games.

Above I have outlined the important bricks for building an understanding of educational use of computer games. To limit the scope of this dissertation I will concentrate on the particular challenges of the school setting, which despite all is still a prominent site for education. This delimits the more informal and incidental learning processes around computer games that have earlier been a topic of research for example by Vandeventer (1997), Jessen (2001) and Gee (2003). It may be that in the end I will find more similarities than differences, but initially this limitation will simplify things.

Terminology

I have throughout this introduction used some terminology that typically causes great confusion. In the following the most important terminology is listed going from general to more specific. There is also an expanded list at the end of the dissertation that the reader can refer to:

- *Educational software*: The concept refers to all computer programs with an educational aim. Educational software is, therefore, a broader group than educational computer games and the applications are quite different in that they do not necessarily have game elements. When they have game elements, it is seldom an integrated part of the experience, but rather small separate activities. Educational computer games are often included under the heading educational software.

- *Educational computer games*: Computer games developed for educational use or titles often finding their way to educational settings both the fake, bad, ambitious and superb. This includes edutainment but is not limited to it. In this dissertation educational computer games often implicitly exclude edutainment when used.

- *Edutainment*: Edutainment is a sub-group of educational computer games that are heavily criticized. Typically edutainment titles are characterized by using quite conventional learning theories, providing a questionable game experience, simple gameplay and often produced with reference to a curriculum.

- *Educational games*: Refers to traditional non-electronic game-like activities developed for educational use spanning board games, simulations, role-playing games etc.

It should be recognized that the terms are not used consistently in the research field.

Problem statement

The problem this dissertation overall solves is the fragmented nature of the research field educational field. This implies building a framework for the research field educational use of computer games extending from the following key elements: experience-based, engagement, educational quality, safe environment, student autonomy and emotional investment. The problem posed is solved through the completion of these steps:

- Overview the current research area, hereby identifying important problems while building a terminology for future work (part 1).

- Identify the specific learning elements in educational use of computer games focusing on a school setting (part 2+3).

- Use the learning elements identified for building a theory on educational use of computer games (part 4).

The dissertation's method

Naturally, the building of a framework for educational use of computer games was not within the reach of a few empirical studies that I carried out in connection with this PhD dissertation. To build the above framework I used previous research and my own empirical studies, ultimately combining these to a theory on educational use of computer games that bring together all the pieces of the dissertation.

The actual process started with an initial overview of the field both concerning educational theory in general, the research on non-electronic games and in particular research on educational use of computer games. Early on, I focused on experiential learning as the basic educational theory, as it was used in previous game research, and it on a basic level challenged the underlying educational theory behind edutainment. The overview of previous research uncovered a number of key areas, described in chapter 4 and 5, which served to inform the empirical studies. Initially, the intention was to build the framework by bringing together all theory relevant to the subject. Although, this never proved feasible the framework remains grounded in a broad theoretical foundation which will become clear in the later chapters.

Two empirical studies were conduced with several purposes: Open exploration of the appropriateness of the selected educational theory, examine structural properties for educational use of computer games, examine current gaps in the research area and provide a practical grounding for the final theory.

The first empirical study, in chapter 3 of teachers' expectations consists exclusively of descriptive statistics with a sample size of 43 teachers. This study uncovered the structural properties for using computer games in schools supplemented with existing theory, as this is mostly missing in the research area. The second empirical study is the most central, examining educational use of the historical strategy game *Europa Universalis II* through qualitative analysis and statistical analysis (see appendix for an in-depth description of the game used). The goal is to achieve an understanding of how computer games are actually perceived, used, engaged with and learned from by students. The second study is made up of 72 students and two teachers. It includes both qualitative and quantitative measures of students' experiences by using computer games in history teaching.

Each of the empirical studies is unique and has no earlier counterparts. The second study is especially distinctive as it operates with a control group and designs the computer game experience around the existing limits in a school setting. In that sense the empirical study aspires to sidestep the potential critique of experimental teaching styles. Experimental set-ups often make the actual experiences gained unfit for wider use in the educational system.

The focus on commercial computer games

This dissertation will have a stronger focus on commercial computer games than one might initially expect. This is a logical consequence of the perception of computer games presented earlier, where I saw computer games as having a stronger inherent claim to learning than other media forms. It makes sense to treat most computer game genres as potentially educational depending on the framing although the educational quality has different degrees. Thus, the basic premise for using commercial games is met, but a number of other factors for choosing commercial games should be mentioned.

First of all, the majority of educational computer game titles on the market are lacking in quality and, therefore, make questionable examples for researching educational potential. The titles are mostly produced on a low budget, sold at low retail price and constantly on sale (Buckingham & Scanlon, 2002; Leyland, 1996; Taylor, 2003). As senior designer Margo Nanny of the company Interactive Learning states:

> Both the gaming industry and the educational software industry are acting in a short sighted fashion by driving their product design entirely from the latest software fad and short term bottom line.

> (Stern, 1998:1)

The rationale for using a commercial computer game was that this way I had a proven commercial title. I knew it worked gameplay wise and could concentrate on its educational potentials. With most educational computer games, I would have been concerned with whether the results were contaminated by a flawed gameplay that would altogether make the computer game of little interest to students. It remains a constant problem whether studies on educational use of computer games are addressing the lack of a specific title or the educational use of computer games in general. On the other hand, the commercial game title might fail because it lacks support for the learning experiences and is not specifically developed for educational purposes. The choice of a commercial computer game for the empirical study leads to speculations concerning the external validity of studying the use of computer games for educational purposes in general. However, I decided to use a commercial computer game because the existing educational computer games seemed to disqualify themselves on both accounts, neither working as education nor computer games. This was especially evident for the target group I wished to address; educational titles were practically non-existent for high school classes. Studying an older group of students in the educational system provided some clear advantages as they can better give feedback, the computer game can be more complex and the older students have more background information for playing a computer game.

Commercial computer games, therefore, remain central to this dissertation both reflected in the theoretical approach and the empirical studies carried out to support the development of the field. A question that arises is how to choose an appropriate commercial title for educational use. A question not easily tackled, but some guidelines can be identified, although they have been kept in the appendix in this dissertation.

Overview of dissertation

The end-goal is to explain the educational use of computer games through a theory, which can be summarised as follows: In educational use of computer games the student is playing and constructing knowledge through interaction with the game universe. Slowly building on top of existing knowledge from previous experiences arising from inside the game universe and other spheres of life facilitated by instruction. It is an experience-based hermeneutic exploration in a safe rich environment, potentially scaffolding the student while maintaining student autonomy and ensuring a high emotional investment in the activity.

Part 1: Background

This part outlines the broader context for educational use of computer games by outlining its history, the market conditions and adjoining influential disciplines like educational media and educational games. The results used later are primarily the ones on the structural conditions and practical barriers in relations to educational use of computer games. Primarily, the goal of this part is to ground the framework for educational use of computer games.

Chapter I: The history of educational computer games.

Here the background for educational media use is outlined with a focus on the emergence of educational use of computer games. The chapter presents characteristics of the titles, the influential forerunners and sketches recent trends in the approach to educational use of computer games.

Chapter II: Looking back on research into educational use of games and simulations.

This chapter examines the research conducted on simulation and games in respect to how it points forward to important research questions in research on educational use of computer games.

Chapter III: Empirical study on school use of computer games.

This chapter examines what problems and barriers teachers perceive in relation to educational use of computer games and the current levels of use in the educational system. This is a good starting point for further inquiries into the barriers experienced, when actually using educational computer games.

Part 2: Theoretical foundation

This part forms the foundation for the empirical studies and the final theory on educational use of computer games. The focus is on the variety of studies, looking at the educational potential of computer games supplemented with basic theory on education, learning and teaching.

Chapter IV: Standing on the shoulders of giants: An overview of the research on educational use of computer games.

The area of educational use of computer games is vast and it is, therefore, necessary to address different paradigms and sub areas before venturing further in the dissertation. This chapter presents the most important contributions and a grid for overviewing the area. Research on computer games and education is limited, although the numerous different approaches to studying educational potential of computer games have a good share of common problems.

Chapter V: An initial framework for studying the educational use of computer games.

Here the educational theories that steer the empirical studies including educational theory, computer games theory and media theory. The chapter establish the necessary terminology for examining educational use of computer games in the following chapters and prepare the way for the final theory in chapter 10.

Part 3: Main empirical study

The main empirical study primarily focuses on the problems encountered when introducing computer games in a high-school history course.

Chapter VI: Method considerations concerning main empirical study.

Here I present important method considerations in connection with the empirical study focusing, on the sampling, validity, reliability and naturalness of the research design. The procedure, purpose, method problems and tools for gathering data are also presented in this chapter.

Chapter VII: Practical barriers and perception of history.

Here the empirical results are presented, focusing on different student groups' trajectory through the course and the role barriers played for the course. In addition, the chapter discusses the fight between different understandings of history present among the students and its impact on the learning experience with computer games.

Chapter VIII: Issues in teaching with computer games.

The chapter will outline, analyse and discuss the characteristics of teaching with computer games as it was experienced by history teachers during the main empirical study. The focus is on the progression among students increasingly applying the entire spectrum of learning history: appreciation, exploration and linking.

Chapter IX: Evaluation of the learning outcome.

Here the empirical results on the learning outcome of using computer games will be examined. The traditional approach to learning outcome and measurements will be criticized for not taking into account the special characteristics of computer games.

Part 4: Combining empirical findings with existing theory

This is the final part of the thesis, bringing together theoretical work and empirical findings, resulting in a theory on educational use of computer games.

Chapter X: Theory on educational use of computer games.

Here the ends meet with a coherent theory for understanding educational use of computer games. The focus is on how use of computer games in an educational setting can provide concrete experiences that teaching can extend from to provide a stronger and richer educational experience.

Chapter XI: Final thoughts

The last chapter presents a summary of the results and some final thoughts on the scope and implications of this dissertation.

Part 1: Background

This part outlines the broader context for educational use of computer games by outlining its history, the market conditions and adjoining influential disciplines like educational media, military use, business games, and educational games. The goal is to ground the framework for educational use of computer games in history to avoid repetition of previous research, making sound choices concerning theories applied, and achieve an inclusive understanding of what an educational computer game can be.

Chapter I: The History of Educational Computer Games

> Unlike the scripted, paper-driven exercises of the past, computer simulation has become a must. In fact, it may be the only way to represent the complexities of future warfare.
>
> Lieutenant General Eugene D. Santarelli
> (Quoted in Aldrich, 2003:22)

This chapter is the historical background for the framework of educational use of computer games, and as such does not have a direct bearing on later parts of the dissertation. The chapter is, nevertheless, important to ground the framework historically. Especially, since, researchers often lack an understanding of the realities of life, when considering the educational potential of computer games. There tends to be a fantasy that with the right knowledge of how to produce educational titles better titles will appear almost by magic. However, one should be careful to automatically consider the low availability of high-quality educational titles as a result of limited knowledge of producing educational titles as market forces have also clearly influenced the face of educational titles.

The goal of this chapter is to situate educational computer games in an historical context by presenting the related influential areas, describing the historical significant events and outlining the market conditions. The starting point is the strong traditions within the business studies and the military for using games for educating people, dating back to the 18th century. The military perspective is interesting to document that educational use of computer games is not merely a new, hyped phenomena. After the overview of military and business titles the similarities educational use computer games share with other educational media are examined. The similarities have heavily influenced the current face of educational computer games. The last step is to examine how the educational computer games developed from the Wild West to being dominated by edutainment titles.

It is concluded that educational media increasingly came to shape the form educational use of computer games took, although historically there have been other, more ambitious, attempts at developing educational computer games. Edutainment becomes dominating in spite, or perhaps because, of its conservative approach to education, and questionable game titles.

The military's educational use of computer games

The earliest formal roots of war games are *Chaturanga*, the Indian forefather of chess, but the formal introduction of games into the military starts with Helwig in 1780, refined later by Lieutenant Von Reisswitz. During the 19th century the German military seriously begins to use *Kriegsspiel* as a way to simulate strategy on the battlefield. This becomes the first organized effort to use games for a direct educational purpose in Western culture. In 1824 the game was recommended for training officers and a copy of the game distributed to every regiment in the German army. The use also spreads to the rest of the world (Avendon & Sutton-Smith, 1971; Leeson, Unknown).

The US military starts to use commercial computer games for training with a modification of *Doom* called *Marine Doom* back in 1998. The impact of the military is by some considered paramount for the computer game industry's current focus on warfare and violence (Kline, Dyer-Witheford, & Greig, 2003). Earlier in the 1980's the military tries to use the computer game *Battlezone* for eye-hand coordination, but fails. However, the military had a long tradition for using games, and it was not about to give up (Macedonia, 2003).

Instead, the military took a new starting point with the traditional German board game called *Kriegsspiel* and developed other types of computer games. Instead of concrete simulations computer games were conceived broader. The real rationale for using computer games became team tactics, decision-making, conflict resolution and strategy. This is the idea behind using *Doom, Delta Force 2, Guard Force and Joint Force Employment* in the military today (Plotz, 2003; Prensky, 2001a; Social Impact games, 2004). There are still computer games used for more low level skills like *Bottom Gun* for torpedo firing through periscope readings but they are fewer in number and are more precisely described as simulations rather than computer games.

The military's use of computer games has increased over the last years most noticeable with *America's Army, Full Spectrum Warrior, Close Combat Marines and Full Spectrum Command.* It has become more affordable to tweak existing commercial computer games for use in military setting and it has increasingly been possible to hire game developers for developing a specific game title, often in the form of so-called modifications (mods). Mods refer to computer games built on existing commercial computer game engines, but with certain characteristics tweaked.

The military is often hailed as true champions of educational use of computer games (Prensky, 2001a), but access to its findings and results are for good reasons often limited. The direct influence on educational use of computer games is harder to asses, but as mentioned above a significant amount of titles are developed for military training. Still, the military has a number of characteristics that makes it less interesting to look at their experiences with computer games. The military area deals with very different target groups, quite alternative settings for playing and to say the least serious consequences for not learning from the game well. It may be hard to maintain the importance of play, when we consider military training games. Some of these characteristics are also shared by another influential area, namely business games and simulations.

Educational business simulations and computer games

Previously, I have hinted that business simulations and games were early used for teaching a variety of business-related topics, including the general operations of a company, the management of a specialized business or specialized parts of the business area. The area is too large to ignore altogether, and a few words proving its existence is important to construct an overall inclusive framework of educational use of computer games.

Business simulations and games has long been a natural part of especially American business schools, whereas computer games with business content are still mostly found at more introductory levels (Faria, 1990). The area of business simulations and games have not until recently seriously begun to influence the research into educational use of computer games although sparks, flew between them over the years.

In 1956 the US Air Force simulation *Monopologs* let players become inventory managers managing the Air Force supply system. One year later *Top Management Decision Simulation* made its way into a business college class at the University of Washington. Thus, the way was paved for thousands of business games and simulations[5]. Although games and simulations also spread to other areas they remained strongest within business studies and the military, where games and simulations originated (Woods, 2004). The area of business games and simulations have never really joined forces with educational use of computer games, probably because business didn't seem the first priority to teach younger children who quickly became the major target group for educational computer games.

From early on, computer games with a business theme have been labeled like any other commercial computer game, although the high complexity often pointed to a bit older players. Almost any business area have been the topic of computer games, like running a Railroad company

---

[5] Especially business education has taken games to its heart best exemplified with the following web-site for non-computerized classroom-games for college listing more than 130 games www.marietta.edu/~delemeeg/games.

in *Railroad Tycoon*, being a Oil Tycoon in *Oil Imperium*, running an airline in *Airline tycoon*, building up a car company in *Car tycoon*, making a pizza empire in *Pizza Tycoon*, leading a worldwide company and learning the basics of the market in *Capitalism II* (**Error! Reference source not found.**). The actual use of these for more formal learning is, however, more uncertain, but many of these titles are quite successful, perhaps showing a way for an alternative to edutainment with integrated and engaging gameplay – although not always state-of-the-art computer games.

Educational Media: The forerunner for educational computer games

Computer games follow other media surges almost perfectly. Every new media invention is bound to go through a stage of being considered of potential high value for educational purposes, where you combine the magic of the new medium with the traditional need for conveying knowledge to new generations. Unfortunately, the optimism is mostly followed by pessimism, when new media forms are brought into educational settings without delivering the promised salvation. Often the first attempts are based on existing media practice, which has indeed been the case with computer games. The theoretical winds from educational media have shaped, inspired and influenced educational use and research into computer games – maybe building the very foundation for perceiving educational computer games as a species in its own right (Calvert, 1999; Cuban, 2001; Saettler, 1968). Educational media maintains its strong grip and continues to influence the form educational computer games take, especially the manifestation of edutainment. Ultimately the strong ties with other educational media is part of the explanation for the emergence of edutainment that only realizes a quite limited part of the potential for using computer games in education. It is, therefore, also worthwhile to look at educational media to track some of the characteristics brought into educational use of computer games.

Educational media research distinguishes between educational media from at least two perspectives. On one hand it may contain direct academic content like spelling, math, history, geography and science. This is the traditional perspective on educational media, but often it has been broadened with a pro-social perspective. In a pro-social perspective educational media is expanded to also encompass social and emotional development of children. This second perspective is opposed by Calvert (1999), stressing that educational media should address specific curriculum goals. Calvert's approach is continued in the dominating approach to educational computer games, namely edutainment. The narrow focus on curriculum is problematic because it implies a narrow perception of education, which I opposed in the introduction to the dissertation. Interestingly, the curriculum focus has triumphed over the years, right from the first instructional films to current edutainment.

Instructional films make their mark

The first attempts at using educational media were carried out at school museums as early as 1890 in New York City with instructional films without sound. The use expanded up during the 1910's with some suggesting the integration of instructional films in schools. However, this was cautioned against by Cohen in 1918. "This impression that we are ready to supply just what the schools need in the way of educational picture […] is quite general and absolutely erroneous" (Cohen, quoted in Saettler, 1968:97). Still it was introduced in many schools subsequently causing a lot of problems. Finally, in the 1930's the instructional films market crashed, not just due to the general depression, but as a consequence of deep structural problems. A lot of the problems formulated in an evaluation by McClusky in 1937 to turn things around echo some of the concerns that are with us today, when we look at educational computer games.

The problems identified by McClusky (Saettler, 1968) were among others the widespread scepticism against combining entertainment, commercial interest and education. Instructional films were considered low culture and below the dignity of both educators and educational institutions, although educators on the surface might seem positive towards the enterprise of educational media. Another well-known problem was a lack of seriousness in the instructional films produced and a tendency for aiming at fast profit. The sales methods and propaganda used by proponents of instructional films alienated educators and eroded the confidence in the instructional films. This was also supported by regular technical problems, copyrights issues and confusion regarding restrictions of use. The commercial operators had on their side been hit hard by competition from subsidized production resulting in a saturated market. A lot of universities, school museums and companies engaged in both distribution and production of subsidized instructional films directly or indirectly with government funding. Also present in early attempts was a clash between commercial interest, directors of movies and the subject experts who were consultants on the production. What worked in a film wasn't necessarily in accordance with curriculum. McClusky suggested a market of independent developers to solve the problem with a strong committee to advice and validate products. Nothing became of it (Saettler, 1968).

The concerns discussed above related to instructional film are increasingly being raised after the consolidation in the edutainment business during the 1990's, where the big companies began dominating the market (see appendix). The structural problems remain a part of educational computer games even today. Indeed, all of the problems from the instructional films in the 1930s are found when considering the dominance of edutainment in the current market. Before looking closer at edutainment's path to power a look at how educational television rejuvenates instructional films is relevant. Educational television experience similar problems as edutainment, and influence the educational approach favoured in edutainment.

Educational television dawns on us

The first educational television was delivered by the University of Iowa in 1933. The first many years educational television was aimed at college students with a slow pace and one-way communication. The result was often boring and somewhat ineffective educational programs with

Picture 1: A picture taken from the first Sesame Street shows at Prairie Public Broadcasting History.

the exception of more concrete programs in science subjects. In science you could visualize processes of driving, show pictures of space and dynamic presentations of systems. The first slow years were succeeded by more active years from 1967 when legislation enforced broadcasters to air educational television (Calvert, 1999; Federal Communications Commission, 2003). This legislation also led to more attempts at reaching younger age groups, however, with little success until Sesame Street (Picture 2) was launched on November 10th, 1969.

Early on problems related to the inconsistent knowledge of viewers' initial knowledge, the age variety in viewers, the wish to run the programs live and not being able to build on earlier programs (Calvert, 1999). You couldn't assume that all viewers had seen the last episode. Some of these problems are clearly present in relation to educational use of computer games, which also aim at a broad target group. Computer games also give very different experiences through dispersed patterns of play and more choices for the player. Sesame Street solved some of these problems and, although somewhat criticized, became the model for future educational programs as it won the hearts of the viewers.

Interestingly, educational media almost disappeared from broadcast television in the United States during the 1980's as a consequence of new legislation. It would take several new legislation attempts before educational television would re-emerge in the mid-1990's. Educational programs have now become popular and some stations specialize in educational content i.e. Nickelodeon, Discovery Channel, History Channel and Animal Planet (Calvert, 1999; Miller, 2002).

According to Calvert (1999) the evaluations of the effectiveness of educational programs are controversial, but in general lend support to educational media as preparing children for school. Some of this effect is due to a general appreciation of learning in the home, when educational programs are viewed. Children from middle-class families are especially inclined to view educational programs. This suggests that educational programs may actually widen the gap in preparedness for school between social classes rather than bridge the gap. The middle-class families secure and extend their head start by using the educational programs that are relatively speaking more expensive for lower classes. The educational programs are also more easily embraced by middle-class culture, where education is closer to parents' heart (Calvert, 1999).

The appeal of computers for educators

Interaction with the audience is from the birth of television seen as an important characteristic implemented through live shows. The potential of computers was, however, soon to dawn on educators. Although, television through live shows came one step closer to interacting with the user compared to books, the computer was believed to take it at least several steps closer. As Loftus & Loftus state,

> Educators began to realize that the computer, with its powerful interactive abilities, might be used to aid in instruction. Thus the concept of computer-assisted instruction (or 'CAI') was born.

(Loftus & Loftus, 1983:116)

The 1960's saw massive investments in CAI for example 4000 students during 1967-68 completed 300.000 arithmetic lessons. The lessons were mostly on simple math like addition and fractions, but most importantly it seemed to work (Cotton, 1991; Loftus & Loftus, 1983; Willis, Hovey, & Hovey, 1987). The expansion continued up through the 1980's and 1990's with the appearance of a range of terms covering the use of computers in school for educational purposes, i.e. computer-based education (CBE), computer supported collaborative learning (CSCL) and computer-based instruction (CBI). Computer-based education refers in the broadest sense to the use of computers in education, but the sub-area that historically most clearly affected the use of educational computer games was CAI.

The term computer-assisted instruction (CAI) is actually quite a narrow term and refers to drill-and-practice, simulation or tutorial activities offered as stand-alone activities or with limited guidance from teachers. The area has been heavily researched and although early studies showed that CAI worked (Cotton, 1991; Loftus & Loftus, 1983; Willis et al., 1987); it has more recently been noted by Soloway & Bielaczyc, (1995:1) that, "By and large the impact of computers on education has been minimal". Educational computer programs continue to be caught in restrictions imposed by learning theories, hardware limits, structural problems and market conditions. A point also vigorously pursued by Cuban (2001) This is perhaps especially true for CAI, where drill-and-practice remains one of the most significant trademarks.

Although CAI has been shown to improve learning it is unclear whether CAI is more or less effective than conventional teaching. The common conclusion is that a combination is preferable (Cotton, 1991). Still, CAI is often caught in the drill-and-practice approach to learning. Developers have apparently consistently found it hard and cumbersome to construct real alternatives to drill-and-practice programs that can work in school settings. This is interesting as the drill and practice model used in early CAI is apparent in the early educational computer games and continues to be present in a lot of the popular educational computer games titles (Brody, 1993; Miller, 2000). The easy way out.

However, most of the current titles use an adventure game format to contextualize the drill-and-practice. This has led to the critique of educational computer games as sugar-coating learning (Egenfeldt-Nielsen, 2003e; Healy, 1999). The major difference between educational computer games and CAI is primarily the role of motivation for engaging the students. Computer games are primarily seen as being able to offer both stronger intrinsic and extrinsic motivation. From the start this is the major ambition of educators and researchers turning to computer games - to alter educational computer programs so students become more motivated. This is where Thomas Malone's research in the early 1980's starts and this is the real birth of educational computer games. Over the years motivation becomes the sole alibi for producing educational computer games instead of other educational software.

Parallel with educational computer games maturation, educational software increasingly turns towards multimedia learning studying the advantages of integrating different media forms. The term multimedia learning is coined in the 1990's to describe the advantages of computer-mediated learning from a primarily cognitive perspective influenced by modern thinking in cognitivism like Howard Gardner (1983). The overall conclusion in multimedia learning is that the different modalities give a better learning experience when the content is encoded in different modalities: text, pictures and sound. Furthermore, theorists within multimedia learning stress the opportunity for different cognitive learning styles to be nurtured in multimedia learning (Mayer, 2001).

The emergence of a market for educational computer games[6]

Naturally, the success of educational software and educational media was used, when educational computer games appeared both in terms of the form and content of the titles produced, but also the market approach. Over the years this resulted in educational computer games turning into a limited manifestation – edutainment.

Despite the early discussions and search for educational potential of computer games the area's history has for years been conspicuously missing in the mainstream computer game research community. The long line of articles and books on computer games history largely ignores educational computer games (i.e. Hunter, 2000). One exception is Broderbund's highly acclaimed series *Where in the World is Carmen San Diego* (i.e. DeMaria & Wilson, 2002). The industry lacks a coherent perception of what signifies important game titles in the history of educational use of computer games. We need good examples for reference and a shared terminology to address recurring elements in failed educational titles. The first step is to identify some of the more successful and influential titles over the years and how specific companies influenced the development. There is an abundance of interesting titles that have been more or less designed for educational purposes, as the market was earlier not as structured into tight little boxes as now. For example, the game designer Chris Crawford could go from producing *Patton Versus Rommel* a war game with little educational appeal to, *Balance of the Planet*, an ambitious attempt to educate people about the environmental problems facing our time (Crawford, 2003).

---

[6] A variety of sources weew used gather the information in this section. Information were scattered among different sources, some of questionable quality. Information derives from general descriptions of companies, titles and historical events from a variety of web-sites grown by volunteer gamers supplying bits and pieces of information and different mailing lists Serious Games, Becta and Games Network). The computer games mentioned as important have been identified as significant in the development by at least two independent sources. The most influential sources are: www.terc.edu/mathequity/gw/html/gwhome.html, www.mobygames.com, www.the-underdogs.org and www.classicgaming.com

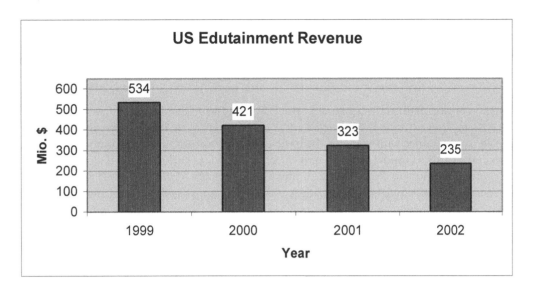

US Edutainment Revenue

Table 1: Shows the decline in edutainment revenue over several years (Taylor, 2003; The ESA, 2003).

As mentioned previously the current market of educational computer games suffers from a good deal of the problems also present in the 1930's when the instructional films market crashed. This is not to say that a crash is imminent, but it explains the falling and stagnating market (table 1) that Buckingham & Scanlon (2002) also point to. In the words of senior designer Margo Nanny from Interactive learning, when speaking about pitching a concept, the market is quite conservative. She quotes a publisher for saying "All we're interested in now is 'meat and potatoes' which is essentially reading and math with a licensed character" (Stern, 1998:1). However, it was not always only meat and potatoes.

The history of educational computer games

It is interesting to examine how edutainment came to dominate the area of educational use of computer games, while making explicit the germs latent in the area's history that can point to other alternative manifestations of educational use of computer games.

The early years

The first years were influenced by research project that later led to some of the most successful educational titles. In 1971 the Minnesota based research centre MECC produced *Oregon Trail* which remains a bestseller today. Also the famous *Lemonade Stand* came from MECC. It took the journey all the way up to the hyped 1990's. In the late 1980's the research centre was sold to a North American venture capitalist for merely $5 million. When The Learning Company a year later bought MECC the price was $250 million (Educational Software Classics, 1999; Lauppert, 2004).

In 1973 a project named Plato emerged with a focus on math and educational software. Computer games played a central role in this project, which opposed the beginning tendency to construct drill-and-practice educational software. The inspiration for this project was not behaviourism but rather the found of

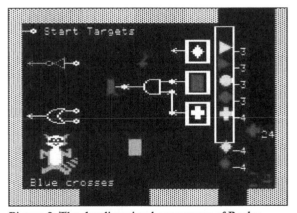

Picture 2: The dazzling visual appearance of Rocky Boots – it was impressive back then in the 1980's.

cognitivism Jean Piaget and educational philosopher John Dewey. The inspiration manifested itself in attempting to teach math through more everyday math examples. Instead of relying on abstract algebra like 2+2 you would have questions like; if you have 2 bananas and get 2 bananas more how many do you then have. The measures of effectiveness in evaluation studies indicated a significant positive effect on math achievement and attitudes towards math (Olive & Lobato, 2001)

The approach favouring math and science was later continued with The Learning Companies' two popular titles *Rocky Boots* (Picture 3) from 1982 and *The Robot Odyssey* in 1984, where children had a chance to make acquaintance with some of the basic concepts of math and programming. *Rocky Boots* won several awards, is fondly remembered by many educators and children, thus paving the way for later interesting potentially educational titles as *The Incredible Machine* in 1993. *Rocky Boots* was described as, "a visual simulation that made it possible for upper-grade-school students to design simple digital logic circuits, using a joystick to move around circuit symbols on the screen and plug them together." (Robinett, 2004:1). Thus, *Rocky Boots* was among the first educational software tittles with simulation as key to the learning environment. Although, *Rocky Boots* wasn't the first educational game, it was certainly one of those with the greatest impact in the early years. The integration between the educational content and game mechanism was quite successful. According to the author it ended up selling more than 100.000 copies (Robinett, 2004).

A title among the first commercial educational computer game was *Basic Math* from 1977 that is among the first titles exhibiting the characteristics of edutainment. It is followed by a similar title in 1979 *Electric Company Math Fun*, which is closer to an actual computer game. In, *Electric Company Math Fun* two players each control a gorilla competing against each other. The more right answers the faster you progress through the jungle. If you fail an answer your gorilla is thrown in the river and cannot get up before answering a new question correctly.

From the beginning of the 1980's the educational computer games wave came rolling, indicated both by the large number of released titles (Willis et al., 1987) and research beginning to target the area. Looking at the titles described at two leading sites for game documentation The Underdogs and Moby Games the trend is clear. Educational computer games were seriously contesting traditional computer games for a place in the shopping bag of ambitious and worried parents. A worry not decreased by the continuous debate on the risks associated with mainstream computer games (Egenfeldt-Nielsen & Smith, 2004).

Educational adventure games take the lead

Snooper Troops (Picture 4) was one of the first examples of a successful educational adventure game that became one of the preferred and dominating genres for the educational computer games market. Here children would play detectives, solving different assignments. The game primarily based its educational value on the ability to facilitate better problem-solving skills like many later titles. It was followed by several other educational adventure games, which is hardly surprising as this was the decade of the adventure games. A not so classic educational adventure but influential title was *In Search of the Most Amazing Thing* from 1983, where you have to explore a science-fiction universe with your long-lost uncle Smoke Bailey.

It is clear that *Snooper Troops* from 1982 along with *Where in the World is Carmen Sandiego* and *Oregon Trail*, both seeing the commercial light in 1985 (Picture 5), offered alternative

educational computer games - edutainment had not taken over. This probably accounts for the success of the latter titles, now, even 20 years after. Although these titles are still

Picture 3: Ready to solve puzzles in the popular Snooper Troops.

focusing narrowly on transferring information from the computer to the player, it is less mechanistic. They also have a closer integration between motivation and gameplay in line with Malone's theory discussed later. The player must work for the knowledge, solve meaningful puzzles and travel through a meaningful game world. The tie between the play experience and the learning experience is also stronger. The tool for a closer integration of learning and gameplay is mostly the adventure genre, which experiences its best days up through the 1980's and early 1990's. The success of the adventure games is promoted by new technology and the introduction of the graphical user interface. The market leader Lucas Arts and Sierra both produce educational game titles with some success. Among these were *Winnie the Pooh in Hundred Acres Wood* from 1984, *Mickey's Space Adventure* in 1986 and *Troll's Tale* coming out in 1984. Several of these games were produced by Al Lowe, who later went on to make the classic *Leisure Suit Larry* series. The success of educational computer games peaks in the mid-1980's with the two most famous titles *Oregon Trail* and *Where in the World is Carmen Sandiego* (Picture 5). The Carmen Sandiego series continues for years and has spanned several sequels. The integration of geography in the gameplay wins it an educational reputation.

Picture 4 and 5: Showing the two triumphant educational computer games in the 1980's, Where in the world is Carmen Sandiego (1985) and Oregon Trail (1985).

Oregon Trail was an early hit for the company, Broderbund, and has been republished several times in refurbished versions; the latest is version 5 from 2000. The basic gameplay doesn't change significantly. You follow in the footsteps of the early American settlers and have to make decisions concerning the journey. Through the game school children learn about the American pioneer spirit.

> You can almost smell the dust from the wagon train! Kids will build real-life decision-making and problem-solving skills as they choose their wagon party and supplies, read maps, plan their route and guide their team through the wilderness.
>
> (Broderbund, 2003:1)

Despite the promising description there is not really any evidence to support the claims for educational value. While some of the highlights in educational computer games see the daylight the term edutainment is coined.

Edutainment begins to make its mark

The well-received and popular game, *Seven Cities of Gold*, from 1984 was the first game title to be described as edutainment, although not really having the characteristics of edutainment. The legend goes that it was Electronic Arts founder Trip Hawkins who coined the term. *The Seven Cities of Gold* sold 150.000 copies across several platforms and won several design awards. The game had an educational touch with its exploration, strategy and actions taking place in a historical setting (Mamer, 2002).

In 1987 follows something of an oddball, not really being a game but with extreme success, adhering to the edutainment formula. Not only may the title *Mavis Beacon* make you wonder but also the gameplay. In the game you can set up different races against time as you type the best you have learned. Although some might hint that most children could have learned it just as well on a traditional typing machine it was a success and continues to sell. This concept has been reproduced several times over the years; perhaps most famous is the more recent morbid title, *The Typing of the Dead*, from Sega in 2000 (Picture 6).

Picture 6: You have to punch the right key combinations to get a high score.

The edutainment title, *Reader Rabbit* from 1989 also enjoys success, attempting to teach you about spelling and reading, paving the way for toddlers' future schooling. This brand continues to serve The Learning Company well in the market today with a number of different instalments over the same brand. The graphics have improved, but the gameplay is pretty much working in the same way. As will become evident in the following, educational computer games over the years go from innovative titles to re-hacks of old classics. In comparison the remaining game industry's talk of sequels, licenses and betting on the same game seem like wild exaggerations. When we look at the most popular titles identified over the years more than 75% of these are sequels (see table 2) and this number increases as the edutainment industry consolidates through the 1990's.

The current historical presentation runs the risk of underestimating the impact of edutainment titles as they are often not fondly remembered, contribute no real innovation and are, therefore, not mentioned in historical accounts. It is, therefore, worth stressing that the edutainment market grows and slowly becomes dominating pushing other types of educational computer games out of the market. It is noticeable that the use of edutainment has from the beginning been driven by business and market interests rather than by the needs of educators. Arguable, the edutainment genre has become home for a lot of questionable titles, developed by hopeful amateurs or gluttonous business people seeing a chance to capitalize on parents' wish for educational computer games. The criticism of edutainment has, of course, weakened the appeal of using the label edutainment. Currently edutainment titles are sold at discount price in a stagnating market with more critical consumers (Buckingham & Scanlon, 2002; Facer et al., 2003; Leyland, 1996; Mamer, 2002)

This development happens despite Lucas Learning emerging as a separate company in 1998 with *Star Wars DroidWorks*. However, in general the game industry gives up on educational computer games. *Star Wars DroidWorks* use a first-person shooter game engine from Lucas Arts' other commercial computer games. The idea is to make "solid educational content to create something different: a thoughtful game that's actually fun and helps kids to learn within the game medium" (Blossom & Michaud, 1999:1). However, initiatives like Lucas Learning are rare and the general change is best indicated by leading educational computer game developer The Learning Company ending up under the educational publisher Riverdeep with little room left for manoeuvring and innovating. The tendency for less innovation in a harsh market is increasingly being bemoaned by people in the edutainment industry who see little change over the years despite an outspoken desire for better titles (Children's Software, 1998).

The move of production of educational computer game industry from the computer game industry to educational publishing is bound to influence the approach taken to designing educational computer games – in consequence, strengthening the edutainment's grip on the market.

Educational publishers look to other educational media and adopt similar business models and educational thinking for all their educational products (Buckingham & Scanlon, 2002). The decline is accelerated by adventure games in general becoming less popular among players. This influences the development of educational adventure games with quality suffering, educational adventure games becoming less innovative and produced on small budgets (Sluganski, 2001-2004).

Educational computer games go out of fashion

Through the 1990's educational computer games, as a consequence of edutainment's dominance, begin to acquire a bad name with commercial game developers avoiding explicitly labelling their computer games as educational. Educational computer games are increasingly seen as low-budget titles aimed at pre-school or early-school children – not competing with the still fiercer market for commercial computer games. Nevertheless, some of the educationally most interesting titles are produced in these years, interestingly never marketed as educational.

Around 1990 a couple of quite interesting titles are released although most are not explicitly educational computer games. These developers avoid being put into the same category as the increasingly criticised edutainment titles, presenting the titles as commercial AAA titles. The most noticeable are *SimCity* (1989), *Lemmings* (1990), *SimEarth* (1990) and *Civilization* (1991). Most of these computer games should be well-known. *SimCity* is about starting a city and maintaining its growth as mayor. In *Lemmings* you must help some misguided Lemmings to the end of the level by arranging Lemmings in just the right way. *SimEarth* lets you tinker with the development of Earth from pre-historical times till today, whereas *Civilization* starts with the first civilizations emerging. In *Civilization* you must win by managing different key area of a civilization including warfare, technology, trade, city management, diplomatic relations and economic planning.

The credibility of educational computer games was still somewhat intact and *The Incredible Machine* in 1993 didn't change that. However early critical voices were beginning to grow stronger as the edutainment formula became more dominating (Brody, 1993). At Sierra the aspiring game designer, Jane Jensen, later well known for the *Gabriel Knight* series throws the player into the role of ecologist Adam in 1992. In *Eco Quest 1: The Search for Cetus* the player must through the dolphin Cetus save the ocean from man's destruction. The game is characterized by a very fine mix of gameplay elements and educational information you have to acquire.

Title	Year	Edu-game	Series	Genre	Subject
Basic Math	1977	Yes	No	Puzzle	Math
Electric Company Math Fun	1979	Yes	No	Puzzle	Math
Word Fun	1980	Yes	No	Puzzle	English
Rocky Boots	1982	Yes	Yes	Puzzle	Programming
Snooper Troops	1982	No	Yes	Adventure	Cognitive
In Search of The most Amazing Thing	1983	Yes	No	Adventure	Cognitive
Mule	1983	No	No	Strategy	Cognitive
Winnie the Pooh	1984	Yes	Yes	Adventure	English
Seven Cities of Gold	1984	Yes	No	Strategy	Social studies
The Robot Odyssey	1984	Yes	Yes	Puzzle	Programming
Balance of Power	1985	No	No	Simulation	Society
Lemonade Stand	1985	Yes	No	Strategy	Math
Oregon Trail	1985	Yes	Yes.	Adventure	Social studies
Where in World is Carmen Sandiego	1985	Yes	Yes	Adventure	Geography

Math Blaster	1986	Yes	Yes	Puzzle	Math
Mavis Beacon	1987	Yes	No	Action	Typing
Hidden Agenda	1988	No	No	Strategy	Social studies
Life & Death	1988	Yes	Yes	Simulation	Health
Reader Rabbits	1989	Yes	Yes	Puzzle	English
SimCity	1989	No	Yes	Strategy	Social studies
Balance of the Planet	1990	Yes	No	Simulation	Environment
Designasaurus I+II	1990	Yes	Yes	Adventure	Geology
Lemmings	1990	No	Yes	Puzzle	Cognitive
SimEarth	1990	No	Yes	Simulation	Geography
Super Munchers	1991	Yes	Yes	Action	Trivia
Civilization	1991	No	Yes	Strategy	History
Castle of Dr. Brain	1991	Yes	Yes	Puzzle	Science
Crystal Rain Forrest	1992	Yes	No	Puzzle	Programming
The Incredible Machine	1993	No	Yes	Puzzle	Science
Caesar	1993	No	Yes	Strategy	History
Dinopark Tycoon	1993	No	No	Strategy	Geology
SimHealth	1994	Yes	Yes	Simulation	Society
Freddie Fish	1994-	Yes	Yes	Adventure	Cognitive
Millie's Math House	1995	Yes	Yes	Puzzles	Math
Backpacker	1995	No	Yes	Adventure	Geography
Putt Putt Saves the Zoo	1995	Yes	Yes	Adventure	Cognitive
MS Magic School Bus Explores	1995	Yes	Yes	Adventure	Science
Logical Journey of the Zoombinis	1996	Yes	Yes	Puzzle	Cognitive
Pajama Sam	1996-	Yes	Yes	Adventure	Science
Dr Seuss Preschool	1999	Yes	Yes	Puzzle	English/Math
Roller Coaster Tycoon	1999	No	Yes	Strategy	Society
Virtual U	2000	Yes	No	Simulation	Administration
Lightspan	2000-	Yes	Yes	Adventure	English
The Sims	2000	No	Yes	Simulation	Society
Globetrotter 2	2001	No	Yes	Adventure	Geography
Freddi Fish 5: Creature of Coral	2001	Yes	Yes	Adventure	Math
Math Missions	2003	Yes	Yes	Adventure	Math
Jumpstart Study Helpers	2003	Yes	Yes	Adventure	Math/ English
Disney Learning 1st and 2nd grade	2003	Yes	Yes	Adventure	English

Table 2: Important titles over the years

Edutainment defines the market

In the mid-1990's some of the big edutainment brands that are still with us today are established and come to dominate the market: *Freddie Fish* (1994), *Putt Putt Saves the Zoo* (1995), *MS Magic School Bus Explores* (1995) and *Pajama Sam* (1996).

The titles that dominated the end of the millennium are hard to single out and many of them built on earlier well established brands. I will not go into detail with them, but mention the most important ones from a somewhat US-centric point. The edutainment games are now mostly centred upon pre-school children and early school age. They cover basic areas like arithmetic, reading, typing and, spelling. Most titles have close adherence to school curriculum in most major countries suggested by titles from the US, the UK and Sweden (Buckingham & Scanlon, 2002; Softbase, 2004; Veta, 2004). The most noticeable series and games are *Dr Seuss Preschool* (1999), *Oregon Trail* (2000), *Reader Rabbits* (2000), *Bioscopia* (2002), *Math Missions* (2003), *Jumpstart Study Helpers (2003)* and *Disney Learning* (2003). The brands formed in the mid-1990's also continue to be marketed. The majority of these titles fall under the edutainment label although some older republications are an exception.

Picture 7 and 8: Showing two of the best-selling educational computer games in the current market: Jump Start Study Helpers (2003) and Math Missions (2003).

The infatuation with fitting the educational computer games to existing curriculum has hardly helped the creative development in the market. The market is definitely suffering from a bad image and conservatism.

The twitch speed generation

In the mid-1990's the idea that computer games might fit well with the demands of a new generation is gaining momentum. It slowly gains a stronger foothold with the general enthusiasm for children's knack for digital learning and comes to challenge edutainment's narrow focus on curriculum content, but ends up promising even more doubtful potentials of educational computer games than proponents of edutainment. Supporters of the new twitch-speed approach talk about a Nintendo generation and twitch speed learning reflects this development (Gros, 2003; Hostetter, 2003; Papert, 1996; Prensky, 2001b; Provenzo, 1992).

The basic proposition is that new media is changing a generation's way of learning. The twitch speed generation is not comfortable concentrating on one task at a time, but is engaged in a variety of tasks at the same time. The traditional educational system is not challenging enough and is in opposition to this new way of learning. The following ten points are listed as characteristic of the new generation: twitch speed, parallel processing, graphics first, random access, connected, active, play, payoff, fantasy and technology-as-friend.

> This game generation is used to a twitch speed, parallel processing, active, fantasy world. Games have changed the learners' cognitive skills so that the game generation can process a lot of information at the same time. Video games are an excellent

learning tool because the computer can adjust its difficulty according to the player's preference or need

Hostetter (2003:1)

It has been suggested, although with little research backing, that computer games are well equipped to become learning devices for this new generation for example in relation to game's difficult levels (for a criticism of advantage of difficulty levels see appendix). Prensky (2001a) has especially been the proponent of this view in his book *Digital Game-based Learning*. The most important characteristics of computer games are their knack for engagement and interactive learning. The way these are put together is the real trick and Prensky sees a true potential in computer games for revolutionizing the educational system (Prensky, 2001a, 2004). This approach is currently the most optimistic and reflects a general increased interest in computer games for educational use. The main idea is that players through computer games learn important skills that are necessary to navigate in modern society, to cope with the increasing information bombardment and to acquire an alternative learning style. However, similar to edutainment the arguments lack substantiation and especially when applied to computer games glances over the challenges, focusing only on the potentials.

Edutainment is dead – long live educational computer games

In research circles there is emerging an understanding that in order to produce educational computer games beyond edutainment you must combine commercial game developers, educators and subject matter experts. This is reflected best with the initiatives of Education Arcade and Serious Games who aim to bring developers, educators and subject experts together through seminars, web-sites, conferences and joint development projects. Arguably, in the long run children are probably too smart to be cheated by the discount games that edutainment often are. If we look at computer game titles in general, that dominate the commercial hit charts, it is clear that these are not discount games, but are the result of state-of-the-art in all areas necessary to make a game.

Overall it actually seems like the educational computer games including edutainment to some degree are dying as a separate breed. Edutainment lives on through old brands, gameplay forms and is increasingly being seen as educational software. The links to the computer games industry have become weaker with the mergers over the years (see appendix). This process is probably also part of the explanation for the current lack of explicit focus on the gameness of edutainment. The structures they operate within are educational software, and this is an entirely different breed than computer games – to name a few important differences: educational software lacks the coolness of the game industry, the state-of-the art technology, the constant innovation in gameplay, but perhaps most importantly the basic desire to produce entertaining products beyond anything else.

Serious Games: A new movement in educational computer games

The starting point for modern educational game researchers is often a critique of edutainment as it manifested itself up through the 1980's and its continuing domination of the market. Such critique is important for building a better educational foundation for computer games. Edutainment started as a serious attempt to create computer games that taught children different subjects through computer games. Arguably, it ended as caricatures of computer games and a reactionary use of learning theory. The conservatism in educational computer games seems to be maintained by a vicious cycle leading to a still smaller target group: Limited investment results in little innovation and low quality eroding the market, which subsequently results in less investment (Egenfeldt-Nielsen, 2004).

However, in the new millennium a broader approach to education and computer games is becoming stronger, and educational computer games are re-emerging on the agenda as a serious topic. This is perhaps best illustrated by the increasing number of initiatives in the United States, the United Kingdom and the Nordic Countries[7]. These initiatives may provide the impetus for more innovation and higher quality products that can drive the market forward and get investors to take a new interest.

In the United States the Serious Games initiative is regularly hosting conferences between developers and researcher to discuss new roads for educational computer games and this is supported by another separate initiative, Education Arcade, with a similar agenda. Not least the Games-to-Teach project at MIT has put educational computer games on the agenda. Also the group of researchers at the University of Wisconsin-Madison including James Paul Gee and Kurt Squire is forming the field.

In the United Kingdom initiatives have been pushed more by government funding through Becta and Nesta Future Lab resulting in interesting new research and collaboration between industry and research. At the University of London several projects aimed at educational use of computer games are in the first phases, for example *The Making Games Project*. This is a three-year project that tries to develop author-ware for school children so they can design their own computer games (Facer, 2003; Oliver & Pelletier, 2004).

In the Nordic Countries Learning Lab Denmark is establishing a centre for educational games as an extension of several ambitious educational game products produced in collaboration between researchers and industry. At Malmö University in Sweden a project is also underway between a medical company and researchers to produce an educational computer game dealing with ethical dilemmas in the medical industry. At the IT-University of Copenhagen a research project to develop a new form of serious games is underway. The project centres on developing the prototype Global Conflicts: Middle East examining the problems in the design process of games that combine education and entertainment.

Most researchers in these projects share the belief that it is possible to go beyond earlier educational computer games with dubious learning experiences and limited technical platforms. The hope is to avoid common pit falls like separating learning content and computer game by focusing on a close integration of gameplay and learning experience. There is also a broader conception of the educational experience around the computer game. Rather than seeing educational computer games as operating in a social vacuum a socio-cultural understanding of the surrounding environment's importance is emerging. The learning experience is not limited to the interaction between player and game. This is most distinct in research by Gee (2003) and Squire (2004). There are several reasons why educational computer games are back on the agenda. A variety of sources serves to push this new order both on a society and individual level.

The first claim concerns the general increase in awareness and knowledge of computer games in the public. People are more subtle and open towards computer games and their influence on several levels. This is a consequence of the general higher percentage of the population playing computer games (The ESA, 2003). It means teachers are less sceptical, in-experienced and stigmatised when approaching computer games for educational use. Parents will also be more open towards educational computer games and the necessary competences to critically choose between good educational titles and less good ones are becoming more common. This forces the publishers to reconsider their 20 year old edutainment formula.

A second major influence is the general level of research in computer games, which is to say the least booming. Since 2001 we have seen the establishing of the Digital Game Research Association and an increase in conferences dedicated to research in computer games. The number has increased from zero to more than five conferences the culmination for the time being the first Digra conference – Level up in the Netherlands (Utrecht). We have seen the launch of the peer-reviewed journal Game-studies and the emergence of numerous research centres (see also the

---

[7] For links to the different initiatives see link section in appendix.

current state of games research in chapter 0). This general trend rubs off on research into educational computer games. Indeed, 2004, has seen more than five conferences relating to the educational potential of computer games and it does not seem to slow down.

Thirdly and this is perhaps the most controversial claim, given the game industry's obsession with better audiovisuals, game technology has reached a level, where we can make decent educational computer games within a reasonable budget. This discussion is wider but is supported by the establishment of the Games-to-Teach project's collaboration with Microsoft. This to some degree runs contrary to the general development in the game industry, where computer games are becoming increasingly expensive to produce (Newman, 2004; Vogel, 2001).

The fourth factor is the changing learning environment, where learning is expanded to the home and to the entire lifespan. The coining of terms like home learning, lifelong learning and supplementary training indicates a more flexible approach to learning (Aldrich, 2003; Buckingham & Scanlon, 2002; Egenfeldt-Nielsen, 2001). This calls for learning products that are capable of engaging people in more entertaining ways, as learners can choose to abstain from dedicating time to learning. In competition with other spare time activities, learning must live up to its best.

Conclusion: Edutainment is prevailing for now

This chapter has staged the scene for educational computer games outlining its roots, the significant changes, important titles and the current market conditions. The market is defined by the dominance of edutainment extending a long tradition from educational media. Since the 1980's edutainment has slowly overtaken the market, increasingly, giving less room for innovation and resulting in declining revenues. Educational computer games are fighting many of the same problems of earlier educational media and have still not found its form. These last few years we have seen new initiatives on the horizons that may change the nature of the market and its products, a development especially carried forward by a new research interest in the area.

Chapter II: Research into Educational use of Games and Simulations

> Some educators feel that the content of these games has educational value. Others are sceptical about the content of "pure" electronic games but acknowledge that the motivational game format could perhaps be the perfect packaging for otherwise mundane educational content. The idea of using games to package content predates electronic games altogether.

> (McGrenere, 1996:82)

The previous chapter looked at the influential ancestors to educational computer games, and outlined the history of educational computer games. However, one area deserves more attention, namely the research into educational use of non-electronic games. As indicated in the introduction this research tradition is quite strong and can help build a foundation for educational computer games use. The goal of the chapter is to identify the significant theoretical findings and discussions in research on educational use of games, which is recyclable for building a framework for educational use of computer games.

The chapter evolves around three key areas that are identified as the most important in previous research. The first key area is the *learning environment* for games, which is found to often have a number of unfortunate characteristics complicating the educational use of games. The second is the role of *personal learning factors*, which is found to be an overlooked area. Last, the *learning outcome* is examined, which shed light on the problems with measuring learning outcome from games.

It is concluded, that especially in relation to the more practical problems of teaching, one should be careful not to underestimate the difficulties. Problems like lesson plans, physical space, learning theory, importance of debriefing, and teacher qualifications are well described in the literature. In relation to learning outcome it is found that games may have something to offer, but we should not settle for just asking whether you learn from a game. Rather, we should ask the harder questions: who, what, why, and where do games work – this is equally important for computer games.

Several relevant insights are carried forward to the empirical study - we do not need to start from scratch when researching educational use of computer games.

Traditional games make their way into school

One of the first social studies games is the *Inter-Nation Simulation* from 1958 about international relations, where you play one of 5-7 hypothetical nations. Another one aimed at 11-years olds is *The Sumerian Game* from 1961, where you learn about some of the economic elements in Mesopotamia around 3500 BC. These are commonly referred to as simulations to differentiate them from games and stress their educational nature. In reality, however they are very close to our definition of games and share a lot of the same dynamics and problems, which was also discussed in the introduction (Gredler, 1992; Lee, 1994; Seidner, 1975; Wolfe & Crookall, 1998).

Simulations were not really in keeping with the trends within learning and education in the 1950's, when they started to appear. Simulations and games extended from learning theories prioritising appreciation of the underlying dynamics and processes of events rather than rote memorization of facts and principles. Games became a strong supplement to teaching by virtue of their concrete experiences leading to learning. Instead of being taught about topics students engaged with these topics and played them out. Thereby students make their own experiences and get feedback on their specific actions in a safe environment. This is believed to give a stronger experience drawing on especially the theories of David Kolb and John Dewey, which I will return to in chapter 5. Overall, games were believed to increase motivation, focus attention and change the teacher's role. The teacher is no longer the authority but facilitates the learning experience (Abt, 1968; Coleman, 1967; Coleman, 1973).

Another premise of educational use of games is the complex nature of games that potentially prepare students for the challenges in modern society. Traditional teaching methods are not conceived as capable of preparing students for the increased complexity in society and the learning skills necessary in real life. This overall approach to games' potential for facilitating alternative learning experiences is also clear in the previously mentioned twitch-speed approach to learning. The rationales for using computer games are often quite similar to the arguments brought forward above, when games were initially introduced in schools (Coleman, 1967).

Earlier research on non-electronic games: similarities and differences

The implications of using games for educational purposes have over the years been examined in numerous studies. The overview below attempts to identify some of the important trends that we should also look for when considering educational use of computer games. One of the main problems with the findings below is the problems with actually evaluating games. It has been questioned if it is at all possible to use traditional methods for measuring learning outcome, which will be addressed towards the end of the chapter (Druckman, 1995; Saegesser, 1981).

A frame for reviewing learning through games

The following examination of different important aspects of games promoting learning is based on the categories in earlier review studies. It has not been possible to go into detail with separate studies, but instead I aim to present the results from the most important overview articles over the years (Bredemeier & Greenblat, 1981; Clegg, 1991; Dempsey, Rasmussen, & Lucassen, 1996; Dorn, 1989; Druckman, 1995; Randel et al., 1992; Van Sickle, 1986; Wentworth & Lewis, 1973). It should be noted that the reviews are quite dated, which is perhaps a sign of the decline of research into educational games in favour of research on educational potential of computer games as argued in the introduction. I will supplement some areas with research studies of newer date to expand on areas not covered sufficiently in existing overview articles. The review is split into three areas. Each of these areas will be presented and discussed to give a status for the research field. They are also reflected on and used in the empirical studies presented later in the dissertation.

- Learning environment: What properties of a learning environment have a bearing on the learning outcome and what variables are important?

- Personal learning factors: What personal factors can play a role for the learning outcome of a specific game experience and how significant is the impact?

- Learning outcome: What are the effects of using games for learning within different areas and in relation to different domains of learning?

Before entering into the specifics of these areas it is worth considering more overall factors of the research like the type of games used in educational settings and prevalence within different subjects. It seems obvious games could lend themselves better to some subjects and that not all game genres have been equally used. Early on there were few studies comparing different game genres (Roberts, 1976) and this remains a problem. In a search for what game genres were encountered in research articles on simulation and gaming Dempsey et al. (1996), covering both computer games and traditional games, found 43 simulation games, 26 others, 10 adventures, 4 puzzles and 1 experimental. They attribute the large number of simulations to the history of the research area, which grew out of business and military training. The problem with their distinction is that the simulation category is quite broad, as simulation is in a majority of games an almost intrinsic property. Especially when we turn to computer games this category becomes very vague.

The scourge of the setting

The setting for educational games use is often the school and this holds certain problems related to the quite rigid structure of the educational system. Saegesser (1981; 1984) and Coleman (1973) point out that the time schedule, physical space, learning theory and existing role scripts hinder the use of games and this potentially influences the learning outcome. The time schedule in schools is not structured to accommodate games that stretch for hours and may be hard to keep within a specific time limit. Also the actual physical classroom causes problems, when you suddenly have more than 25 students playing actively. The existing theories of learning and teaching are neither very adapt for games as they favour for example classroom teaching. The precise impact of these factors is hard to access; however, we should be alert to implications derived from the overall structure in current educational systems.

Furthermore, Bredemeier & Greenblat (1981) and Dorn (1989) state that the attitude of the instructor towards games influences the outcome and that the instructor's knowledge and skill in using the game is also a factor. Also the concrete use of the game can change the outcome if the instructor uses a variation of the gameplay or introduces the game differently. For example, it is far from trivial whether a game is introduced as a competition or a joint exploration. The game experience can also suffer if it is regularly jeopardized by the teacher's lack of knowledge about the applicable rules in different game situations. It seems that the importance of the learning setting has been somewhat neglected in the research in the later years perhaps as a consequence of the more rich hunting fields in adult learning, especially business and military training. Here the constraints and traditions of learning are less tainted by the factors put forward above.

In his interesting article Dorn (1989) draws on earlier research to outline some factors for instructors to ensure that they achieve the best setting for facilitating learning when using games. Dorn stresses that games should not be the only teaching style in a course, but should be supported by other teaching methods having clear educational aims. Depending on the use and timing of games in a course, they can serve different purposes, for example games at the beginning of a course can serve to introduce theory, core concepts or provide some shared concrete experience, while giving the students a way to know each other. More specifically the instructor should have some experience with the games used, be skilled in administering the game, have a desire to use the game, keep in mind the role scripts in the class, be able to perform debriefing, evaluate different games and be aware of the physical limits with regard to time and space in school. These seem like basic and reasonable demands, however they may prove much harder to implement in real life (Dorn, 1989; Elder, 1973).

The complexity that opens up with the many variables in the learning environment is staggering and quite overwhelming for anyone with a practical focus. Even though they might not all be cleared away they are certainly worth considering, when planning on teaching a course with computer games or setting up a research design on educational use of computer games.

Personal learning factors

The role of personal characteristics has been examined to some degree although Dempsey et al. (1996:12) find that in reality studies are "very unclear in reporting these characteristics". In their review the most frequently reported variables were gender, age, academic ability and to some degree race. The limited reporting of such characteristics is quite interesting as the early work in the field stress the importance of individual differences (Greenblat & Duke, 1981). These individual characteristics are interesting by themselves but also important in examining a sample to minimize method problems related to matched samples research design (Remus, 1981). The matched samples design is often a given experimental set-up as you must conduct the study within the existing class structure in schools, where randomisation of sample is difficult. The fact that basic factors like age, race, gender and academic ability are only cited in approximately 25% of the studies indicates that the problem is not very high on the research agenda.

It is argued that games might be a way to reach students with weaker academic abilities. According to Coleman et al. (1973) games are more effective for students with high academic ability. However, Bredemeier & Greenblat (1981) find more mixed results and point out that games *may* be able to reach less advantaged student groups but this depends on a variety of factors. They especially point out that the prior attitude of the student towards games plays a role. In consequence it seems the less advantaged students may benefit from games, but primarily if they are initially favourable towards educational games – maybe not that surprising.

Other indications of the role of personal factors are the structure of the group in relation to size organization and relations between students. The argument is that the composition of the group facilitates different learning experiences while adding to the dynamics in both the environment and for the specific student, for example winners and losers of the game have very different experiences. It seems that the initial group cohesion is quite important for the performance in a game environment and remains relatively stable as the game progresses. Some studies indicate that the initial attitude of the students is of limited consequence for the performance, whereas group cohesion is central (Bredemeier & Greenblat, 1981; Clegg, 1991; Wellington & Faria, 1996).

One area that has received little attention is the importance of earlier experiences with games, which could be expected to play a role for the learning outcome. Knowledge and experience with playing games makes it possible for students to concentrate on playing the game, and, consequently spending less time mastering a new learning form. This is an area that becomes even more relevant in relation to computer games with more complex interfaces and larger variations in student experiences with computer games.

A Procrustean bed: assessing learning outcome

The question of the precise learning outcome from educational use of games is one of the areas, which has received the most attention over the years within the research area of educational use of games: How can we measure the learning effect of games on students? As I have implied in the introduction this question is far too broad and needs to be qualified with: "For what purpose, under what conditions and how can we be sure" (Bredemeier & Greenblat, 1981:307). This also implies that the interesting question is not whether we learn from games, but rather if this learning experience is better under some conditions, for some users, for some purposes and if the nature of what we learn is different. I have tried to clear the way for these questions in the sections above and try to give a general verdict on the learning outcome associated with games in the following.

The list of claims for what games can do is very long, even as early as 1981 when Greenblat sums it up. Greenblat's (1981) list is too long to reproduce here, but in short forms it spans two pages with 30 different claims. The 30 claims and other claims over the years[8] have been hard to document due to problems with measuring learning in a school context and to construct methods for measuring learning from games in accordance with existing dominating theories on learning. It has also been pointed out that several studies in general are flawed, challenging the findings on learning outcome so far (Dorn, 1989; Wolfe & Crookall, 1998). Evaluation problems have been clear from early on, but continue to influence the research.

Bredemeier & Greenblat (1981) and Dorn (1989) point out the necessity of awareness towards the basic learning theory we ascribe to and what assessment is feasible to confirm learning outcome within the chosen theoretical frame for understanding learning. One choice relates to what signs of learning we accept and as Saegesser (1981) points out, many learning theories with strong backing

---

[8] For example the claims at Educational Simulations' web-site www.creativeteachingsite.com/edusims.html

in schools put external signs of learning over more subtle forms. Although these notions of warning are more than 20 years old, they still hold true although the theoretical landscape of learning has changed. We still run the risk of not realising the full potential of games if we try to put them into the Procrustean bed of specific learning theories. On the other hand we need to be specific about the learning outcome we expect and identify alternative ways for measuring learning. Otherwise the learning may become repetitive, undocumented, confusing and point in different directions, which is a very real risk when using games for teaching (Elder, 1973).

The assessment of learning has given rise to numerous problems over the years. One of the most persistent is the lack of taking the most basic factors into consideration when conducting a study. Wolfe & Crookall (1998) have argued for more qualitative methods and a more critical stance towards an automatic acceptance of traditional research designs for educational research, which is also stressed by Bergman (2003). Others also encourage the establishment of a basic foundation for pursuing research, for example a clear definition of games and a shared taxonomy of games. Some within the research field also find that researchers with educational research backgrounds are in short supply although such a background is found necessary to conduct rigorous research on educational use of games (Wolfe & Crookall, 1998).

Wolfe & Crookall (1998) list nine goals that draw on traditional research methods in educational theory, but are less suitable for studying games. Some of the principles that are challenged when studying games are control groups receiving placebo, all course sections being identical and that tests should be administered under optimal circumstances is questioned. They conclude that this is almost impossible in relation to games due to their open-ended and flexible structure. Problems may however arise from this approach. The principles are important because the validity and reliability of the study is otherwise compromised. Or in other words, you might just as well not perform the study because you won't know what you are studying and if your results are just a fluke.

There is some consensus that three areas need to be measured to gauge learning outcome in a given game. The overall variable is substantive learning, which can be both learning about a subject or about oneself (cognitive and affective). When assessment of learning outcome is divided into cognitive and affective we can distinguish between different domains of knowledge and learning methods extending from the outline in the introduction. The split between cognitive and affective is also sometimes seen as the division between on one hand specific skills and on the other hand more general principles, concepts and orientations. The problems with distinguishing between these two areas have influenced game research from the start and the problem is shared with other educational research (Bredemeier & Greenblat, 1981; Elder, 1973). The two other areas that as a minimum should be assessed are those having a bearing on the overall variable learning outcome. These are motivation to learn and the relation between students and teacher. Most of these variables are taken into consideration in serious new studies (i.e. Kashibuchi, 2001).

The outcome of cognitive and affective learning

The reviews are not consistent in their conclusions on learning outcome, but in general it can be concluded from reviews that: In some instances games seem to be more appropriate for affective learning, while cognitive learning in general is found to be as good as other teaching methods (excluding retention over time) (Bredemeier & Greenblat, 1981; Butler et al., 1988; Butler, 1988; Dorn, 1989; Druckman, 1995; Lee, 1994; Randel et al., 1992; Van Sickle, 1986)

The review by Dempsey et al. (1996) following Gagne's taxonomy[9] show that the cognitive ability problem-solving is the most researched learning outcome followed by the more general affective

---

[9] The taxonomy includes attitude, motor skills, cognitive strategy, problem solving, rules, defined concepts, verbal information, and other skills.

ability attitudes. This implies that in general much of the research has been aimed at identifying learning outcome in more overall competences and not necessarily the learning outcome of facts and concepts. This also ties well in with the overweight of research in social sciences, where problem solving and attitudes have traditionally been an important area (Abt, 1968:70-71).

The success of math games reported by Randel et al. (1992) runs to some degree counter to this, as math is a subject that also teaches very specific skills. The review concludes that the most successful learning outcome is achieved in games with very specific required skills. This implies that it may be relevant to revisit games for learning more specific skills, for example in algebra, physics, chemistry and grammar rules. However, positive findings on specific skills may also be due to the methods used for measuring learning outcome. As discussed above measurement of learning outcome tends to favour specific facts and skills over more complex knowledge acquired in more general games as discussed previously.

The increased retention over time of learning appears to be one of the most consistent findings within the research areas (Bredemeier & Greenblat, 1981; Randel et al., 1992; Van Sickle, 1986); however Dorn (1989) challenges this claim, citing older studies that show no difference in retention over time. However, the newer and more thorough study by Randel et al. (1992) supports the claim for better retention over time. Although not all the studies in the meta-analysis by Randel et al. (1992) examined retention over time the ones that did, in general found a better retention over time compared to traditional teaching methods. This leads to different speculations to the origin of this increased retention. When considering retention most of the above researchers relate better retention to the higher motivation, interest and relevance experienced when using games for educational purposes.

Conclusion: Implications for researching educational use of computer games?

We have seen that games are used in very different subjects with varying degrees of success. You may end up concluding that games have been used in almost every imaginable setting, subject and age group and you would not be entirely wrong. I have painted a somewhat positive picture of the area and it is worth remembering that the reviews of the area are somewhat contradictory especially in relation to learning outcome.

One explanation for the conflicting results is that we are talking about an object of study that is too wide. The difference between role-play games and simulations is not trivial. When we approach computer games we should be alert to this problem. It does matter what genre of games we are studying and, furthermore, we can have a large number of badly designed games. We should be careful not to equate a specifically bad or extraordinary game with a general claim for using games for learning. A lot of the early studies on educational use of games were based on titles developed by fiery souls and with little training in designing games. The designers of these first educational games were learning as they went along and the results are still with us today. These results may not show problems with games for education per se, but rather with specifically badly designed games.

There are still a lot of problems left, when we look at the research on learning and games, but it would be a shame if we didn't build on the rich results from the early days to achieve a strong foundation for studying educational use of computer games. The above review does indicate that educational computer games may be a worthwhile area to study as the research into educational simulations and games in general is quite positive. We should, however, be alert to some of the problems that transfer from games to computer games in an educational setting. The findings below should be taken into consideration when approaching the field of computer games.

Domain	Factors to consider
Learning environment	Awareness of the impact of time schedule, physical space, debriefing, learning theory and existing role scripts.
	Teacher's attitude, general skill, specific knowledge.
	Variations in gameplay and introduction of the game.
Personal learning factors	Individual in relation to gender, age, academic ability, race and game experience.
	Group matters in relation to size organization and relations between students.
	May promote underachievers more than traditional teaching methods.
Learning outcome	Methods for measuring should be game specific, problems with basic principles for quantitative designs.
	Assesses basic influencing factors on learning outcome: motivation and student-teacher relation
	Different domain of learning i.e. cognitive and affective
	Learning theories favour overt signs of learning

Chapter III: Empirical study on School Use of Games in Denmark

Teachers are responsible for providing an opportunity. Students are responsible for learning.

David Ellis

This chapter provides the last piece of background for the dissertation by looking at teachers' perception of advantages and disadvantages in relation to computer games in education, and collecting teachers' experiences with the educational use of computer games.

From the previous chapters we have little feeling for the actual use of computer games in educational settings, and how teachers perceive computer games. Therefore, it seems natural to gather information through a survey on precisely how and to what extent computer games are used in the educational system. There is a belief in some circles that computer games do not play a role in education; however, this primarily derives from anecdotes and educated guesses. We lack precise information on the actual educational use, which is probably partly responsible for the somewhat glorified picture concerning the educational potential of computer games. A survey of the existing practice will result in indications of the limits and potentials of educational use of computer games, which so far have remained buried.

The survey was taken by 43 teachers with a broad background within the Danish educational system. In general, the experiences with computer games are quite limited, and happen without changing teaching practice. The main advantages are the increased motivation and the alternative presentation of computer games. The disadvantages are mainly the quality of the titles, and teachers feeling they lack knowledge of the relevant titles. The chapter concludes that the use of educational use of computer games is limited, and that so far the disadvantages outnumber the advantages. The results are found to be in line with a study conducted by British researchers (McFarlane, Sparrowhawk, & Heald, 2002).

Method Considerations

The results are obtained through a short quantitative survey administered over the internet. The survey is kept short so all teachers feel comfortable completing the survey. Only participants who have answered the majority of questions (above 75%) are included in the data analysis.

Participants

The participants are randomly selected by sending out letters and e-mails to schools found through www.krak.dk (a Danish electronic phone book). The geographic distribution is satisfactory, representing most areas of Denmark.

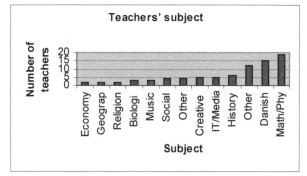

Figure 2: Shows the subjects the participating teacher's taught. Teacher could choose more than one subject.

It should up front be stressed that the sample is relatively small and more than anything describes Danish teachers' expectations as many of the participant did not actually have experience with using computer games. The participants were 43 teachers from elementary schools (6-16 years) and secondary schools (15-20 years). The survey indicates a higher preference among math/physics teachers to participate in the survey. The participants could choose more than one subject that they taught, usually teachers have 2-3 subjects they teach (Figure 2).

The age mean of the participating teachers was 45.5 years with a standard deviation of 10.1. Gender is relatively equally distributed with 24 men and 19 women, although male teacher were not expected to outnumber female teachers.

Method problems

The study failed to really gather a lot of information on concrete experiences with teachers' use of computer games in an educational setting. Of the 43 participants only nine have concrete experience with games. Among these only one has concrete experiences with actual educational use of computer games, while the other teachers refer to game-like applications. The survey primarily shows how teachers perceive computer games and why they don't engage with them. Few of the participants can be said to have deep knowledge of teaching with computer games. We should, therefore, be careful to interpret the data beyond describing teachers' initial experiences and preferences for using computer games for educational purposes.

There is a small overweight of male math/science teachers in the sample, which indicates that the sample is somewhat skewed. Math/science teachers do not make up the majority of teachers in the Danish educational system. This is probably due to self-selection and may influence the results, for example technical problems connected to using computer games for teaching may be less clear in this study, as math/science teachers often have higher proficiency in information technology. Earlier studies have found that math/science teachers in general have embraced information technology to a higher degree than other teacher groups. Furthermore, they are more positive towards information technology than other teacher groups (Egenfeldt-Nielsen, 2001). There also exists a historical affinity between math/science and computer games due to the technical challenges involved in producing computer games. It has been suggested that the predominance of male players to a certain degree arises out of this relation between math/science and computer games (Cassel & Jenkins, 1998). Therefore, it is more likely that this group of teachers will have private experiences with computers, computer games or programming, which gives them a head start in understanding and using computer games for education.

We should also notice that there may be an overweight of teachers interested in computer games, although reduced by offering small cash prizes for recruiting teachers. The incentive for teachers with no computer games experience was also stressed in the letters, e-mails and posters distributed.

The low response rate, considering that the letters and e-mails were sent to 150 schools, typically with between 20 and 40 teachers, is also a problem and to some degree probably reflects the cultural position of computer games, as, despite significant changes over the years, a teenage, violent and waste-of-time phenomenon.

The educational prevalence of computer games and experiences of teachers

The survey indicates that most uses of commercial computer games in Denmark are on an experimental level, for example the use of *Counter-Strike* and *The Sims* at Højby School. Other research projects involving computer games have been Learning Lab Denmark's *Brainbuilders* and *Tracks*, where you try to introduce science in a meaningful way through role-play and computer games simulations (EMU, 2004). Attempts have also been made that take a cross-curricular approach and integrate computer games in the existing curriculum. One example of this trend is the production of the Danish teaching material titled *Behind Computer Games* consisting of background book, idea catalogues and web-site with web resources on computer games. The teaching material is cross-disciplinary and attempts to draw on existing methods and content in different subjects (Egenfeldt-Nielsen, 2003a). Another recent attempt is the national game industry trade organisation's launch of a web-site with a similar goal (Multimedieforeningen, 2004). Also the 5th dimension project conducted on an youth centre in Denmark utilized computer games as one activity to engage children with learning in alternative ways (Sørensen, 2001). There has also been made an accompanying teaching material to the Danish commercial adventure game *Blackout* with some success. Another group of educational use evolves around health organisations' attempt to reach schools, for example with the games *Foodman* and *Cell Fight*. Another similar example is the marketed of a computer game by the national council on electricity to teach children better habits when using electric appliances. Finally, there is the game *Global Island* that attempts to teach students about globalisation and democracy (Mellemfolkeligt Samvirke, 2003).

Despite a number of attempts with computer games the qualitative data from the survey indicates a lack of experience in using computer games in an educational setting. The experiences are often related to quite simple use of computer games or few limited experimental attempts at using computer games for a specific topic. Few really have experience with computer games in school and especially experiences beyond running 1-2 courses with computer games are lacking.

According to the survey there is a lack of excellent teaching experiences, although all teachers are fairly positive. The positive experiences are mostly related to use of computer games that are easily integrated into the current teaching practice and some quite basic simulations developed by the Danish educational publisher UNI-C. The examples below are from the survey, where teachers' described their experiences with educational use of computer games in an educational setting:

> Teacher A: I have in Physics used different games in connection with electricity laws and nuclear physics. It is my experience that most students easier understand the physical laws in the mentioned topics, when they are allowed to play with them.

> Teacher B: I have done a course in Danish on computer games with special focus on the Danish produced game Blackout (Deadline) four times. Every time it has been a satisfactory success. Only technical problems (mostly at home with the students) have led to difficulty.

> Teacher C: Religion: Expedition in the Bible: It takes a very long time… Most students thought it was both educational and funny. Students who played themselves were very quick.

> Teacher D: I regularly use game-like language exercises.

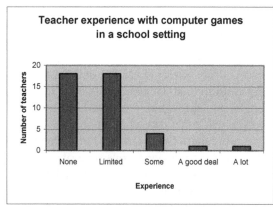

Figure 3: Shows the number of teachers that has experience with using computer games in a school setting.

The general computer game type in educational experiences found in this study falls within one of four somewhat arbitrary categories: Simulations, language practice, adventure games and edutainment. Except for one educational experience all the computer games used are specially designed for an educational setting.

The group of teachers who play computer games see themselves as quite capable, although not expert players. It seems necessary to have some knowledge and liking for computer games to introduce them in teaching. Playing computer games is not widespread among teachers both reflected in weekly play (Figure 3) and qualitative statements like Teacher E who states "It is seen as unconstructive nonsense by some colleagues". Even when teachers do play computer games the genres played differs from students. The genre preferred by teachers is strategy followed by simulation, which is not the most popular among students. Here we find a higher preference for action, although the preference of students changes as they grow older (Egenfeldt-Nielsen & Smith, 2000).

Figure 3 and 4 show that use of computer games is still trailing somewhat behind the use of non-electronic games (Figure 4). It is especially clear that there is a group of teachers who have been using non-electronic games to a great extent as the category 'a lot' is different for games and computer games use. This might indicate that they find non-electronic computer games less cumbersome and overall easier to fit into the school setting. Obviously, the technical barriers are not present with traditional games compared to computer games. However, the teachers using games might have changed their teaching practice to better fit using games and could prove a good group to target if educational computer games are to become more widespread.

Figure 4: Teachers' experiences with non-electronic games in a school setting.

Most teachers in this survey actually seem to be quite unaware of the special demands on teaching with computer games. In general, they perceived computer games as fitting within the current teaching practice. This parallels experiences with information technology where teachers would only later experience how computers changed the balance between teacher and students, the role of teacher and the perception of what constituted knowledge (Egenfeldt-Nielsen, 2001; Lopez, 2002; Veen, 1995).

The prevalence patterns of use in Denmark are similar to findings from a study in United Kingdom by the government-sponsored body, Becta. Kirriemuir & McFarlane (2002) summed up the different uses of computer games and the titles used for different purposes. They found that the following characteristics applied to the use:

- Edutainment was the most prevalent computer game type.

- Simple simulations games were used in some places.

- When commercial computer was used it was pc-games opposed to console games.

- Computer games were mostly common in schools in US, mainland Europe and Australia. UK use was mostly described as experimental.

The survey on Danish teachers presented here had smaller prevalence of edutainment. Still edutainment is quite dominant, and most alternatives to edutainment mentioned by teachers adopt the same basic learning approach. It should be noted that the somewhat limited use of edutainment in Denmark can have several explanations. First, the UK has a larger market for edutainment due to its population and edutainment needs to be tailored to the curriculum and translated to fit into a specific national educational system. The transfer and adaptation is hard in Denmark (and most other small countries) with a smaller population than the UK. Second, the Danish educational system has quite a small tradition for digital educational material targeted at specific curriculum goals compared both to the UK and the US. Third, the UK experiences a push for using computer games to deliver content represented by for example the *MaxTrax* and *Runner* games used for bringing people back into the educational system (Kambouri, 2003), and partly the approach taken by Teachers Evaluating Educational Multimedia (McFarlane et al., 2002) for providing information on computer games with useful curriculum content.

Next, we will look at what advantages and disadvantages teachers saw in relation to educational use of computer games. This will shed some light on why the prevalence of educational use of computer games remains quite small.

Teacher perception of disadvantages in using computer games in education

According to the teachers in this study the primary drawback to computer games is the quality of the available titles on the market (Figure 5). A third of the teachers consider this a disadvantage and this is strangely enough in some opposition to the second disadvantages, the lack of knowledge of computer games.

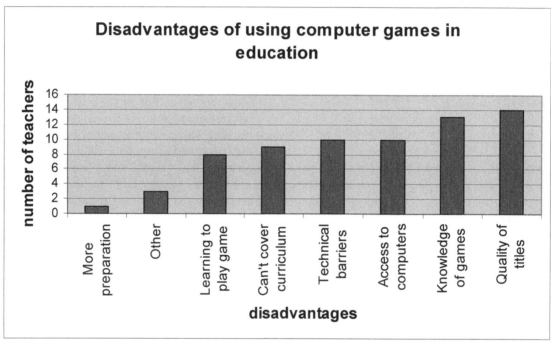

Figure 5: Show the disadvantages as they were perceived among the teachers in the empirical study.

It is interesting that even though teachers know little about games, they still know enough to say that the quality is too low. This is clearly a wake-up call to the producers of educational game titles. However, relying on better titles may be a too limited approach that echoes the earlier discussion on the lack of computer games for girls. For a long time there was a too narrow focus on computer games not addressing the interests of girls, being a male universe. Despite heavy research and specific girl titles this did little to integrate girls into computer games (Cassel & Jenkins, 1998; Egenfeldt-Nielsen & Smith, 2000). There exists a connection between computer game titles and cultural positions, not changed over night. The producers of educational computer games would certainly design different titles if there was a market; on the other hand the market needs these titles to push the development.

There seems to be a bit of a deadlock where educators are very much conceiving educational computer games within a simple framework, not willing to change teaching practice. Teachers' conservatism makes it hard for other types of educational titles to penetrate the market[10]. Other

---

[10] I have elsewhere described this as the edutainment market's vicious cycle (Egenfeldt-Nielsen, 2004)

types of computer games will be more advanced and demand more changes to teaching practice. Technical problems and access is already a big problem and will probably increase if edutainment titles are exchanged for more advanced titles. The more advanced titles demand better hardware, have a steeper learning curve and are usually more complex to use (Vandeventer, 1997).

Teachers also mention the problem about covering the curriculum when using computer games and this may point to the cultural perception of computer games in large not being relevant to education. It may also reflect the problems with using computer games designed for other purposes. However, the best explanation is perhaps the tendency for computer games in some sense to focus on a narrow part of curriculum. Computer games will focus on some aspects and let you play with these, but ignore other elements. On one hand this gives you a deeper understanding of the simulated aspects in the computer games, but it also implies a superficiality as you will miss elements that would otherwise be presented in traditional teaching. This conflict was also clear in the later empirical study, where it will be more thoroughly addressed (see chapter 8).

In the qualitative comments teachers in a British study (McFarlane et al., 2002) continuously mentioned the attitude and perception of computer games. The pressure from other colleagues and the reservations towards the relevance of computer games were marked. It was also suggested that the gameplay would be prioritised above the subject, a well-known problem from other research (see chapter 4). A final very down-to-earth barrier mentioned is the cost of class-sets, which is at least the same price as books. This can be further complicated by existing school licensing agreements that may have certain restrictions of exclusivity.

The above results are also supported by British studies (Kirriemuir & McFarlane, 2002; McFarlane et al., 2002). The disadvantages and problems with computer games have recently been studied quite intensely in a study by the organisation TEEM (Teachers Evaluating Educational Multimedia) (McFarlane et al., 2002). The results from this study are more qualitative, but support the findings above. Related to teachers' expectations and overall barriers Kirriemuir & McFarlane (2002) find that many teachers recognized the learning potential of computer games, but the cultural position of computer games held them back. Concerns also surfaced around learning new hardware and maintenance issues. These areas seemed to be an important hindrance, which was also clear in my study.

Teacher perception of advantages in using computer games in education

Despite the many disadvantages teachers also find a lot of advantages. The most consistent attraction of using computer games was found to be motivation, which was selected by almost half of the teachers. Still this is apparently not the Holy Grail for all teachers, which is somewhat surprising considering the continuing emphasis on motivation in the research literature (Gee, 2003; Malone & Lepper, 1987a; Prensky, 2001b, 2004). Motivation is still the main incentive, but apparently not for all, and most of the teachers mention other advantages along with motivation (Figure 6).

The advantage mentioned by second-most teachers was perhaps surprisingly the ability of computer games to present material in another way. This is a broad topic, but it is interesting that computer games are not only perceived as a way to make students more motivated and things more interesting. It is appreciated that computer games can be used for something else than other teaching material, a quality that seems necessary if computer games are to get a firmer grip on educators. This finding is not really supported by other research on teacher experiences where the presentation of subject material in computer games is mostly found problematic and superficial. In the study by McFarlane, Sparrowhawk & Heald (2002) the focus on computer games is mostly on motivation, increased interest and collaboration around the computer games.

The third most selected advantage is the interest in the topic, which runs along the same lines of motivation, but is more related to the subject taught. Interest also has a more long-term and broader effect than motivation that goes beyond the actual use of the computer game. Motivation is more limited to the concrete playing experience here and now.

The fourth advantage relates to the general learning environment as being more favourable. It is interesting that learning environment, peer-collaboration and student autonomy is not seen as an advantage by more teachers as it is prominent in Danish research circles (i.e. Jessen, 2001; Sørensen, 2000). This indicates that the teachers are very much conceiving the use of educational computer games within a quite traditional framework, where the focus is on the concrete relation between player and game. Computer games are not seen as a new potential teaching practice informed by the unique characteristics of computer games. Teachers do not expect computer games to be capable of supporting the social interaction that is often stressed as one of the traits of computer games culture and which is increasingly becoming a part of educational computer game research (Jessen, 2001; Newman, 2004). On the other hand, they do see the potential for computer games presenting material in alternative ways. But this is very much related to the computer game in itself, not to a different teaching practice.

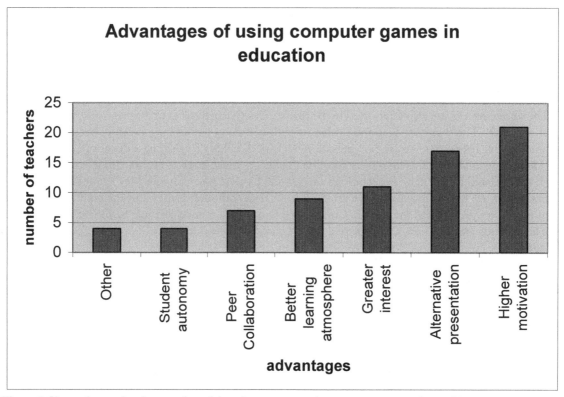

Figure 6: Shows the teachers' perception of the advantages to using computer games in teaching.

Other advantages mentioned in qualitative comments by different teachers were greater depth in a given topic, the simulation aspects in computer games and other ways to 'tell' a story than the traditional literature.

Conclusion: Low prevalence, conservative use and many obstacles

Summing up we can conclude that the educational use of computer games is not very widespread and mostly within a somewhat simple framework. A number of different structural limitations exist in the school system: Teachers' competences, technical barriers, administrative boundaries and general perception of computer games in society. This may be painting a grim picture, but nevertheless we need to realize that computer games are not neutral objects that can seamlessly be inserted into schools. The next chapter will build a theoretical foundation for understanding different kinds of educational use of computer games.

Part 2: Theoretical foundation

This part forms the foundation for the main empirical study and the final theory on educational use of computer games. The focus is on a variety of studies, looking at the educational potential of computer games supplemented with basic theory on education, learning and teaching.

Chapter IV: Standing on the Shoulders of Giants: Overview of the Research on Educational Use of Computer Games

> Research into the use of mainstream games in education is relatively novel, but growing rapidly. Research is mainly concerned with the development of related competences and literacies during game play or the role of games in the formation of learning communities either while gaming or related to game play.

> (Kirriemuir & McFarlane, 2003:3)

Part 1 gave the background for building a framework for educational use of computer games, but without really getting much into the specific research on educational use of computer games. The findings presented in this chapter are important pieces in establishing the field of educational use of computer games, while informing the empirical studies and theoretical work later in the dissertation. The area is split into several themes that have influenced the area and they represent very different approaches to the object of study. More than anything it illustrates the breadth and potential of educational computer games. The chapter's goal is to present an elaborate overview, contributing to developing an appreciation for previous research results, and identifying the key areas for understanding the use of computer games in educational settings.

The chapter starts by looking at the early research in the area, which extends from instructional technology with a strong focus on motivation. Edutainment extends from this research, but simplifying the results of instructional technology. The conservatism in relation to learning theory and gameplay makes edutainment a winner commercially but increasingly unpopular among researchers. Researchers, looking at math and science, challenge edutainment with inspiration from constructionism. Other researchers turn to adventure games for a different learning experience. However, over the years both of these research groups become less of a challenge for edutainment. The latest research approach, named 3rd generation, extends from a socio-cultural and constructionist starting point, where educational use of computer games is not seen as located in the educational title. Rather, educational use of computer games is seen as an activity that is accomplished in the interplay between game, student, context, and teacher. Based on the upcoming overview the following six key areas are identified: 1). Learning vs. playing, 2). Drill-and-practice games vs. microworlds, 3). Transfer vs. construction, 4). Teacher intervention vs. No teacher intervention, 5). Depth vs. superficiality, 6). One subject vs. cross-subjects.

The chapter concludes that the research into educational use of computer games has gone through three generations, although not in strict chronological order as the generations overlap. The 1st generation maintains a narrow focus on learning as the computer game filling players up with knowledge. The 2nd generation perspective is more inclusive, trying to understand the more complex processes between player and computer game. We are now beginning to see the 3rd generation become more dominating, where player, computer game, teacher and context all become important element for understanding educational use of computer games.

Do we need an overview of studies on educational use of computer games?

There exists few attempts at overviewing the field of educational use of computer games and most are dated, aimed at a specific area or have a profound skewedness towards educational use of traditional games. The field is scattered without internal consistency, few successful applications and questionable research. The first overviews of the research areas have appeared within the last 10 years, but have not delivered much in terms of overview (i.e. Cavallari, Hedberg, & Harper, 1992; Dempsey et al., 1996; McGrenere, 1996). Some of the obvious problems within the field, even the more serious attempts are: 1). A lack of division between different ways of using computer games. 2). Weak theoretical knowledge of computer games. 3). Underdeveloped theory for facilitating learning. 4). Confusion about the educational area. 5) Incomplete literature due to the variety in terminology, publication places, and researcher backgrounds. Lately, we have seen some more ambitious attempts at surveying the area however they suffer from the same problems, only covering parts of the area although coming further down the road than previous reviews (i.e. Bergman, 2003; de Freitas, 2005; Kirriemuir & McFarlane, 2003; Mitchell & Savill-Smith, 2004).

There are good reasons for the lack of overview, mainly the cross-disciplinary nature of the field encompassing a wide area of disciplines. To make matters worse the closest established research field, computer game research, is still just learning to walk and remains fragmented despite converging trends (see introduction). The area of education and learning has a longer, more solid tradition, but is overwhelming to overview and hard for researchers to get a handle on. In effect the area of education and learning supports the fragmentation. One researcher may use a constructivist approach, whereas another will draw on behaviourist theories, both without knowing the opposite theoretical background.

The overview could have been structured in different ways, but I choose to maintain the thematic areas that slowly surfaced during the research to show the different satellites around the research field, educational use of computer games (Figure 7). This is also to underline that these areas do in fact have next to no exchange of findings between each other.

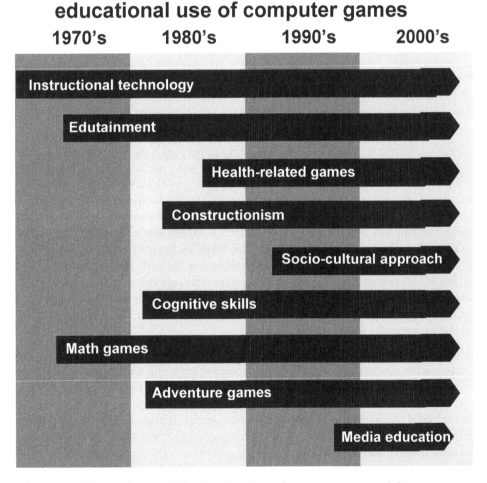

Figure 7: Shows the different themes within educational use of computer games and there emergence.

The early basic research on educational use of computer games

This research overview starts by looking at the early insights into educational use of computer games from instructional technology research and how these insights slowly become more twisted in edutainment.

Instructional technology launches the research interest

When computers were first introduced in classrooms in the United Stated the learning principles were drawn from behavioural theory and thinking and inspired by previous experiences with television for education. The first computer games for educational purposes were naturally strongly coloured by the learning approach to computers, which instructional theory attempts to change by examining educational use of computer games in their own right. Over the years instructional technology strongly influenced educational computer games research, although the somewhat narrow focus on motivation has gone a bit out of fashion in research circles.

The theoretical background for instructional theory was supplied by the American educational psychologist, Edward L. Thorndike, in the beginning of the 20th century. His work initially concentrated on animal learning, but was expanded to human learning. His major achievement was the introduction of the concepts reward and punishment. Not content with the narrow focus on practice or repetition he stressed that feedback was a strong tool for shaping the learning experience. Thorndike argues that instruction of a given individual was necessary to support the connection of what should be linked and to discourage things that don't go together. The stimuli presented to the learner should not be random, but based on the learner's experience and feedback adjusted consequently (Saettler, 1968). Thorndike's account of future progress in instruction from 1912 is strikingly similar to educational software today:

> If, by a miracle of mechanical ingenuity, a book could be so arranged that only to him
> who had done what was directed on page one would page two become visible and so
> on, much that now requires personal instruction could be managed by print.

Thorndike in 1912 (Quoted in Saettler, 1968:52)

Thorndike believed books and teachers each had their place in education. Teachers should not be used for conveying information that a book might as well supply. Instead a teacher should through insight and sympathy guide the student (Saettler, 1968). The importance of social context was, although somewhat appreciated, not well-integrated in his theory. Reflection was neither very explicit in Thorndike's thinking, but is forcefully introduced by his contemporary John Dewey who attempts to set a new course for education. Dewey influences the early movement in instructional technology, but his contributions are watered down over the years before re-emerging again after the cognitive revolution had slowed down. I will not go deeper into Dewey's thinking here, but the dissertation's next chapter presents him as part of the attempt to reframe our understanding of educational use of computer games.

The design of computer games in accordance with instructional theory somewhat accounts for the rigid and conservative educational use of computer games that is still with us today. The theoretical heritage is apparently hard to throw away, especially because it is an easy starting point for designing educational computer games. Thorndike's prophecy in the quote above attests to the link between instructional theory and educational computer games. It is possible to actually change the feedback to the student playing a computer game or using educational software based on previous input. The educational software, especially computer games with the strong rewards, is the dream of Thorndike come true.

Another trend in early instructional theory is the focus on overt behaviour that Skinner is especially a proponent for, when his theory catches on in educational circles during the 1950's. Only overt actions are interesting in a learning perspective not any thoughts, understanding or reflection that may or may not happen. In 1958, Skinner actually did build a drill-and-practice machine resembling later edutainment titles. Behaviourism implies a narrow focus on the ping-pong between player and computer games – the computer game will ask a question and the player will answer. When the question and answer are linked enough times resulting in reward, learning will occur. The player getting the question 2+3 answering 5 and getting points as reward will learn algebra. There are, of course, a number of problems with the behaviouristic approach, which is the reason why the theoretical learning landscape has changed since those days. A behaviouristic approach is most useful, when we are studying less complex learning phenomena. The complexity involved in figuring out a riddle cannot be boiled down to a number of random attempts of which one will slowly be conditioned as when a pigeon learns that pressing the lever at the right time leads to food (Gleitman, 1995). Some kind of reasoning or understanding is necessary, which becomes increasingly important when considering educational use of computer games beyond a 1st generation perspective.

Instructional technology discovers computer games

The behaviouristic approach never really manifests in the research area educational use of computer games, but is quite evident in edutainment titles. Before turning to edutainment it is worth presenting some of the early instructional technology research that extends from a cognitivist approach. The research area of instructional technology into computer games primarily becomes active in the 1980's in relation to computer games. Over the years it is represented by researchers like Thomas Malone, Mark Lepper, Richard Bowman and Marshall Jones. Contributions especially focus on the value of computer games for motivating students and how educational computer games can be built to harness these qualities. The basic idea is that drill-and-practice software is not satisfactory by it self, but needs strengthening by enhancing the learner's motivation through different mechanisms and taking into account player attention, focus, curiosity and fantasy pointing forward to a 2nd generation perspective, where the player becomes a more important part in the learning equation.

Thomas Malone (1980) is not as such interested in the educational features of computer games but is interested in providing more efficient educational software in general. He especially focuses on intrinsic motivation defined as what makes an activity fun or rewarding in its own right, rather than through external rewards. In his early work he suggests that the essential characteristics of good computer games can be captured in three categories: challenge, fantasy and curiosity (Malone, 1980). He later expands these in collaboration with Mark Lepper (Malone & Lepper, 1987b) to five categories. Through this collaboration he also expands his work to encompass computer-based instruction in general with strong ties to computer games (Malone & Lepper, 1987a). Malone & Lepper (1987a; 1987b) identify a number of categories that should be considered in designing drill-and-practice computer games to enhance learning.

- **Challenge**: The activity should be of appropriate difficulty level for the player. This is done through clear both short-term and long-term goals, uncertain outcome and facilitating investment of self-esteem through meaningful goals. Furthermore clear, constructive, encouraging feedback is essential.

- **Curiosity**: The information in the game should be complex and unknown to encourage exploration and organization of the information both in relation to the sensory area and the cognitive area.

- **Control**: The player should gain the overall feeling of being the controlling party. This is done through a responsive environment, high degree of choice in the environment and by equipping the player with the ability to perform great effects.

- **Fantasy**: The activity can increase intrinsic motivation by using fantasies as a part of the game universe. These should appeal to the target group emotionally, serve as metaphors for the learning content and be an endogenous part of the learning material.

- **Interpersonal motivations**: This refers to the increased motivation resulting from the social context of the computer game most directly competition and collaboration with peers. Also the recognition of your peers will serve to motivate.

Malone & Lepper (1987b) distinguish between extrinsic and intrinsic motivation to distinguish between different forms of drill-and-practice computer games. Intrinsic motivation refers to a motivation that arises directly from doing the activity, whereas extrinsic motivation is a motivation that is supported by factors external to the activity. Intrinsic motivation is for example the students spending hours learning how to play *Counter-strike* whereas extrinsic motivation would be parents' approval of their offspring playing an edutainment title to learn spelling. In edutainment the activity in itself is rarely motivated. On one hand Malone & Lepper (1987b) argue that a long list of educational computer games have extrinsic game-elements, which can be in the way for the learning experience. These correspond to the heavily criticized edutainment titles, where there is no connection between the computer game and the learning part. The game part is mainly used as a reward for doing some learning activity. However, Malone & Lepper (1987b) argue that intrinsic use of game elements in drill-and-practice computer games can facilitate enhanced learning and sustained interest for a given topic over time. However, the importance of integrating learning elements into the game-play doesn't make it into most educational computer game designs, evident from Konzack's (2003) analysis of a number of titles and several more common sense observations by researchers (Leddo, 1996; Leyland, 1996).

According to Malone and Lepper (1987a) a drill-and-practice perspective assumes that anything else than the learning material in a learning experience is noise and potentially a hindrance for learning. The graphics, narrative, sound or ad hoc activities in a computer game are in the way for learning. From this perspective it hardly makes sense to call edutainment drill-and-practice, as edutainment is ripe with qualities opposing a clean drill-and-practice perspective. However, edutainment is usually described as drill-and-practice due to its adherence to behaviourism, which will be pinpointed later in this chapter.

Lepper & Malone (1987a) also bring up classic problems in using computer games for educational purposes. They point to the problems between time-on-task, motivation and computer games. Depending on the learning context the question of motivation may be more or less important. Assuming we have a number of fixed school hours to spend on an educational computer game the additional features for increased motivation may turn out to divert the students from learning the relevant material, decreasing time-on-task. In a home setting these additional features will, however, sustain the interest of the player and result in time spent on educational content that is an extra supplement. Here any time-on-task is an extra benefit. Related to this is the question of whether it makes a difference that the learner feels in control when learning through a motivating educational computer game compared to traditional teaching methods. Malone & Lepper (1987a) point out that this may be a choice between superficial learning and in-depth learning. When learning is driven by the student's own discovery in computer games the quality of learning improves, but not necessarily the number of topics covered.

Malone & Lepper (1987a) acknowledge that the real challenge is how to balance the wish for learning specific content, attitudes or skills with the discovery-based approach in computer games. They also envision great problems in matching the open environment with learners with different abilities. They refer to the academic level of students but with the increasingly complex computer games (compared to that time) it also becomes a question of catering for different levels of game literacy among learners.

The research on computer games from an instructional technology perspective has also shown a sustained interest in the theory of Csikszentmihalyi's concept of flow. It has received a lot of attention within computer game research, but is generally not well integrated. According to Csikszentmihalyi, in order to achieve a flow experience a person's full attention must be centred at an activity, and you must feel at one with it. An important point is that the flow experience is so strong and intense that people will engage in it without any other rewards, incentives or reasons. It is these characteristics that lure game researchers to, as flow theory might explain the infatuation with computer games. Csikszentmihalyi (1992:49-66) identifies eight characteristics of the flow experience:

- Feeling you can complete the given activity

- You can concentrate on the activity

- The activity has clear goals

- The activity provides fast feedback

- Deep involvement in the activity

- A sense of control over the actions necessary to perform the activity

- Self-awareness disappearing during flow

- Sense of time is altered.

Marshall Jones' (1998) work is often cited as the theory of flow in relation to educational use of computer games. Jones finds that the flow theory to a large degree explains the motivational aspects of computer games and they should be catered for when designing educational computer games. Jones' research somewhat echoes Bowman (1982) describing, how computer games are constructed in a way that facilitates flow.

Bowman (1982) takes a more direct look at, how computer games perceived through the flow theory have a direct bearing on school practice. Through interviews with players he identifies some of those mechanisms that create a more engaging and intrinsically motivating learning experience in arcade parlours compared to classrooms. The most interesting are clarity of task, choice in problem-solving strategy, possibility for self-improvement, balance between skills and challenges, clear feedback, enjoyment while learning and lack of fear of failure. He concludes that some of these characteristics cannot be extended to teacher's practice while others are transferable. The characteristics reflect the flow theory, and it is stressed how altered teacher behaviour may facilitate more engaging and motivating learning experience for the benefit of all parties.

When looking at instructional theory, especially Malone's work has over the years served as a guide to many researchers and designers. However, the theory's focus seems too narrow on the relation between computer game structure and player. The latest revisions of the theory try to integrate the collaboration around computer games as an additional increaser of motivation identifying cooperation, competition and recognition as important motivators. However, the social context for educational computer games is primarily considered in relation to interpersonal encounters that increase motivation; not as a potential mediator and tool for learning as suggested by for example Squire (2004).

The legacy of edutainment

> To this point computer games with 'educational' features have not fared well in the marketplace. The 'educational' content tends to come at the expense of the gameplay and control is taken out of the hands of the player… Game buyers (as opposed to concerned parents) are wary of edutainment.

(Leyland, 1996:1)

Edutainment is inspired by the instructional approach, behaviourism and later cognitivism. It tries to focus on simple computer games and the delivery of straight-forward information to the player. Many early popular educational computer games have a different understanding of learning and do not fit the label of edutainment. However, continuously there is an undergrowth of edutainment titles building on the instructional technology approach supplemented with especially behaviourist learning theory. Other educational computer games are slowly outmanoeuvred by edutainment which encompasses a more conservative approach to learning with its promise of simplicity appealing to parents as discussed in chapter 1. An exploration of edutainment's nature is important as it will show the characteristics and problems of current edutainment titles that I wish to avoid in my later empirical work and theory of educational use of computer games.

Edutainment is potentially a broad term which covers the combination of educational and entertainment use on a variety of media platforms including computer games. The term edutainment is quite elastic as a lot of games are put into this category, and game companies are so inclined as to strengthen the appeal for parents, although the brand edutainment is not as attractive anymore (Konzack, 2003). Parents appreciate the combination of entertainment and education, preferring play that teaches children something. This links well with the common rationalizing of children's play pursued by adults as argued by Sutton-Smith & Kelly-Byrne (1984). There is a distinct tendency for both educators and parents to cast play in developmental terms. Children should not just play for the sake of playing, but in the process preferably nurture other skills. This wish for rationalizing play is extended to edutainment and used for creating a new market. Although, there are theoretical good arguments for using play for learning as I will discuss in chapter 5, it seems these are mostly left behind in edutainment.

Edutainment is a subset of educational computer games that is easily recognizable with a clear reward structure separate from the gameplay. Usually you use the game part as a reward for giving the right answer. In *Math Blaster!* the players must shoot down the right answer and on success ones balloon will move towards a needle. The player that first pops the balloon wins. It is assumed that a constant shooting of the balloons will automatically lead to a conditioned response no matter the learning, context or previous experience. In the recent *Math Missions Grades 3-5: The Amazing Arcade Adventure* by Scholastic, you earn money for every correct answer. This money can be spent on buying arcades and you even get to run the arcade. Here the rewards are still used as a way to push the learning forward without really being related to understanding the learning experience as such. There is not really any connection between the arcade games and the math questions. It is not different from a mother promising the noisy child an ice cream if he will be quiet and do his homework.

We should not think of edutainment as a fixed genre but rather as different titles which share some assumptions about motivation, learning theory, learning principles and game design while being produced, marketed and distributed differently than commercial computer games. The characteristics are outlined below drawing on the above discussions and chapter 1.

- *Little intrinsic motivation*: Edutainment relies more on extrinsic motivation through rewards, rather than intrinsic motivation. Extrinsic motivation is not really related to the game but consist of arbitrary rewards, for example getting points for completing a level. Intrinsic motivation would for example be the feeling of mastery from completing a level.

- *No integrated learning experience*: Usually edutainment lacks integration of the learning experience with playing experience, which leads to the learning becoming subordinated the stronger play experience. The player will concentrate on playing the game rather than learning from the game. One example is the skipping of text about the pyramids and going straight for the mini-games located in the game universe.

- *Drill-and-practice learning principles*: The learning principles in edutainment are inspired by drill-and-practice thinking rather than understanding. This means that you will constantly get arithmetical problems like 2+2 memorizing the results, while not necessarily understanding the underlying rules that make 2+2 = 4.

- *Simple gameplay*: Most edutainment titles are built on a simple gameplay often from classic arcade titles or a simple adventure game with a world you can move around in.

- *Small budgets*: Edutainment titles are often produced on relatively limited budgets compared to commercial computer games and with less than state-of-the-art technology.

- *No teacher presence*: Edutainment never makes any demands on teachers or parents. Rather edutainment assumes that students can simply be put in front of the computer with the edutainment title and learn the given content or skills. There is no required teacher or parent guidance, help or involvement.

- *Distribution and marketing*: They are distributed and marketed differently than commercial computer games for example through bookstores, supermarkets, schools and family magazines.

Edutainment games probably do learn children bits of things, but mostly edutainment is simple in its facilitation of learning experiences. Rote learning in relation to spelling and reading for pre-school and early school children may see some gains from edutainment. However, edutainment does not really teach the player about a certain area, but rather lets the player perform mechanic operations. This will lead to memorization of the practices aspect but probably not a deep understanding of the skill or content – it will be parrot-like not really grasped by the student and although this may work for some limited areas, like spelling and reading, this is a quite limited scope. In general, the parrot-like learning will result in weak transfer and application of the skills as it is not fundamentally understood, but only memorized as a mechanic action in the game environment (Gee et al., 2004; Jonassen, 2001; Schank, 1999). This may show up on assessment which formulates questions that are very close to the aspect learned, but not if the assessment strays away from the specific aspect learned.

There is also common agreement that edutainment fails to integrate the learning with the computer game. Hence, a change of focus in the learning experience from the educational part to the game part. This result in weak learning experiences especially if you consider the time-on-task issue – the player won't spend a lot of time on educational experiences, but rather gain a lot of game experience. (Brody, 1993; Fabricatore, 2000; Facer et al., 2003; Vandeventer, 1997). In general, the information in edutainment is fed to the player in chunks separated from the games like in the Swedish game *Chefren's Pyramid*. Here you start with a presentation of Egyptian history and an overwhelming amount of facts that you scroll through and *sometimes* read. Then you start the 'game', where you walk inside a Pyramid finding different puzzles or small games like *Backgammon* – but these game dynamics have no connection to Egyptian culture, which the game is supposed to teach the player about. Most players will learn to play *Backgammon* though.

Edutainment is also criticized for supporting a superficial and problematic construction of learning in the new generations. As Okan (2003:258) asks "Should learning be fun?" This is supported by Healy (1999) and Kafai (2001) who ask whether we in our eagerness to revolutionize learning are undermining the very foundation for learning. Students need to be able to endure frustration during learning and stay on track despite problems. This is argued to be rare in edutainment titles and that may be right, but it is certainly not a feature of computer games in general. Frustration and challenge is central in Gee's (2004b) account of the learning qualities of the commercial computer game *Rise of Nations*.

The dynamics found in edutainment are also apparent in the e-learning industry, where low budgets, high amount of mediocre contents and craze for ease of use has led to the lowest denominator. There is put little weight on the quality of titles as the market is unable to evaluate the products. The decision-makers buying the e-learning tools are not the ones using them (Aldrich, 2003). This parallels the parents' choosing the educational titles for their offspring. Although a few parents will sit and play the educational title with their children, they are still quite detached from the playing and most engage superficially with the computer game (Buckingham & Scanlon, 2002).

Overall the shortcomings of edutainment has let to an overall negative attitude towards edutainment titles. There is, to put it mildly, widespread scepticism towards almost any aspects of edutainment. The gameplay, learning principles and graphics are all criticized heavily by users, both children and parents, really starting with the mergers in the early 1990's (Brody, 1993; Buckingham & Scanlon, 2002; Leyland, 1996).

Learning outcome from educational use of computer games

One question which until now has escaped our attention is the broader question of the learning outcome from educational use of computer games. It seems there may be some benefits on the general skills. We have touched on the effectiveness of traditional educational games in chapter 2, but there are not yet any attempts at reviewing the effectiveness of educational use of computer games for learning. All the studies described below lack examples of previous research, but some preliminary findings seem to emerge.

Author(s)	Year	Genre	N	Subject	Results
Levin	(1981)	Action	-	Math	Computer games are motivating, engaging and ultimately successful in teaching children the planned math concepts. Computer games may be especially suitable for teaching different ways of approaching math that caters for individual differences.
Dowey	(1987)	Puzzle	203	Dental health	Children learn best from a combination of teaching and computer games but although they learn about dental hygiene this does not transfer into change of everyday practice.
McMullen	(1987)	-	37	Science	The drill-and-practice computer game was not found to have any effect on the learning, neither short-term nor long-term. However the students playing the computer game indicated that they thought they had learned more.
Jolicoeur & Berger	(1998a; 1998b)			Fractions Spelling	You learn from computer games, but educational software is more effective.
Wiebe & Martin	(1994)	Adventure	109	Geography	They find that there is no difference in learning geography facts and attitudes between computer games and teaching activities not involving a computer.
Sedighian and Sedighian	(1996)	Strategy	200	Math	The learning outcome is critically affected by teachers' integration of computer games and traditional teaching, but computer games prove highly effective.
Betz	(1995)	Strategy	24	Engineer	Finds that computer games increase motivation and learning
Thomas et al.	(1997)	Adventure	211	Sex education	Students learn from playing the computer game both on specific knowledge items and in self-efficacy.
Brown et al.	(1997)	Action	59	Diabetes	The study finds that children can learn about diabetes from computer games changing everyday habits.
Klawe	(1998)	Adventure	200	Math	Computer games are effective in teaching students about math.
Adams	(1998)	Strategy	46	Urban geography	Computer games increase motivation and teach students about the role of urban planners (affective learning)
Noble et al.	2000	Action	101	Drug education	Students taught by the computer games, found the experience motivating and wanted to play the computer game again.
Turnin et al.	(2000)	-	2000	Eating habits	Computer games can teach students about eating habits and lead to significant change in everyday habits.
Feng & Caleo	(2000)	-	47	Spelling and math	Children that played computer games learned better than peers not using computer games, mostly in spelling.
Becker	(2001)	Action	-	Program.	The study testifies to the increased motivation in connection with computer games. Games are found to be more effective and motivating than traditional teaching
Lieberman	2001	Action		Asthma, diabetes,	A review of a number of research projects that support that you can learn from computer games.
Rosas et al.	(2003)	Action	1274	Reading and maths	Computer games increase motivation, and there is a transfer of competence in technology from using the computer game.

McFarlane et al.	2002	-	-	All subjects	The study finds that teachers in general are sceptical towards the learning of content with computer games. However the learning of general skills was appreciated.
Gander	(2002)	Strategy	29	Program.	The study finds that computer games are effective for especially teaching specific knowledge.

Table 3: An overview of the studies into the effectiveness of educational use of computer games

The table above presents an overview of quantitative studies on educational potential of computer games. It should be stressed that many of the studies below use computer games as the sole teaching style. The studies examine whether computer games work as a viable supplement primarily during school time. Especially the studies related to health matters take a broader approach looking at computer games' educational potential in them selves, compared to traditional teaching and in combination. In general, the studies of health related educational use of computer games are also stronger than other areas. Overall one must say that the current findings are actually more positive and promising than educational use of traditional games (table 3), but it is hard not to be sceptical as the method flaws are severe. We can certainly say that you learn from computer games but the support for saying something more valuable is weak. The current studies do in most instances not compare computer games with other teaching styles, which is really the ultimate test. This would support necessary extra investment on a larger scale in the area.

In the following I will focus on the studies that cover strategy games and have some relation to teaching of social studies, mainly to illustrate the problems with existing research within the area. Furthermore, this genre is also the one that lies closest to the computer game used in the later empirical study. I have only located two studies which qualify for increased attention. Both of them examine *SimCity 2000*, which have from its release been emphasized as ripe with learning potential (Becta, 2001; Pahl, 1991; Prensky, 2001a).

The most interesting study on the effectiveness of using computer games for teaching is by Betz (1995). It is characterized by operating with a control and experimental group, actually comparing educational use of computer games with a different teaching style. The participants in the study are freshman students in an engineering technology course with one class assigned as experimental group; another freshman class is the control group. The computer game is presented as a computer simulator and two weeks before the reading assignments the experimental group gets a head start to ensure they play the computer game. Both of the groups get the same reading and test after the study. The correlation is tested with the Mann-Whitney test, and show that the experimental group does better in the test ($p < 0.05$). The survey results from the experimental test were also quite positive as most students preferred the computer simulator, used it more than the reading, enjoyed it more, tended to discuss it with friends, thought the computer game was less hard and found that the computer game helped them understand the reading. Interestingly, they also found that the computer game helped them understand the reading. Overall the positive aspects of the experience were overwhelming and support use of computer games.

The study, however, does have some methodological flaws on closer examination that seriously challenge the validity, reliability and generalization of the results to commercial computer games in general. First of all, the manual for the computer game is quite dense on the topic urban planning. It actually points to relevant reading, which hardly can be said for most commercial computer games. The extra material point to the game designer Will Wright's special interest in providing an educational experience. The random sampling is problematic as it consists of classes, which are not normally considered acceptable as a random sampling (Coolican, 1994). A class may have different established dynamics or other hidden variables, which influence the results. These problems are aggravated in Betz's study as little effort is done to examine if there exists basic differences between the classes, especially a pre-test exam to establish the academic level would have been critical to raise the scientific quality. This is, however, often hard in an educational setting and a pre-test could also steer the students in a particular direction, challenging the validity of the study.

The most serious flaw is however that the results don't really measure computer games compared to other teaching, but rather as an extra supplement. The experimental group and control group get the same reading, but the experimental group also plays the computer games. It is hardly surprising that extra time-on-task within a somewhat related area that also sparks discussion and interest, increases learning. On the other hand, it is of course interesting that you can get students to spend more time on a subject through computer games. Still, the real question is whether the time used on the computer game is sufficiently legitimised by increased learning, compared to other teaching methods. In other words the study doesn't show us how big the impact of the computer games is and it fails to show if the same result could have been obtained by reading an extra hour instead of playing. Of course the extra hour provided by the computer games would perhaps never emerge with traditional teaching material.

In another study of *SimCity 2000*, Adams (1998) also finds support for using computer games within the subject urban planning. Adams takes a more structured approach to teaching, with the computer giving the students different experiments to carry out in the game. The outcome of the study was evaluated through essays and the student's preference. The course was voted a favourite project by 48% of the students, outperforming the 8 closest projects significantly. The study, however, lacked more systematized evaluation of learning with a control group or pretest-posttest set-up. All the problems in Betz's study reported above, also holds true for this study. Although the study finds the students to learn from computer games, it is quite unclear what the exact effect is and how it compares to traditional teaching styles.

Overall the 17 studies in table 4 above overwhelmingly support that you learn from computer games, and that most students appreciate games in educations. However, the studies in general do not ask the hard questions concerning educational use of computer games. None of the studies actually compare computer games to other teaching methods or activities, to examine whether computer games are worth the initial efforts in learning the interface, setting up computers and the other problems that will be documented in the remaining part of this chapter. Most of the studies are one-shot studies with a lack of knowledge of the characteristics of computer games and with weak connections to earlier research. As was stressed in chapter 2 on educational use of traditional games, we need to raise the bar for educational use of computer games by asking under what circumstances do we learn and how do computer games compare with other learning experiences. It is hardly enough to establish thabt we learn from computer games as this is essentially true for any activity we engage in. The real question is what computer games offer that set them aside from existing educational practice.

Computer games as cognitive and audiovisual challenges

When establishing that players can learn specific knowledge from computer games turns out to be hard, some researchers instead eagerly suggest that there might be other benefits to playing computer games – some general skills. Eye-hand coordination, spatial ability and problem-solving have especially received attention in that respect. These do in general not have the same serious method problems as the studies on learning outcome previously mentioned in general.

Early on eye-hand coordination is popular to connect with capable players of computer games (Egenfeldt-Nielsen, 2003d; Greenfield, 1984; Loftus & Loftus, 1983). However, from the start, most studies of eye-hand coordination in video games yielded negative results in the sense that video games did not seem to improve eye-hand coordination. The number of studies on eye-hand coordination is limited, but add up to the following conclusion: There does not seem to be any differences between non-players and players in respect to eye-hand coordination (Funk & Buchman, 1995; Gagnon, 1985; Griffith et al., 1983). The failure to find long-term effects has resulted in few short-term studies on the effect of eye-hand coordination. In a recent pilot study on *Super Monkey Ball*, no effect was found on eye-hand coordination (Egenfeldt-Nielsen, 2003d). Some have sarcastically noted that humans train eye-hand coordination every time we pick up something or perform an action and computer games can hardly compete with that frequency (Loftus & Loftus, 1983)[11].

The area of spatial ability is better researched than the question of eye-hand coordination, and positive effects of computer games have been found. This has both been on a long-term basis (Gagnon, 1985; Green & Bavelier, 2003; Greenfield, Brannon, & Lohr, 1996; Lowery & Knirk, 1983) and short-term improvement through video games (Dorval & Pepin, 1986; Gagnon, 1985; Green & Bavelier, 2003; Lowery & Knirk, 1983; Okagaki & French, 1996; Subrahmanyam & Greenfield, 1996). However, there are some studies with opposing results (Okagaki & French, 1996; Scott, 1999), which could be attributed to the measurement of different areas of spatial skills.

One of the major controversies is the issue of whether you can transfer skills learned in video games to areas outside video games and although the area of spatial skills gives some indications of transfer, there are method problems. A frequent source of error in the studies on spatial ability is the measurement methods undermining the findings: The test of spatial skills is conducted on a computer screen, which is the same platform as computer games. Hence, the test is administered in an environment favoured by the computer game players. The favourable results for the computer games group may, therefore, be a consequence of familiarity with the test platform, instead of general improved spatial ability. Furthermore, the closeness between test platform and activity does not really test transfer to everyday activities.[12]

The area of problem-solving is often linked to adventure games and the idea is very popular among teachers, journalist, parents, players and researchers in relation to adventure games (Greenfield, 1984; Herring, 1984; Whitebread, 1997). Problem-solving has received much constant research attention over the years (Curtis, 1992; Gee, 2003; Greenfield, 1984; Grundy, 1991; Jillian et al., 1999; Kirriemuir & McFarlane, 2002; Ko, 2002; McFarlane et al., 2002; Pillay, Brownlee, & Wilss, 1999; Quinn, 1997; Walker de Felix & Johnson, 1993; Whitebread, 1997). Most of these studies are not very solid, but the general conclusion in the best performed studies relate problem-solving to computer games. Problem solving might be improved between computer games, but it is hard to transfer the improvement to other contexts than computer games. It is also found that good general problem-solving skills predict better performance in the computer game, so computer games may potentially be used to test problem-solving (Ko, 1999).

The results in this overall research area are mixed, but do lend some support to computer games having a connection with spatial skills, problem-solving and to a very limited degree, eye-hand coordination. However, the transfer of improvements obtained in the computer game context to other areas of life have been notoriously hard to document, although a recent study lends some support to possible transfer in the spatial area (Green & Bavelier, 2003). I will not dwell too long with this research area, as more in-depth discussions call for more thorough theories on the exact nature of problem-solving, spatial ability and eye-hand coordination, which is beyond the scope of this dissertation.

Subjects where computer games have been studied extensively

The overview of studies on learning outcome was not equally distributed across all subjects and neither is the remaining research on educational use of computer games. The educational use of computer games is favoured within the most basic subjects like math, science, reading and spelling. It is worth spending more time on these areas as this is where there is some aggregation of results. There is little actual research on how much computer games are used in educational settings. However, McFarlane, Sparrowhawk and Heald (2002) asked students whether they played computer games in school. Depending on age level a rather large number did play computer games

---

[11] For an overview of especially eye-hand coordination the article by Egenfeldt-Nielsen (2003) can be consulted.

[12] See also Greenfield & Cocking (1996) for especially cognitive effects of computer games.

in school, fewest at the highest keystage (table 4). This is in line with edutainment being strongest in the pre-school and early school area as discussed in previous chapters.

Keystage Level	Age group	Percentage playing computer games in school
2	7-11 years	63.4%
3	11-14 years	70.8%
4	14-16 years	23.2%

Table 4 The statistics are from McFarlane, Sparrowhawk and Heald (2002:28)

The study is unclear in reporting whether the playing is part of teaching or purely entertainment, in breaks or in after school activities. However, it seems unlikely that it should exclusively be educational use as the difference between boys and girls is quite significant; indirectly pointing out that this is partly a voluntary activity.

The obsession with math and science

> Most of the early mathematical computer games focused on drill and practice of simple number operations and concepts. Such games are easy to develop. Moreover, playing such games are an effective and motivating method of increasing fluency for many students. However, drill and practice is only one of many components of mathematics learning and can also be achieved via a variety of non computer-based methods.

(Klawe, 1998:9)

There has been a significant amount of research projects dedicated to using or constructing computer games, which can rejuvenate the teaching of science subjects and especially math. This has partly been facilitated by a political interest in increasing the interest in natural science in order to stay competitive in the global educational race. The increased interest and preparedness for using computers and hence computer games, among teachers in natural science subjects, has also played a role (see chapter 3). Finally, the early educational computer games within math (in reality mostly edutainment) may have provoked, more as a red rag than as state-of-the-art games. Researchers convinced it could be done better.

Over the years a surprisingly large number of projects have focused on this area, and compared with other subject areas it is quite well-researched. The studies which approach topics of general interest to the use of educational computer games will be overviewed in chronological order starting out with the Plato project.

The Plato project from 1973 yields positive results in relation to using computer games for math, and these results support initiation of later research into the field. This was for example clear in the research by Levin (1981) on using computer games to learn alternative and everyday arithmetic. In Levin's perspective we need a new way of learning arithmetic, as the current models are not appropriate when we have calculators and microprocessors to do most of our math in everyday life. Levin (1981) constructed the two educational computer games *Harpoon* and *Sonar* in 1981, based on the *Darts* game from the Plato project. They are intended to facilitate new understandings of arithmetic closer to everyday needs. They prove motivating, engaging and are ultimately successful in teaching children the planned math concepts. Based on the results it is suggested that computer games may be an appropriate approach for teaching different ways of approaching math that caters for individual differences.

Up through the 1980's the educational programming language Logo is the favourite flavour within maths and attempts are also made to combine it with earlier progress on computer games. The approach is especially formed around children designing math games themselves. Here the results were also encouraging, as the students engaged with designing logo math games outperformed the control group (Kafai, 1995; Kafai & Resnick, 1996; Olive & Lobato, 2001; Papert, 1996). We will return to constructionism later in this chapter, as this theoretical approach's bearing on educational use of computer games deserves more attention.

The 1990's are kicked off with the E-Gems study overviewed by Maria Klawe (1998). It is impressive in its findings, and is probably one of the first cross-disciplinary academic research groups dedicated to studying computer games. They focus on two educational math computer games they design in connection with the research project: *Super Tangrams* in 1996 and *Phoenix Quest* in 1997 (Picture 8). These are the basis of several empirical studies where different variables are

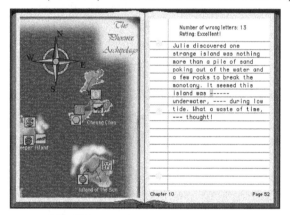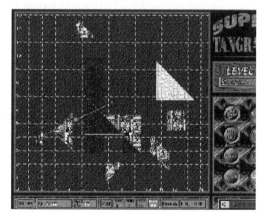

Picture 8: The first picture is of Phoenix Quest (1997) and the other is of Super Tangrams (1996). They are very different game genres, but try to use the same principles.

manipulated to determine the most active elements in facilitating the learning process. The results are particular strong as they are replicated by different research designs and research teams. The total number of students in the empirical studies is also quite impressive as approximately 200 students participated in the controlled studies of *Super Tangrams* and a similar number in the research on *Phoenix Quest*. On an overall level the computer games produced in the project proved motivating, popular and highly effective in teaching math to students *(Klawe, 1998; Sedighian & Sedighian, 1996, 1997).*

Klawe (1998) sums up the results of the E-Gems project and stresses that computer games should be used for math activities that are otherwise hard to introduce in a classroom. Special attention should be aimed at elements in computer games that are particular strong like unlimited amount of activities, visualization, manipulation, symbolic representations, adaptive sequencing, feedback and meaningful, contextualized activities. These elements are not believed to be limited to educational math computer games, but should apply to all educational titles. The generalization is not based on research, but connects well with earlier ideas of intrinsic motivation and flow theory.

In the discussion of the challenges during the game design process, Klawe (1998) raises some of the central problems with educational computer games. Most of these are backed up by an earlier study by Sedighian & Sedighian (1996) the researchers responsible for the Super Tangrams part of E-Gems. Klawe points out that the immersive effect of computer games lead to a lack of awareness of the mathematical structures and concepts integrated in the computer game. This result is weak transfer of game experience to other contexts. In an earlier study by Klawe & Phillips (1995), the use of paper and pencil during gameplay is found valuable for transferring computer game math experiences to other classroom practice. In the same study debriefing and shared discussions is also stressed. They do not draw on research from the simulation & gaming community presented earlier, but findings are in line with the heavy focus on debriefing in educational game research.

Klawe (1998) argues that transfer can especially be improved through careful game design, where the math elements are integrated echoing Malone & Lepper's previously discussed work. Also, it seems that a teacher's explicit and constant probing of the educational relevance during playing computer games, will increase the value. She suggests that both *Super Tangrams* and *Phoenix Quest* solve the problem, but at least one study challenges the ability of *Phoenix Quest* to make explicit the math concepts and structures (Jillian et al., 1999). This transfer problem appears in most research into educational use of computer games, and we will continuously run into it[13]. It seems to be an unsolvable double-bind. On one hand it is assumed that the learning must be stealth and undetectable by children. This is based on the premise that an educational computer game should resemble a traditional computer game. It shouldn't give itself away as children will then shy away from the educational title (Brody, 1993). The learning elements should be integrated in the game experience and not stand out. On the other hand it seems that if the players are not aware of the learning elements, it will undermine the learning experience and especially the transfer value (Bransford et al., 1999).

The idea of stealth learning, and the close overlap with commercial computer games runs contrary to the emphasis placed on debriefing in research on educational games, which was discussed in chapter 2. Especially in E-Gems, the problems with implicit learning elements become problematic. They are not only concerned with teaching the students basic arithmetic so often encountered in drill-and-practice educational titles, but aspire to using computer games for more advanced math concepts and structures. These concepts and structures are more complex and can be hard to automatically uncover in a game context. It can also be argued that these concepts require a more reflective process than the rote learning of arithmetic. This may also be generalized to other more complex topics presented through computer games.

Another basic problem addressed by the E-Gems project, is the clash between the player's control when playing and the need to scaffold the learning experiences. Again there seems to be a conflict between the computer game medium and pedagogics for facilitating learning. The solution suggested by Klawe (1998) is to carefully integrate a reward system that will steer the player in the right direction. However, this seems to entail some problems considering the classic time-on-task issue. Even with a proper reward system, the student will sometimes take the wrong path and may experience failure and waste valuable time on an insurmountable problem. Depending on the concrete learning experience and your theoretical background, it may be a complete waste of time or one of the essential factors of computer games. According to for

Picture 9: Show the Logical Journey of the Zoombinis (1996) with the Zoombinis about to cross the bridge.

---

[13] Indeed most educational research struggles with the transfer problem (Bransford, Brown, & Cocking, 1999).

example Gee (2003) the students will in such hopeless situations, often in the long run, learn how to steer clear of too hard problems and frame a problem sufficiently precise to avoid problems in the future. This may sometimes be possible, but it also seems that this may be the reason for the relatively simple simulations and representations in computer games. They mostly require a minimum of skills and knowledge from the outside world to be played. It may be necessary to reconsider this approach if we want more complex educational computer games than just drill-and-practice. Today it is unthinkable for most players to read the accompanying manual to a computer game, but this doesn't mean that it might not in fact be more efficient as computer games increase in complexity. Interestingly, many players will after some play consult the manual expecting to find more information on different game areas. This can point to good points of departure for introducing an educational perspective.

The research project Through the Glass Wall has a slightly different focus than E-Gems, as it takes the role of supporting the concrete educational use of computer games for math more seriously. They review existing educational math computer games and set-up guidelines for educators and parents to choose better educational computer games (Kliman, 1999; Murray, Mokros, & Rubin, 1998). The project results in less research findings and there is not the same kind of iterations as the E-Gems project, but they have some interesting findings. The focus is on an educational title called *Logical Journey of the Zoombinis* from 1996, which somewhat resembles the classic computer game *Lemmings*. The *Logical Journey of the Zoombinis* was developed as an out-spring of educational math research and took as starting point children's own experience and fun with math related issues. Their approach could be described as learning math in another way through computer games (Hancock & Osterweil, 1996). The developers of the *Logical Journey of the Zoombinis* share this ambition with other research projects in this area. The Through the Glass Wall project suggests that compared to traditional educational math titles the math is an integrated part of playing *Logical Journey of the Zoombinis* (Picture 9) and encourage math-related reflection, thinking and discussion (Murray et al., 1998; Rubin et al., 1997) They stress the importance of the narrative frame and the gender neutral game universe. They also find that the game teach the children basic math concepts although they do not compare it directly with other teaching methods. However, the results from the Through the Glass Wall project are hard to generalize as they build on limited qualitative data and what accounts as learning is quite vague. They do not really measure the difference between different educational computer games, but purely observe the dialogue around the computer game. The results of playing, reflecting and discussing are never really examined. Furthermore, the critical question of transfer is not tackled. The problem of recognizing and transferring the math skills is also a real issue here, where math is never really mentioned in the computer game, and a debriefing context is never established.

Despite the large number of research projects within the math area, it is also tainted by a lack of awareness of prior research. Each project starts from the assumption that little or no earlier research has been done, each reinventing the wheel. They do draw on larger theoretical frameworks but not specific research into educational math computer games.

The dominance of educational adventure games

The most consistent claim on the educational potential computer games is in relation to adventure games, especially promoted by Australian researchers. This link may be due to an integration of computer games in the curriculum goals in the Australian primary schools as early as 1989, which is still maintained (Beavis, 1999a; Cavallari et al., 1992).

The support for adventure games is expressed by researchers, journalists, educators and parents. Additionally, the amount of research into adventure games is larger than any other genre. Adventure games are bestowed with the ability to increase problem-solving as a basic part of its puzzle-based structure. The success criteria in adventure games is often identified as logical thinking and puzzle-solving (Cavallari et al., 1992; Egenfeldt-Nielsen & Smith, 2000), which are well respected qualities in the educational system. Also the close relation to reading a text when playing adventure games is appreciated by educators (Heaney, 1989). The relationship between text and narratives is considered a strong educational feature, although the increasing graphical representation somewhat diminishes the direct parallel to more classic text forms. However quite few studies have actually been done with purely text-based adventure games, with Grabe & Dosmann (1998) being an exception. One could easily claim that adventure games are the 'easy' transition from traditional teaching methods in the softer subjects (i.e. English, history and geography) to game-based learning. Adventure games offer a close connection between existing theories within a subject field and computer games.

Cavallari et al. (1992) sums up the claims in educational circles for adventure games as teaching knowledge, skills and attitudes which are transferable to other contexts. It is stressed that most adventure games are not explicitly educational, but that they "provide opportunities" for interested teachers. The teacher's role is perceived as imperative for the learning experience. Cavallari et. al (1992) encourages the teacher to consider the following options, although weakly documented: Use adventure games across curricula and do not be limited to one subject. Encompass the adventure game within an overall topic that the students have preferable already knowledge about. Furthermore, provide additional resources concerning the topic to extend the scope of the computer game. The last point on providing supporting material is strongly supported by later research on a strategy game by David Leutner (1993).

A majority of the researchers in the early 1990's end their papers by calling for more research directly comparing use of adventure games with traditional teaching methods. Such studies are still scarce within the adventure games area, but an interesting study by James Wiebe & Nancy Martin (1994) supports the cautious attitude by the majority of researchers. In their study they use the classic adventure game *Where in the World is Carmen Sandiego* for teaching geography. They compare the students playing the adventure game with a group of students learning through non-computer games. They find no significant difference between these two groups, and this leads them to question heavy investment in educational computer games. The study has some flaws though, especially the short time span of 40 minutes for both groups. In this period half of it was dedicated to non-geography related activities to control for Hawthorne effect (the potential bias arising from researcher's interest in the study). However, that only leaves 20 minutes for the computer game to have an impact, which is a short learning experience in traditional teaching, but especially with computer games that usually spans longer periods of play. You need to start up the computer game, learn the interface and link the game to geography. This is a type of empirical design that Wolfe & Crookall (1998) would warn against, as the results are jeopardized by not really taking into account the special characteristics of computer games.

Another study answering the call for studying educational use of computer games is by Shirley Grundy (1991), and interestingly she is studying the same game, namely *Where in the World is Carmen Sandiego*. She examines the game through mainly qualitative methods, focusing on student competences and student decision-making processes. The educational potential of the game is initially described as knowledge about computers, feeling of success, factual knowledge, literacy skills and problem-solving. These potentials are in opposition to Wiebe and Martin (1994), as they do not focus narrowly on one subject, but take a cross-curricula approach, which we have previously seen supported in this chapter by other researchers. The findings are not quantifiable but emerge through systematic data analysis of student interaction around the computer game. The authors do not find support for students gaining more knowledge about computers. They find that *Where in the World is Carmen Sandiego* could support a wide area of relevant topics, but learning these is not an integrated part of the game. Most students had successful experience with the game, ending up solving the assignments. Overall, students draw on earlier subject experiences and the computer game fits well in with the current theme in the course that is about different countries all over the world. The background information from earlier work in the class was used heavily. However, the game's almanac was only used to a limited degree as it proved too cumbersome. It was also clear that knowledge and information provided by the computer game that are not perceived as directly applicable to the specific computer game situation in question, was not considered relevant and interesting enough to spend time on. The learning was therefore only superficial; exposing,

> a real need for the program to utilize information provided in the information frames in the early game, so that students learned the benefits of remembering and assimilating the knowledge.

(Grundy, 1991:49)

This problem is a returning problem in the research literature (i.e. Jillian et al., 1999; Squire, 2004) and challenges the very notion of using computer games for learning, as the relevant educational material may be quite limited.

Furthermore, the students had a blind belief in the computer game's ability to present accurate and valid information. When students experienced a contrast between own knowledge and information presented in game – they stuck to the game. The superficial approach to knowledge was also present in the general reading of the text in the game, which was superficial and most students skipped the text or glossed through it. This was also made worse by problematic game design. The clues in the game were presented in short sentences, but always as the last word - the unfortunate consequence was that the students skipped to the end. Not surprisingly, they put the game goals higher than the learning goals, which we could put down to bad game design, but it seems to run deeper. You can say that students lived up to the principles for playing the game – complete the assignments as fast as possible not thinking about the educational goals (Healy, 1999; Magnussen & Misfeldt, 2004). Another game design might have changed, this but the suggestion by Grundy (1991) that the game should have mechanisms that drew on information presented earlier in the game is not easily implemented. A computer game consists of a quite basic gameplay and it is almost impossible to get even a fraction of the background information to have a bearing on the game. In the strategy game *Civilization* there is an encyclopaedia describing a range of objects, events and inventions and most have at least a ½ page description. This is also so for the Colossus of Rhodes, however the game effect of the Colossus is to double your trade in the city, where it is built. This is the real impact it has and this is what most players will learn. Squire's (2004) analysis of the strategy game *Civilization III* have similar examples.

Grundy (1991) concludes that although limited explicit learning potential existed in the computer game, it offered many implicit learning possibilities that the teacher can harness. Alternatively, the computer game should be redesigned to support the learning experiences closer. Grundy ends up cautioning against investing heavily in the area with so few clear advantages.

A more fine-grained approach to the learning process in adventure games and the potential implications for transfer, is presented by Oluf Danielsen, Birgitte Olesen and Birgitte Holm Sørensen (2002). They set up three different potentially active dimensions of learning in the computer game *Miljøstrup* (Environtown): informative, attitude and action. Each of these dimensions gives a different optic for understanding how the computer game can facilitate learning. The informative dimension is concerned with the facts presented in the computer game and the comprehension of this information. The action dimension looks at the learning that occurs, when the students do something in the computer game and whether this transfers to actual everyday environmental behaviour. The attitude dimension refers to learning that results in reflection or alteration of attitude to game-related environmental themes.

Unfortunately, they do not adjust their method approach to match the different learning dimensions: informative, attitude and action. All of the results are based on qualitatively methods, and for example the conclusion, that children do acquire some specific knowledge of environment, is left hanging in the air: What information, by whom and to what extent? The same is true for the attitudinal dimension, where they also find that the engaging experience with environmental content in the computer games have made students' attitudes more favourable towards environment. The really interesting part is their observations and interviews with students in their home environment, where they determine whether the knowledge obtained through the computer game is transferred to everyday activities. They find that this is the case for some students. These students are characterized by already having a home environment that can facilitate the experiences with the computer games. As the researchers conclude,

> Each pupil may well build up knowledge and attitudes about correct environmental behaviour and healthy food habits supported by computer games. But if there is no space for action, the acquired knowledge remains in the individual as potential physical action competence. For many children the learning will thus remain isolated and tied up with the game if it is not picked up and connected with everyday actions, for example initiated by the teacher at school and/or the parents at home.

(Danielsen et al., 2002:78)

Overall the study points to important distinctions in accessing learning outcome and different types of knowledge in computer games, which is further addressed in chapter 5. There is a close connection between adventure games and computer games as a way to teach media literacy. Often adventure games are used to discuss what makes computer games different from more traditional media forms.

Computer games as a way to media literacy

Computer games as media literacy has strong roots in the research on adventure games, but broadens the scope more and sees computer games as an interesting medium in its own right. How do media, including computer games, play a role in relation to literacy, culture, curriculum and society (Buckingham, 2003). Computer games are seen as tied to children's culture and as such, potentially relevant to reflect upon to increase literacy in new media.

The closest example of a representative for computer games in media education is Catherine Beavis (1997; 1999a; 1999b) who has extensively examined the relationship between using computer games and new forms of literacy. She stresses that computer games in general are a way to engage with new culture forms prevalent among children and youngsters. The educational system should not be limited to transferring a classic high culture vision of society.[14] This claim is seldomly used as an argument in itself for using educational computer games, but it holds interesting perspectives for general use of computer games. It is reasonable to suggest that new media culture (including movies, TV-shows and computer games) could benefit from a general higher critical awareness. This should be supplied by the school and, therefore, computer games have a place in the curriculum, which is also the case mirrored in the national curriculum of Australia and Denmark, where games are explicitly mentioned in recent curriculum descriptions.

Beavis (1999a) argues that there are great advantages of integrating computer games into teaching, because they are complex, engaging and well-known by many children. However, she warns against perceiving computer games as neutral. Their closer connection with everyday life, current media practice and culture in general lead to anything but neutral objects of study. They are violent, stereotyped, ideologically loaded and will be very differently approached by different students. Still, this just underlines the relevance of engaging with the media and Beavis (1999a) suggests the following approach based on two studies in Australian schools:

---

[14] There have been similar discussions in Denmark (Egenfeldt-Nielsen, 2003b; Walther, 2004).

How might we work with computer games as part of the literacy curriculum? I suggest we approach computer games much as we do other texts, particularly those to which they seem most closely related, novel and film. As part of the spectrum of texts we examine, we can explore elements in the construction of the texts from aesthetics and structural patterning through to the values they imply and the subject position they seem to ask of their readers. We can discuss with students the appeal of the texts, what they take the dominant values or ideologies to be, how they position themselves in relation to the main characters, particular issues raised by the game and so on.

(Beavis, 1999a:Unpaginated)

Beavis (1997; 1999a; 1999b) is optimistic on the role of computer games in the educational system, as it seems to be a way to approach new literacy forms in a way that is meaningful and motivating for students. There will of course be classic problems, especially in relation to computer game licenses and technological barriers. Since her latest work, these problems have somewhat diminished as computers are slowly becoming a more integrated part of school life and playable computer games demos are wide-reaching enough to serve as object of study. The theoretical work on computer games is also becoming increasingly accessible to teachers making it easier to bridge the gap between existing subjects and analysis of computer games (Egenfeldt-Nielsen, 2003a; Squire, 2003a, 2003b).

The approach to media education should not be confused with the narrow focus on teaching ICT skills in schools. The ability of computer games for teaching these are not widespread, but examined in a pilot project by Becta (2001). Becta also stressed collaboration, motivation and relevant content as apparent in the educational use of computer games, but ICT was the one strongest supported by teachers' assessment.

The titles studied were the *The Sims*, *SimCity*, *Age of Empires* and *Championship Manager*. The skills especially observed to be used were "multi-tasking, switching between windows, and practice at finding and applying rules from menus" (Becta, 20018). This was done with high motivation and interest from all students. The teachers in the study intuitively used computer games for ICT, although they did also find some indication in relation to learning thinking skills, collaboration and some relevant content depending on the specific computer game. The measurements were however quite informal and participating teacher were not entirely representative.

Healthy computer games can change your behaviour

Computer games aimed at supporting more healthy behaviour have some interesting results in this area. Researchers within the field have strengthened their claims by comparing educational use of computer games directly with learning in other media forms. It is also noticeable that studies of health games have the advantages of being able to measure more overt changes in behaviours and external signs of learning.

Educational health computer games are mostly inspired by Albert Bandura's social learning theory, and spans some successful titles along with interesting research findings. Proponents of Bandura's theory assume, that by watching and enacting specific activities, you will learn the activities, especially when enforced by appropriate role-models. Computer games provide a safe frame for these activities and you are able to make children repeat otherwise tedious actions. There are a lot of health games out there, for example *Bronkie the Bronchiasaurus*, *Packy & Marlon*, *Traffic Jam*, *Hungry Red Planet* and *Aids Prevention - Catch the Sperm*.

The area is characterized by thorough empirical studies, when it comes to examining the learning outcome from computer games. This is due to its roots in medical science and psychology, where the documentation of effect is an inherent part of performing research. Most of the results are quite positive and indicate a significant behavioural change.

One of the most interesting health computer games are *Bronkie the Bronchiasaurus*, which is within the action genre, in the sub-genre called platforms games (Picture 10). You control Bronkie that must fight the bad Tyrannosaurus Rex in order to assembling a wind machine to clean the air. The story has minor significance except setting the scene and is quickly forgotten, when you jump over enemies and avoid obstacles that will deteriorate your asthma, trying to make it to the next level. However, in the game a lot of necessary asthma management tools are embedded in the game universes and the activities you perform. The factual knowledge is limited to a few multiple-choice questions between levels, but students will perform asthma management and change their behaviour.

Debra Lieberman (2001) compared playing the computer game for 30 min with watching an educational video for 30 min. The children playing the computer games expressed more enjoyment and learned the same as the children watching the television program. Lieberman stresses that this is interesting, as the video will only be watched one time and have to convey all its information in one chunk. The computer game will deliver a limited amount of factual information in 30 min but will be played for longer periods. Still it measures up on the short trial period.

This hints at a problem lurking beneath the surface, when using educational computer games, namely the computer game's ability to deliver large amounts of information. Computer games consist of basic rules and do not deliver the same density of information as videos or books. It has basic rules covering the most important information, that the game designer or educator wishes to convey about a subject through the game. This information is introduced, re-used and re-applied but seldomly with the same details as for example a textbook. The cyclical nature comes at the expense of introducing large amounts of relevant educational material. The above findings by Lieberman suggest that this might be a pseudo-problem, as children are under all circumstances not capable of receiving and digesting all the information in more classic media like video and books. It is not possible to generalize from such a small study, but it is worth noticing as we approach other studies and consider how to evaluate educational use of computer games.

Brown et al. (1997) found the similar game *Packy & Marlon* (Picture 10) to be quite effective aiming to improve diabetes self-care among children,. The player in the game controls an avatar with diabetes and must monitor level of blood glucose, take insulin injections and choose foods. This is done within the overall narrative of saving the diabetes summer camp from evil rats and mice, who

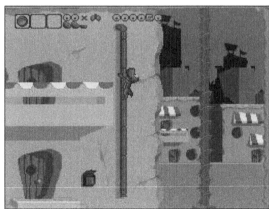 

Picture 10: Packy & Marlon (1997) and Bronkie the Bronchiasaurus (1994) from now departed Click Health.

have stolen the diabetes provisions. The empirical study of the game indicates that well-designed educational computer games can be effective. Players improved on self-efficacy, communication with parents about diabetes, self-care behaviours, and the number of urgent doctor visits decreased. The post-test showed a 77-percent drop in visits to urgent care and medical visits in experimental group compared to control group (Brown, 1997; Lieberman, 2001).

Interestingly the players did not improve their knowledge on diabetes significantly, which links back to the problems with a narrow focus on seeing computer games only in a knowledge acquisition perspective. It also conflicts somewhat with the results described by Lieberman, but the study didn't measure the actual knowledge acquired. Instead the study merely stated that computer games in terms of knowledge acquisition are as effective as an educational video. The effect on factual knowledge may however be limited from both teaching styles considering the general problem of transfer. The classic view on transfer has in general been heavily criticized in educational psychology as relying on a simplified understanding of learning (Döpping, 1995). Alternative approaches to understanding transfer are clear in relation to educational use of computer games. Transfer is seen as quite hard and cumbersome, and computer games will not change this, although computer games seem to include features for enabling transfer (i.e. Gee, 2003; Gee et al., 2004).

The results by Brown et al. are somewhat supported by other research findings (Dowey, 1987; Johansson & Küller, 2002; Noble et al., 2000; Thomas et al., 1997; Turnin et al., 2000) but contradicted by another study that failed to find a transfer of knowledge from the computer game *Foodman* to every day contexts (Sørensen, 1997). This one study on *Foodman*, however, might be more related to limitations in the actual game design than express generalizable results about educational computer games. Foodman's interface is quite arbitrary, hindering the player from understanding the content about healthy food behaviour, and seeing the connection between their actions and consequences. The general challenge in the building interfaces for health-games are partly related to students existing level of knowledge about for example food, which are also recognized in a prototype study (Lockyer et al., 2003).

Getting to 3rd generation: New trends in educational use of computer games

Until now, we have primarily talked about research which relates to computer games in a 1st and 2nd generation perspective focusing on the player and/or the computer game, but this is, as suggested previously, too limited. The following research is less elaborate than the previous themes, but points forward to a 3rd generation perspective that includes player, computer games and context while stressing learning as understanding. In that sense they pave the way for the next chapter, where I will present my educational foundation for understanding educational use of computer games.

Constructionism's dream: Virtual worlds and children as game designers

The theory of constructionism is formulated by Seymour Papert inspired by Piaget's constructivism. The mission is initially to teach children hard subjects like math in alternative ways, but slowly it becomes a well-established overall theoretical learning approach. The most influential tool for constructionist thinking is the programming language Logo. Logo lets students draw computer generated drawings by using mathematical concepts. The concepts are not explicit, but are implicitly used when you draw figures. The so-called turtle, not too different from an avatar in a computer game, can for example draw a square. The student observes the turtle drawing a line and then gives it the command 'turn 90 degrees'. This is repeated three times, and you have a square. The active approach to knowledge and use of external artefacts for facilitating the learning experience is essential for constructionism.

Turning to computer games, these principles have been attempted in several ways. For some constructionist thinkers, computer games are the lost paradise. Here is a universe where the learner can engage with a microworld, and construct different objects and connections (Papert, 1980).

The most noticeable contributions within this field are especially the work by Yasmin Kafai (1995; 2001) which has stood the test of time. Up through the 1990's she develops the idea of children designing games turning children into producers of knowledge, and in a very concrete way let them play with objects in different ways. According to Kafai & Resnick (1996) there is no doubt that you can acquire programming experience through designing computer games, and math used in developing computer games. It is believed that designing computer games makes it possible for the learner to approach a subject in an active way, hereby constructing a personal representation of knowledge by using physical artefacts. The student's learning experience draws on different perspectives giving rise to a variety of actions and in that way giving a fuller understanding of a given topic.

The main focus is the construction process and therefore research has also focused on open-ended games. This has spanned students designing simple games, engaging in virtual worlds, exploring microworlds and playing of other open-ended computer games. The basic assumptions about learning are different in constructionism compared to the dominating edutainment titles. In a constructionist perspective, learning does not come from the computer game, and the challenge lies not in designing an educational computer game with relevant content. Rather the hard challenge is facilitating playing that makes the player engage with the material, discuss it, reflect on it and use the computer game as a means for constructing knowledge. A prerequisite for such constructions may very well be relevant content but the content is far from enough.

The interest in microworlds is therefore also obvious as these are open-ended universes (more or less game-like), where a certain topic is represented in different artefacts. A microworld can be described as a simulation of a part of the world that is simplified and constructed to facilitate the working with concrete objects. When you interact with objects in microworlds, you are learning about these objects' properties, connections and applications. The player can engage and manipulate these artefacts and thereby construct a perception of the given topic. Kafai (1996) notes that the design of these microworlds prove a lot harder than drill-and-practice computer games, as you have to integrate the topic in the microworld. You can't just take a well-tested action formula and use that as the blueprint like in the edutainment genre. The interest in microworlds has especially been strong in relation to math and science (Goldstein & Pratt, 2001; Hoyle, Harris, & Judd, 1991; Hoyles, Noss, & Adamson, 2002; Miller, Lehman, & Koedinger, 1999; Rieber, 1996; White, 1984) but also other attempts have surfaced the use of constructionism as a different approach to computer games (McCarty, 2001; Woods, 2002).

The socio-cultural approach: around the game

Edutainment's narrow focus on computer games as offering the full educational experience continues. It is still strongly supported today by some believers in computer games, as optimal learning machines. Squire's resume of a debate at the Game Developer conference 2002 illustrates the problem:

> Marc Prensky and others argued for the systematic study of learning environments comprised exclusively of gaming activities; in other words, situations where players sit in front a computer, play a game, learn from the game and then walk away. Jon Goodwin responded that, from such an approach, a game would not only be required to provide a robust, compelling context for learning activities but also would need to be able to adjust to individual players' abilities and preferences, provide just-in-time explanations and background material, present divergent problems, include opportunities for reflection and track user behavior in order to assess learning and then adjust learning experiences accordingly. The claim that any game can (or should) accomplish all this is dubious at best.

Since the start of the 1980's there has been an interest in examining the social context around the computer game experience (i.e. Strein & Kachman, 1984). But it is not until the mid-1990's that the socio-cultural approach really starts to influence the area. In the Nordic Countries, Carsten Jessen's (1995; 2001) study of the culture around computer games can be mentioned as an example describing the informal play and learning experiences around computer games that is mediated through especially social relations. This leads to interesting findings concerning peer-learning around computer games and appreciation of the rich social interaction that mediates the game experience. The appeal of computer games to children is found to be closely related to the match between children's existing play culture, and the computer game culture. This research never really goes beyond the informal learning processes surrounding computer games, but points towards the importance of incorporating these. This is strongly supported by Squire's (2004) PhD dissertation, that includes several classes playing *Civilization III*. The explicit goal is to facilitate history through *Civilization III*, especially through the surrounding social environment. This approach is supported in observations and interviews. Squire concludes that

> The most important point in understanding how games engage players in educational environments may be that good games engage players in multiple ways and the interplay between these different forms create dynamic learning opportunities. Different play styles and tastes enriched classroom conversations, often leading to discussions that produce important 'taken-as-shared' meanings. [...] Discussions between different player types drove them to articulate and defend different strategies, even rethinking their orientation to the game as when Marvin, a builder/explorer, implored Joey to rethink waging war.

(Squire, 2004:241)

It is also stressed that computer games do not lend themselves to learning about history as rote memorization. Instead the relationships between variables, events and complex patterns should be the goal.

In a socio-cultural perspective, computer games are tools for constructing a viable learning experience. Computer games mediate discussion, reflection, facts and analysis facilitated by the surrounding classroom culture and the student's identity. This approach is argued to be very useful for understanding computer games with their strong social network (Gee, 2003; Jessen, 2001; Linderoth, 2002; Squire, 2004). Exaggerating a bit, computer games are not interesting for their content, but for their way of initiating new explorations, negotiations, constructions and journeys into knowledge.

Gee (2003) speaking from a socio-cultural perspective, has given one of the strongest theoretical accounts for understanding the learning mechanisms in computer games although not necessarily directly useful in an educational setting. The overarching idea is that children learn to participate in new domains by playing computer games. They learn to make sense of new areas, especially by engaging with like-minded, discussing, reflecting and sharing. A key area in the play activity is the role of critical thinking, which is constantly called for by the social practice the player engage in around the computer game. He presents five main areas of interest concerning computer games, which is also of interest for educational purposes. He sees these as intrinsic qualities of computer games that can be useful in a school setting:

- **Semiotic Domains**: Like other activities in life, computer games are a semiotic domain that you can slowly learn. You learn to make sense and navigate in the domain of computer games, while being pointed to other interesting domains like science. Computer games can also work as a place to reflect on the engagement and processes in domains of practice.

- **Learning and identity**: Computer games give new opportunities for learning experiences, when the student is involved with the material. Computer games are quite good for creating agency and identification and this sparks critical thinking and learning that matters. The learning experience in computer games becomes more effective because you are immersed in the environment. You can make mistakes without real consequences and you are encouraged to keep on trying.

- **Situated Meaning** and Learning: Computer games are well-suited for new forms of learning, where you can interact with the game world through probing, choose different ways to learn and see things in a context. You can interact and challenge computer games and over time build up a more accurate picture of an area.

- **Telling and Doing**: Games can amplify areas, and represent subset of domains so you can practise. According to Gee, games also lend themselves well to transferring between domains. It is possible to transfer what you learn in computer games to other contexts.

- **Cultural Models**: The content in games represents ways of perceiving the world and carries a lot of implicit information. This content also has bearing on other domains of life and can be both good and bad content, depending on your values and norms.

Gee's contribution is currently one of the strongest in the field, but is also symptomatic of the area, as he fails to really engage with earlier research and findings. This makes his theory weaker and supports the fragmentation of the field. To a large degree Gee (2003) makes up for these shortcomings by providing a strong grounding in educational theories. He makes a strong case for a variety of the strong mechanisms in computer games that facilitate learning and we will look closer at these, especially in chapter 7 and 8, where we dissect the concrete learning experience with educational use of computer games.

Conclusion: Key topics in the research area

The approaches above zoom in on different areas of the educational experience in relation to computer games. The instructional technology perspective is valuable for examining the narrow relation between computer games and students focusing on the role of motivation. On a socio-cultural level, we will appreciate and examine the environment that emerges around computer games for negotiating and constructing knowledge. Here questions of collaboration, debriefing and discussion will be crucial to understand how we can construct, mediate and support the knowledge acquired in relation to computer games.

The different research perspectives clearly have something to offer on different levels and although there may be some internal inconsistencies, we have covered the important areas of educational use of computer games. Most previous research, as we have seen, awarded prominence to one or two characteristics in educational use of computer games.

Below I have compiled some of the most consistent claims found throughout the chapter, which document the variation in researchers' claims for educational use of computer games: Increased motivation, more interest in a subject, simulations present material differently, more open-ended approach to information, possible to interact with information, well-known media form from everyday use, a safe virtual play environment to experiment in, more effective learning, more challenging, student has more control, the fantasy world of computer games make students more interested, facilitate a flow experience, increase cognitive skills, a new generation's way of thinking, scaffolding of learning, experience before being told improves learning, better transfer to other contexts than school, through construction in games you improve learning, more peer collaboration and more student autonomy.

More importantly, I also touched on a number of problems that is central and reappear across different approaches to educational use of computer games. The most important discussions that have so far been established are the following:

- **Learning vs. playing**: The basic idea of educational computer games is to combine playing and learning and this never ceases to result in conflicts. It is increasingly suggested, that is should be made explicit that a computer game is about learning a topic and clarified what is expected to be the result. In line with this, the question of control arises. On one hand player control is a critical characteristic in computer games stressed by all researchers, but it is also a fact, that all findings show the benefit of guiding, supporting, scaffolding, introducing and debriefing the computer game experience. This risks taking control away from the player especially in a classroom setting. Another question related to this, is the fear of the implicit message we are sending by using computer games for learning. Learning is not worth sweating for, but must always be fun.

- **Drill-and-practice games vs. microworlds**: All research shy away from a narrow focus on drill-and-practice games alias edutainment, but when we look closer many researchers still indirectly assume that parts of the game have drill-and-practice elements, that can transfer facts and support skills. This may be due to the problems encountered when designing a microworld, it has proven significantly harder than classic drill-and-practice games.

- **Teacher intervention vs. No teacher intervention**: It has consistently been found that teachers play an important role in facilitating educational use of computer games, but in terms of steering the use in the right direction and providing an effective debriefing that can catch misperceptions and interesting differences in students' experiences while playing. This is neglected in edutainment titles, whereas it is central in the socio-cultural approach.

- **Transfer vs. construction**: From one perspective, the challenge of educational computer games is seen as simply transferring information from the computer game to the player. This has been somewhat successful but the use of this information in other contexts have been significantly harder to document. From a constructionist position the simple transfer of information is not enough. You need to facilitate situations where players actively engage in the computer game and construct their own knowledge through the artefacts of the game world. When the player integrates knowledge into existing structures, it is also easier to transfer it between contexts.

- **Depth vs. superficiality**: Indirectly, the question of what kind of learning we are looking for is touched upon in several of the discussions. It seems obvious, that superficial learning is negatively loaded, nevertheless, this is what is encouraged by the drill-and-practice computer games which are still dominating. Bringing depth into use of educational computer games has proven harder as games are built on simple rules, and we should look to the surrounding social context for facilitating a richer learning experience. Computer games may not deliver a lot of information, but they deliver what the student can grasp and ensure that the information is richly supported. Other media may deliver more detailed information on a given topic, but that is of limited value if the students can only engage in a minor part.

- **One subject vs. cross-subjects**: Another general discussion concerns the cross-curricular nature of computer games. Most especially, commercial computer games can't be fitted within one subject. This makes it hard to access the real impact of computer games, and to use them in school settings.

These insights are central, and are later used to ground the main empirical study, to focus the discussions on the experiences with educational computer games use in the empirical study and to build an overall theory for the area.

Learning theories across the different areas

Until now, we haven't really talked about the different inherent learning theories, that the themes above adhere to. In bits and pieces I have presented learning theories like behaviourism, constructionism and socio-cultural approach. But how do they link with broader developments in learning theories? I will make some generalizations below to show that a pattern emerges from the themes presented. Obviously; no area exclusively adheres to for example behaviourism, cognitivism or constructionism, but all of the areas have some kind of core. In the model below some of the important links, are sketched. The idea is to identify different generations' view on educational use of games, which entails the positioning of different learning theories, the historical progression evident in learning theories, and the connection with the educational use of computer games (Figure 8).

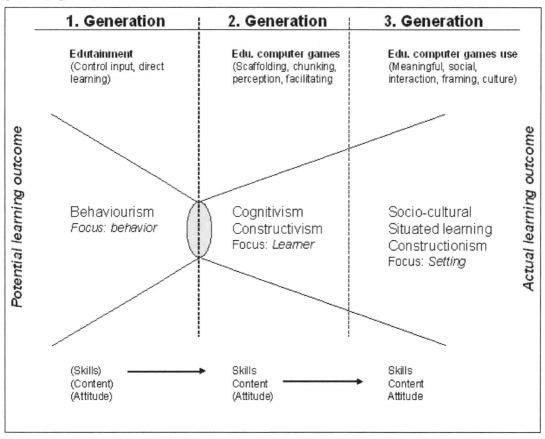

Figure 8: The model shows the different generations characteristics, and how they emphasis different learning theories.

The starting point is a focus on learning through changing the behaviour of students. Behaviourism is only interested in directly observable actions split into a stimuli and a response. The theory claims that you learn by practising skills and contents through reinforcements and conditioning. There is little initial interest in differences between learners, settings and material learned. Through practice you will learn the correct response to a certain stimuli. The 1st generation perspective corresponds with the description of early edutainment that assumes that learning occurs when you unreflectively practise a skill enough times. Some edutainment titles try to differentiate between learners, and take into account different ways of learning, which points towards 2nd generation educational games.

In the cognitivist approach, the learner becomes the centre of attention. The cognitivist approach criticizes the automatic relation presented in behaviourism between stimuli and response. They see the focus on behaviour as skewed, neglecting other important variables, namely the cognitive structures underlying the responses. People have underlying schematas that represent what have been learned. When students approach a new task you need to take into account that they have different schematas. These schematas make up limits and options for each learner that can be addressed through scaffolding information, chunking information, multimedia information, and present material in ways that correspond with cognitive abilities. There are limits to the information you can process, better ways to solve problems and different ways of perceiving information. I call this the 2nd generation approach, using computer games for educational purposes. Here you will try to build educational computer games that present information in ways that are appropriate to this specific learner, and open up different ways of approaching the same topic. The multimedia experience is central for providing these different ways to a topic, and multimedia also supports the player's progression at his own speed and ability. Scaffolding information becomes even more central than in the previous generation. The cognitivist approach and the 2nd generation perspective is also differentiating itself from the 1st generation through its interest in meta-skill: Problem-solving, analysing, perceiving, spatial ability etc. The trend was apparent from the mid-1980's to the mid-1990's where eye-hand coordination, problem-solving and other cognitive skills were heavily researched. It is still found in many educational computer games and educators' preference for the problem-solving abilities that can be harvested from playing computer games.

Constructionism is the bridge between 2. and 3rd generation with a strong focus on the learner, while involving the setting. For constructionists, the artefacts in the environment can be used to mirror the learning processes from the outside. At the same time, the artefacts provide a platform for exploring new material, mostly from an individual perspective, but also in collaboration. This is further stressed in situated learning and the socio-cultural approach, where the learning process is seen as mediated in a social context. In a social context physical artefacts (or tools) are a good facilitator for learning new concepts, as they give a shared starting point and potentially show new ways to proceed (Wenger, 1999; Wertsch, 1991, 1998).

The construction of knowledge, as meaningful through your orientation in a social context, becomes paramount in 3rd generation. Instead of conceiving content, skills and attitudes as residing with the user, knowledge is transferred to culture, tools and communities. Wenger (1999) talks about the interplay between participation and reification, where participants will continuously construct a community through the negotiation of meaning. To support this negotiation reifications are constructed like school culture, agendas, conception of computer games, hi-score tables etc. You learn new things by participating in these communities and appreciating and negotiating what counts as knowledge, skills and attitudes. It is worth stressing, that in this perspective the educational use of computer games ties much closer to the surrounding culture. When you use computer games in schools, the students will draw on a variety of cultural capital to make this experience meaningful. This process is also reciprocal, as the renegotiation of computer games in schools will also lead to new cultural capital being generated, which is useful outside of school. Concretely, this could be introducing computer games as a broader phenomenon than merely action games or changing attitudes towards computer games. Computer games might actually be something else than just fun.

The 3rd generation approach doesn't exclusively focus on the specific computer game, but looks at the broader process of educational use of computer games. It stresses the key role of providing a social context that facilitates asking the right questions and going the right places. Here, the teacher becomes central as facilitator of balancing the educational computer game experience as connected to school, other practices and drawing on other practices to expand the scope of the computer game from 'just' playing to learning.

It should be stressed, that each generation is carried forward to the next, but de-emphasised. The learning mechanisms in behaviourism are still partly at play in next-generations titles and so are the ones from cognitivism but they are conceived in a broader overall frame. They will be more or less adequate for explaining different aspects of learning, for example a socio-cultural approach will have less to say about a student sitting at home playing an educational computer game. Here it will be relevant to look at the interaction between computer game and learner from a more individualistic perspective, like behaviourism or cognitivism.

We can plot the different themes in on a triangle as below (Figure 9), to illustrate how well they relate to the different generations. No theme will fit perfectly, but it still gives a good overview of the development.

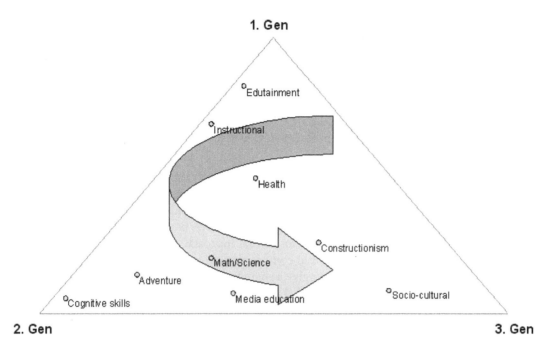

Figure 9: The triangle show how different approaches to educational use of computer games refer to different generations.

The discussion above highlights the need for a broad learning approach to computer games consisting of several layers. We need to appreciate, how content, skills and attitudes are not just transferable and a question of interaction between player and computer game. On the other hand this interaction may very well be severely limited by the concrete implementation of the computer games. An active, interested and strong community that thinks of computer games as its preferred way to learn history, will not get very far if the computer game does not scaffold information, has a problematic interface, assumes existing knowledge nowhere easily found and bombards the students with overwhelming amounts of information. It will certainly also play a role with the basic reward structure, habituation and connecting experience in time. They will be steered in directions by being awarded points, getting a hi-score and beating other players. They will learn that 'sword' refers to the object sword every time they pick up a sword object with text below it. And they will slowly be less impressed by what this specific educational computer game has to offer them.

With a preliminary understanding of how to understand *educational use of computer games* we will expand on this perspective – building the 3rd generation. An important element is a discussion of the relevant educational theories, which is the topic of the next chapter.

Chapter V: An Initial Framework for Studying the Educational Use of Computer Games

We have covered a lot of ground so far getting a fuller understanding of the elements necessary to understand educational use of computer games. The framework built in this chapter relates to the 3rd generation perspective presented in the previous chapter as an alternative to edutainment.

To achieve a more inclusive understanding of educational use of computer games important theory in respect to knowing, learning, teaching, education, computer medium and computer games is presented. The starting point is experiential learning with a strong focus on concrete experiences, which will serve as the framework of this dissertation's later empirical and theoretical work. Building such a framework entails the introduction of the key concepts: *Engagement, play, relevance, experience-based, student autonomy, and representation.*

It is concluded that experiential learning with its focus on experience is a good starting point to achieve a more inclusive perspective on the learning activity, involving player, computer game and context. Normally, concrete experiences will be organized haphazardly in spontaneous concepts, but through instruction scientific concepts can be built. Scientific concepts are what constitute more abstract concepts and thinking, which is central to education. Computer games are potentially a valuable tool for providing such concrete experiences through their rich universe, engaging nature and dynamic presentation of information, but instruction is needed to gain educational relevance.

Different kinds of knowing: Computational view and culturalism

Experiential learning provides an understanding of the *process of learning* but is less interested in the *outcome of learning* and sees knowing as in flux. However, education has an explicit outcome and to some degree work with knowing as a finite size – we have a fixed curriculum that we attempt to hand down to new generations. Before turning to experiential learning I will therefore discuss two views on knowing based on Jerome Bruner's thinking: Computational view and culturalism. I will argue that it doesn't make much sense to grant exclusivity to one on the expense of the other. Although you can of course, depending on your purpose, shift the weight between them as I will do in this dissertation. It is important to build an empirical study and theory of educational game experience, that can acknowledge learning both as a process and an outcome and distinguishing between culturalism and computational view, will help this cause.

The nature of knowing

As have been hinted in the previous chapter, the different generations speak of different kinds of knowing, but what is understood by knowing? I can know a list of kings by heart (content), be able to use a mouse (skill) or know I shouldn't drive too fast (attitude). All of these things are ultimately the result of learning and relates to different types of knowing that I have earlier introduced: content, skills and attitudes. The form of this knowing can however be approached from two sides facilitated by a split between information and knowledge. This split is recognized by Bruner (1996) when he talks about different kinds of knowing, distinguishing between computational view and culturalism.

The computational view operates with information that can be transferred between individuals and stored and retrieved. Information is conceived as a fixed size that do not change as we move between contexts. Bateson (1972) talks about information as the difference that makes a difference. When we draw a map, we select to promote certain differences and although the map is open for interpretation, it does set some affordances for how we as humans read the map. One map will focus on the national differences, another on religious differences and a third the terrain differences. The map provides a form of knowing that is finite and in principle transferable across time and space. From the computational view, to put it bluntly, we can actually ask any student where France is and expect the same fixed answer across time and space. In principle, information denotes any of the above types of learning (content, skills and attitudes); I can tell you about the kings, show you how to move the mouse and tell you that speeding is wrong. The information can be transferred between individuals and contexts.

Bruner (1996) is initially disapproving of this perspective which has roots back to the start of the 20th century's instructional theory discussed earlier and is also apparent in Bloom's taxonomy. He doesn't see the computational view as offering a great many tools for teachers to improve the learning process. To check whether students know France is hardly helpful for improving learning or teaching. We can tell 30 students in a classroom about France and afterwards some are able to answer correctly that France is a republic, whereas others aren't. However, the why seems to escape us. Still, Bruner finds that each kind of knowing offers a relevant perspective for approaching knowing and describing different properties. The computational view to a certain extent views knowing as in a vacuum, and this is helpful if we are to generalize across contexts. It may not really be sensible to talk about humans as acquiring information but it is quite helpful when pointing to artefacts, tools, environments and shared spaces that can be used to facilitate learning. Any of these will in an abstract sense have some difference, that we as humans are likely to find relevant differences through our cognitive apparatus, heritage and socialization.

For culturalism, growing out of constructivism, meaning is central to understand information - understanding the differences that make a difference requires human perception, ultimately resulting in understanding a piece of information. The process of seeing the difference is one of linking pieces across different context by drawing on previous experiences. From the perspective of culturalism, information is constructed, from a given individual's perspective in a specific situation, drawing on previous experiences. An individual will in a learning process approach a given area by drawing on cultural artefacts (including media) and in this process transform information into something meaningful from his/her position - knowledge. From this perspective, knowing requires that a student actively engages in constructing the knowledge. The student acknowledges the right differences and is able to understand the differences by drawing on previous experiences, concepts and narratives. Bruner (1996) tries to reconcile the two positions, but I do not find his compromise entirely appropriate for my purpose.

Instead, I will suggest that these two perspectives point to different forms of knowing. The computational view talks about information detached from individuals as an outcome, whereas culturalism addresses knowledge attached to a situated individual involved in a process. We must be careful not to grant exclusivity to one on the expense of the other, which is what I described as one of the problems with edutainment in the previous chapter. Edutainment assumes a computational view, forgetting how the information is put in play. From a culturalism perspective knowing is personal, meaningful and constructed in connection to more or less generalizable situations, often by using artefacts in a given context. The artefacts including media, set a number of differences, resulting in affordances for the human cognitive apparatus. In some sense it is actually possible for knowing to travel across contexts and individuals as information. This implies that we are capable of transforming knowledge into information and information into knowledge. We do this constantly and with little thought, unless it causes misunderstandings or problems.

Consider the following example that illustrates the two views concerning students playing a historical computer game: "Napoleon led the French forces at Waterloo in 1815". This seems to be a straightforward 'bite' of information that could be part of a curriculum. When one present this in a school class it will, however, take on a number of alternative meanings, although as Bruner (1996) stresses, limited by a variety of general constraints in our cognitive apparatus (i.e. language and human evolution). However, students may have very different backgrounds that will make this sentence meaningful. One may not know Napoleon and take it to be a random general. Another might be well-versed in the Napoleon wars and connect this statement with Napoleon's final defeat after re-emerging as emperor from his imprisonment at Elba. Both interpretations result in learning something. For one student it will support his perception of history in Napoleonic era, while another will gain some factual knowledge of this general called Napoleon.

The information in the specific sentence leads to different constructions of knowledge based on background, context and skills that will change over time. Thus, students transform information into something meaningful for them at a given time. This something is knowledge. The important implication of this, is that we construct knowledge based on earlier presuppositions and the context we are in. However, it also acknowledges that a finite amount of information concerning a topic is presented in a computer game that we built our knowledge on and the quality and scope of this information is an important variable in the learner's construction of knowledge. It is also worth stressing, that the meaning-making of a given piece of information is bound by a number of affordances that support the process of learning (Bruner, 1996; Jonassen, 2001).

Information can also serve as an indicator of learning outcome, although it may be a problematic abstraction to neglect the process the information is layered into. Mostly when you evaluate a given course, you will focus on the information as a finite size and neglect the knowledge of the student. Evaluation becomes increasingly problematic the further you move from information to knowledge, implying that the student is generating the knowledge. There is a difference in knowing between reading a textbook on history with the right answers and playing a computer game where you have to construct the right answers based on your actions in the computer game. With the reading of a textbook you risk memorizing information with few handles for actually using this knowledge at a later time. Computer game experiences will contrary to the textbook experiences provide more handles, as you are building the concepts through actions, providing a richer contextualizing (Schank, 1999).

In summary, I will operate with the concepts *information* (computational view) and *knowledge* (culturalism) to describe different forms of knowing. A narrow focus on information lends itself to a 1st generation perspective on educational use of computer games, where behaviourism is central. My approach will rather build on the 3rd generation perspective outlined in the previous chapter, building on especially constructivism. In my perspective the computational view and culturalism are both important to include, when approaching educational use of computer games. The computational view points to the potential of a given activity, whereas culturalism point to the actual realization of this potential. A computer game, textbook, or historical city walk will present some differences in the world, but these differences need to be appreciated, explored and linked. Next, the process of appreciating, exploring and linking the differences in the world is at the centre of the scene.

An experiential approach to learning

Experiential learning offers an alternative to more traditional understandings of how we in school come to appreciate the differences that make a difference by refining concrete experiences. Computer games are well-suited to support the focus on the concrete experience, as an activity where players are engaged in doing things. Students playing a computer game will point and click, resulting in concrete experiences that are then refined. In the following we will look closer at this process of refinement.

The experiential approach to learning is not a close-knitted theoretical system, but consists of a number of theorists with a shared focus on the importance of experience in any learning situation. The lack of experience-based learning is evident in the educational system, when we consider history, geography, citizenship or religion. We are not actually basing the learning in school on concrete experiences with a given topic, but are primarily relying on students reading or hearing about topics mostly represented by abstract information and concepts with little connection to an actual experience base. This is not a criticism of reading or hearing as these are strong teaching tools, but rather a challenge of the balance between these and other approaches in education. The educational system seems to entertain the fantasy that we can skip the concrete experiences altogether. Instead, reading and hearing about abstract concepts, exclusively reasoning based on these abstract concepts. The experiential learning approach challenges this as a viable path by insisting that learning extends from concrete experiences and that the experiences of students themselves are brought to the centre of the scene.

The strongest proponents of experiential learning are Kolb, Dewey, Piaget, Lewin, Roger and Freire, who are all in some ways opposing the educational system of their time. I will start with Kolb's account in the following as he tries to integrate the different approaches. According to Kolb (1984), experiential learning theorists share a range of assumptions about learning:

- Learning is about *constructing* knowledge not transmitting it.

- Learning should focus on the *process* and *feedback* not the outcome.

- Learning should build on students' *existing knowledge* about a given topic and expand this understanding.

- Learning is fuelled by conflict between *different perspectives* on the world – action, reflecting, feeling and thinking.

- Learning is an *interaction* between the individual and the surroundings. (Kolb & Kolb, 2003)

We will adopt these assumptions, stressing that they represent culturalism that remains fruitful for this dissertation's focus, remembering that the computational view is also a valid perspective.

The experiential learning approach has over the years worked with a learning cycle to stress the hermeneutic nature of learning. Kolb's theory evolves around learning through a four-staged cycle, which historically has roots in similar models by Dewey and Lewin. The model caters for different learning modes, and attempts to present the flow in learning experiences. Different learning modes create a tension that push knowledge forward and in principal take the learner through all four modes. The concrete experience is the basis for the observations and reflections. The reflections transform experiences into abstract concepts, inspiring new forms of actions. The experiences from the new actions are then tested and reflected creating new concrete experiences. The process is then repeated – you will never completely grasp a given area or experience, but continuously explore, closing in on it in a hermeneutic process (Kolb & Kolb, 2003). I will not use the expanded terminology of Kolb, but merely the basic structure to explain the

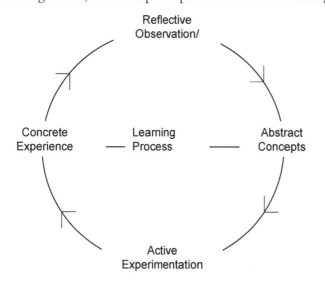

Figure 10: The backbone of experiential learning theory that extends from a circular understanding of learning (Kolb, 1984).

dynamics of learning that are relevant to transfer to educational use of computer games. Experiential learning does not convincingly argue for what drives the learning process forward through the cycle (Figure 10). Drawing on Kelly (1963), I find that humans are constantly exploring the surroundings. Kelly (1963) stresses that the individual is constantly testing and exploring the surrounding world to maintain an adequate perception so that he can act appropriately in a given situation. The basic metaphor and starting point for Kelly is man-as-scientist. He states that:

> Might not the individual man, each in his own personal way, assume more of the stature of a scientist, ever seeking to predict and control the course of events with which he is involved. Would he not have his theories, test his hypotheses and weigh his experimental evidence.

Kelly (1963:5)

This continuing exploration of the surrounding and testing of concepts is impeded by the threat of damage to our perception of the world that can result from the alteration of subordinate concepts (Kelly, 1963). Thus, we are constantly interested in getting a fuller understanding of the world around us, by exploring our experiences while constructing new knowledge, but are held back by the risks associated with new insights. Education is such a safe place, and as we will see later, likewise is play.

Experience and education

Dewey is one of the first proponents for changing school, so it aligns itself better with students' capacity by drawing on their experiences from all spheres of life, and their natural curiosity for exploring the surroundings. Ultimately, this is based on a wish to increase interest and motivation, leading to improved learning by linking learning to students' existing concepts and experiences while making knowledge from school accessible in other contexts. The critique of schooling has increased as the educational system fails to make students capable of actual using their education in everyday contexts. We should remember that ultimately education is merely a subset of learning, namely a planned learning experience facilitated by a teacher. In this sense education must be seen as an attempted socialization of a new generation that can be described in a double perspective: Differentiation and qualification (Ljungstrøm, 1984). The basic goal of the educational system remains one of putting students into the right boxes, while providing them with the proper, necessary knowledge to survive in this box. This double perspective has often resulted in a detached educational system, where you take students out of their everyday context to qualify and differentiate them. On graduation they are inserted back into society in the right places.

The problem of detachness from everyday life is built into the educational system during the formative 18th century as a natural consequence of the differentiation and qualification. Arguably, students always experienced the detachness of the school and failed to see the relevance of learning the finer details of algebra, the American Civil War or German grammar which is certainly far from their everyday life. However, it now makes more of a difference with the changed view on the student role in education. The necessary education was earlier handed down to new generations through authorities that have now been weakened. The lack of authorities makes it hard to maintain the automatic acceptance of the curriculum. The perceived relevance among students, therefore, becomes increasingly important (Egenfeldt-Nielsen, 2001).

It has, therefore, been attempted to put these abstract concepts into everyday contexts or linking them with the student's everyday life. This can for example be algebra questions, like for instance if you have two bananas and Karen gives you five bananas what will you then end up with? This approach builds on Dewey's educational philosophy, and Dewey's thinking can with advantage be used as the framework for educational use of computer games. Dewey elaborates on the role of concrete experiences.

The role of experience

The role of concrete experience in Kolb's cycle is seductively simple, but also quite vague. It is unclear what makes up an experience, but Dewey sheds some light on the concept. According to Dewey (1910), experience is the interaction between humans and their environment including thinking, feeling, seeing, handling and doing. Experiences are equally present whether we are in a real or artificial universe – on the savannah, in the class room or the game universe. In today's computer games you are part of a living, breathing, simulated universe with very concrete self-sustaining experiences –getting still closer to reality (Picture 11).

Picture 11: The left picture is from *Grand Theft Auto 3* showing a very common concrete experience in computer games. The right picture shows rush hour gone bad in *SimCity 4*. Both are clear example of how computer games present very concrete experiences.

What we do, see, feel or think constitutes an experience in any of these places. The insistence on education starting from the concrete experience going to the abstract is also elaborated on by Dewey. He stresses that the concrete should not be confused with a detachness from thinking or a prominence for manual work. Rather the "Concrete denoted a meaning definitely marked off from other meanings so that it is readily apprehended by itself" (Dewey, 1910:136). From the concrete we make links to other similar experiences, building concepts to group concrete experiences. This involves that we should start education from experiences that do not assume a number of links are already in place. The concrete experiences can be seen as objects that through internalization become natural to us like a stone, house or tree. In picture 11 we see how self-sustaining computer games are, there is little need to explain the pictures, although a bit small here. The concreteness of computer games doesn't imply that they lack referentiality, but the referentiality is less of a pre-requisite for understanding computer games compared to abstract concepts delivered through textbooks.

Experiences should not really be thought of in an atomistic sense but, rather as a continuum – experiences do not exist in a vacuum neither in respect to surrounding nor previous experience[15]. However, they can be understood without reference to other concepts. A history teacher starting off explaining the concept of mercantilism will inevitably make a number of assumptions on behalf of the students in terms of existing experiences and concepts. This poses few problems if these assumptions are actually part of students' experience-base. However, the assumptions often match

---

[15] This is also supported by more recent educational research (Schank, 1999)

the teacher's background and not the students' experience-base. Furthermore, the experience-bases that are referred to are not easily accessible to the students.

The continuity of experience is a key in Dewey's (1938) thinking. Earlier experiences will take something from earlier experiences and channel later experiences. In this perspective education becomes a beacon in people's learning environment that can guide them in the right direction by helping them to appreciate, explore and focus on certain aspects in their future experiences. Dewey (1938) stresses that the experiences do not exist in a vacuum and that experiences are formed as an interaction between internal and external conditions.

> Above all they [teachers] should know how to utilize the surroundings, physical and
> social, that exist so as to extract from them all that they have to contribute to building
> up experiences that are worth while.

Dewey (1938:40)

From Dewey's point of view education should rest on experience, but all experiences are not necessarily educational. Dewey (1938) stresses that education tries to facilitate certain approaches to different areas in correspondence with the educator's goals (often set up by a curriculum). The educational value ultimately rests on the "quality of the experience". First of all, the quality is decided by whether it is immediately agreeable to the student, which decides whether the student will engage with the experience. This will depend on the student's ability to connect educational experience with previous or future experience. When a computer game gets started it incessantly builds on previous experiences and instils anticipation in the student that learning something is useful later in the game. Second, some experiences may limit a student's further progress by changing the student's view on a topic or the process of learning in general. Experiences of a high educational quality will on the other hand have a benign effect on future learning processes in general and open the student's mind to other educational experiences. Playing a historical strategy game focusing on war might educate the student in some aspects of history, but may also limit the possibility of adding other important historical facets in future history education orientating the student towards a conception of history beyond war.

In summary, Dewey focuses on educational experiences as characterized by closeness to student experiences and engaging students while promoting future capacity for learning in general and opening up for additional educational experiences. This provides a strong sense of relevance and willingness to engage with a given topic. The student's initial engagement can be thought of as an investment in the object under investigation that pushes learning forward beyond the initial exploration. We continuously invest in a topic linking our understanding of the world, our experiences and concepts to a given topic. This will sustain our interest allowing us to further expand our knowledge of a field, but also make us dependent on our knowing within this topic. You build the relation through exploration of the object over time.[16]

Scientific and spontaneous concepts

So far I have concentrated on the concrete experience in the learning process, but next I extend the framework by elaborating on the role of concepts. The goal is to understand the difference between concepts learned through education, and concepts that emerge more spontaneously in any

---

[16] This assumes that in principle any object holds the same interest for humans. You might as well be a history top-student as a math top-student, although recent research suggests innate topic preferences. History, culture, evolution, situation and predispositions make some paths easier to take (Bransford et al., 1999). However, the point is that beyond the initial curiosity you need to invest in a topic to continue learning about it and this often depends on you linking it to some previous or future experience.

setting. The concepts formed by education have some advantages that should be catered for, when using computer games in an educational setting. Vygotsky's (1986) differentiation between scientific concepts and spontaneous concepts is in that connection useful.

Vygotsky's (1986) two concepts describe different ways of organizing and approaching knowledge. The term spontaneous concepts refer to concepts that emerge from the bottom-up - the spontaneous ordering of experiences. The spontaneous concepts are not systematic and often not conscious, but still used to group experiences. Scientific concepts are in comparison top-down brought around by teaching and instruction. Scientific concepts make the student capable of higher mental functioning and are characterized by being systematic, general, abstract and organizing. The scientific concepts are not possible without an experience-base that gives the scientific concepts the concrete experiences to build the organization on. With no experience base to build the scientific concepts on students will merely learn "parrot-like repetition". To a large degree the strength of a concept lies in drawing on concrete experiences, although over time the concept (as more experiences support the concept) will lose the connections with concrete experiences maintaining only the general characteristics. However, the concept will still be able to activate the experiences under different circumstances, depending on the structuring of experiences and concepts (Schank, 1999). The important point is that it is not hard to teach a student the word mercantilism or give some rudimentary understanding of it relating to trade. However, the concept behind is hard to learn if you have no experiences to build the concept from and especially the transfer to other situations becomes hard (Schank, 1999; Vygotsky, 1986). This is, an increasing problem as school moves further away from the society and as the scientific concepts become more abstract and hard to relate to the experiences of students (Højholt & Witt, 1996). The top-down approach of scientific concepts doesn't imply a direct transfer of concept from teacher to student. Vygotsky (1986) stresses that although scientific concepts are verbal, abstract and systematic they are still constructed by the student linking with previous experiences and concepts (both spontaneous and scientific). It should be stressed that one of the concepts does not have supremacy over the other as they both serve important purposes. Vygotsky finds scientific concepts usually to be ahead of spontaneous concepts if instruction is appropriately based on an experience base.

These observations are clearly relevant to educational use of computer games, where you may downgrade the teacher's instruction letting the experience in the game universe take primacy. This will parallel Dewey's (1938) warning against letting the progressive school (experience-based) lose sight of the teacher's responsibility to guide and extrapolate the essence from experiences. Students will, of course, acquire a number of experiences immersed in the game universe, but these will primarily be ordered as spontaneous concepts and not scientific concepts that can help students see the experiences in a broader perspective, and link it to other related insights within the topic. Indeed, students may, left with spontaneous concepts due to its 'unconscious nature', feel that they haven't learned anything. Especially the linking with other scientific concepts learned through instruction will be hard to connect with the spontaneous concepts. Some random spontaneous concepts risk becoming the only result from using computer games without proper instruction and teaching, which we saw in the previous chapter was mostly the case with edutainment that existed in an instructional vacuum. Edutainment may reinforce some links but not add new links – training rather than learning.

Dewey (1938) cautions us that often school works opposite Vygotsky's implicit intention 'forcing' the scientific concepts on the students, which lacks the experience base to provide the substance to the concepts. Instead of transforming student experiences into scientific concepts the 'parrot like' approach is dominating with scientific concepts being empty vessels. Figure 11 is an elaboration of the abstract concepts in the basic experiential learning model. The abstract concepts comes closest to being a learning outcome that can have two different forms arising spontaneously through actions (spontaneous concepts), or facilitated through instruction (scientific concepts). The question of instruction lies beyond this dissertation, but scaffolding is too central in educational use of computer games to be ignored. Researchers, as we saw in chapter 4, have often stressed the potential scaffolding of computer games. The zone of proximal development is relevant to understand the broader potential of scaffolding in educational use of computer games.

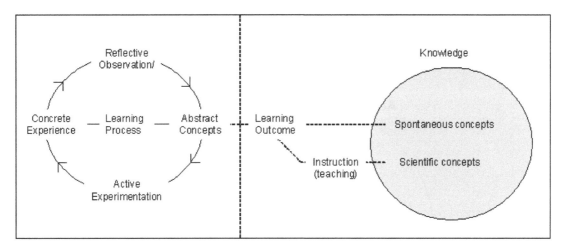

Figure 11: Summarises the connection discussed so far between experience, learning, instruction, concepts and knowledge.

In the introduction to this dissertation I was initially careful not to conceive teaching and instruction as linked to school and even to education. Teaching is on an overall level best conceived in relation to Vygotsky's (1986) zone of proximal development. This theory is originally aimed at children and parents, but is also relevant for teachers.

The theory basically describes the difference between actual and potential zone of development. The actual zone is the development a child or student can achieve by himself, whereas the potential zone is the development achievable with the help of a parent or some kind of tool. Pointing out key elements, reducing complexity or correcting mistakes helps achieve the potential zone of development.

Wertsch (1991) expands on the nature such instruction can take, and finds that a number of tools can also serve this role. Tool is quite broadly perceived including language, book, hammer, theoretical work or computer game. In the following I will expand on how we can conceive of tools in education to understand the potential scaffolding in educational use of computer games. This is central as a computer game can be seen as a tool that mediates the student's approach to a given topic.

The socio-cultural approach: tools, activity and context

The socio-cultural approach focuses on learning as an activity including a closer examination of tools as mediating activities. Furthermore, the socio-cultural approach combined with situated learning can include context, culture and history that is not explicitly included in experiential learning theory. It is especially the work by theorists like Wertsch, Vygotsky, Lave and Wenger that is useful. The differentiation between non-mediated and mediated experiences is important, when we want to understand how education changes with the introduction of computer games as a tool.

Computer games as an embodied tool extend the action of a given agent creating both opportunities and limitations for the agent using it as figure 12 shows below. An activity consists of a relation between a subject and an object, which is mediated by a tool. Tools can be a variety of artefacts found in our social and cultural life that endow us with a variety of opportunities. When we use language we are drawing on a symbolic tool refined through generations. This implies that reading, hearing or writing are experiences that use the symbolic tool language. Language is thick with culture and history, making it useful for a variety of purposes. The same is true when using stories, documentaries, textbooks, blackboards, pencils, calculators, computer games or any other artefact although few have the extensive range of language (Oliver & Pelletier, 2004; Vygotsky, 1986; Wertsch, 1991, 1998). The socio-cultural perspective alerts us to the importance of considering tools and context when thinking about learning and education. Different contexts and tools facilitate a variety of learning experiences, which are also the starting point for situated learning.

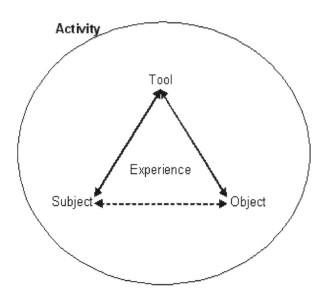

Figure 12: Mediated activity involves the relation between subject, object and tool resulting in an experience. This experience is shaped by the subject, object and tools.

Situated learning insists that to learn is ultimately to become part of a community of praxis. A community of praxis is a somewhat fuzzy term. Wenger goes through great lengths to encircle the characteristics of a community of praxis. The central constitutions of a community of praxis are mutual engagement, joint enterprise and a shared repertoire. The mutual engagement refers to a shared commitment latent in relations towards a given activity. It is not enough to merely be physically located together or be interested in the same topic. The engagement has to be connected in a rich and meaningful way (Wenger, 1999). The increasing engagement in a given community of praxis points you in the direction of how to speak, act, think etc. – ultimately what is important and what is not. In that sense, knowledge becomes socially distributed, not existing inside people, but in their connections, shared artefacts and joint activities. You gain, what Wenger above calls, a shared repertoire around certain activities. Knowledge is continuously produced and reproduced through everyday praxis. "This focus in turn promotes a view of knowing as activity by specific people in specific circumstances" (Lave & Wenger, 1991:52). Remembering my initial differentiation between computational view and culturalism, here is a clear example of knowing from a culturalism point of view.

Knowing and transfer
Situated learning has levelled a hard criticism against the assumed transfer of information as it finds that information does not really become part of everyday life – information is not part of the repertoire we use to engage joint enterprises. From a situated learning perspective we should see

real knowing as grounded in a context. The generalization from a given situation and the forming of spontaneous or scientific concepts doesn't ensure that you can use these concepts in all situations. You have to be able to fit the concepts within a new specific situation (Lave & Wenger, 1991). A radical interpretation of this theory may conclude that we are not capable of transferring knowledge between different communities and contexts. However, this doesn't seem to be the intention behind situated learning. Lave & Wenger (1991) are, nevertheless, showing that the transfer is very hard, and that we should consciously think about creating links between different situations.[17] An approach supported by most modern educational thinking (i.e. Bransford et al., 1999; Schank, 1999). To simply learn the facts and knowledge of a given topic is not enough. You need to apply knowledge to your own life. In that sense situated learning is also sceptical towards current schooling practice and sole reliance on language for learning. In school, knowledge is not connected to the existing practice of students and is often limited to being experienced through language providing few handles for using the knowledge in other different contexts.

When we talk of transfer there is constant debate between the situated learning tradition and the cognitive learning tradition. Initially, these two perspectives differ in where they locate knowledge – fixed in the individual (computational) or fluid in the context (culturalism). From a cognitive learning perspective individuals acquire knowledge that they can bring with them to different contexts. The problem from a cognitive perspective is that the transfer of a learning task and closely related task is often very low. This is usually put down to our limited knowledge about instructional theory and improvements to learning methods are seen as the way forward (Döpping, 1995).

Situated learning is more focused on how knowledge seems to be a part of our everyday praxis and hence is bound to the contexts we engage in. The student fails to generalize from one context to broader application. It is not integrated into the student's existing knowledge structures and is only understood in a quite inflexible way. An analogy to Plato's famous horse example may prove the point. Plato tries to prove the existence of the idea world by pointing to the fact that we can recognize a horse as a horse despite the lack of a large amount of its defining attributes. We still know it is a horse even though one cuts off two legs or take away its mane. According to Plato this proves that we have an idea about the horse that enables us to recognize a horse defying the immediate shortcomings in physical attributes. However, from my perspective the reason why you can recognize the horse is not because of the invisible idea world, but rather because the horse is integrated in a variety of ways in our mind through numerous experiences. This makes it possible for us to generalize from a given set of characteristics to the horse in full – we have the concept of a horse and a number of concrete experiences we can compare when seeing the horse. By experiencing a number of horses we increasingly appreciate the differences that make a difference and are able to ignore the missing legs or mane in the example above.

The discussions above show that we should be careful with our assumptions about how students approach a given computer game. They may very well misperceive information in a computer game and construct limited knowledge of a given area. Constructions may depend on context and slowly change as experiences are connected with more experiences. Ultimately we will have a very hard time actually measuring the educational benefits from game experience because we end of focusing on the outcome neglecting the continuous process involved. We may especially be trapped if we insist on using traditional ways of measuring learning outcome like factual tests that insist on peeling off the layers that according to culturalism make up knowledge. Instead, we should apply methods that are sensitive to both culturalism and computational view, which is also attempted in the later empirical study.

---

[17] This is also the focus of Wenger's later work that examines just how knowledge travels in a community (Wenger, 1999).

Language and everyday experiences

Often we will encounter a reliance on language as *the* tool to teach new generations the necessary content, skills and attitudes to become part of society. We certainly have a preference for lectures, group discussions, black boards and text books that lie quite far from the situations where we are actually expected to make use of many years of schooling. This approach is not the one seen, when we observe the development of children, where different modalities are coupled to guide children: pointing, telling, smiling and showing (Gleitman, 1995; Wertsch, 1998). Preference for language is especially visible in the formulation of curriculum and in the forms of assessment chosen to evaluate students as discussed above. We may go on field trips, set up workshops or other experimental set-ups but mostly we will not consider it valid assessment – here we count on multiple choice tests or essays. The prominence of language is not surprising as it presents one of the most powerful symbolic tools for sharing and transforming experiences. However, language is not *the* experience, but rather a tool for manipulating the narratives that represent our experiences (Bruner, 1991).

Although language is an intrinsic quality of many experiences there is a qualitative difference between experiences that promote exclusivity to language and experiences where language is used to extend the experience. We should, of course, not remove language from the educational setting, which would also be an impossible endeavour. However, we should consider what the limitations are of the current prominence awarded language. Language tends to promote the general principles as it is a tool for generalizing and ordering our world. Language is also especially a tool for manipulating and transforming experiences not necessarily having experiences (Bruner, 1991). Of course, when we read or hear something we are using language as a tool, but the language is never *the* experience. Returning to the difference between spontaneous concepts and scientific concepts we realize that the latter relies heavily on language. Scientific concepts are possible because we can use language to order, share, structure and generalize from experience. Language is the first choice for describing, presenting, analysing and discussing scientific concepts, but this needs to build on some experience-base, and this is often lacking in education. Here computer games may be a way to providing concrete experiences in areas that are otherwise hard. Students can immerse themselves into urban planning in *SimCity*, see the evolution of civilization in *Civilization* and experience Medieval Europe in *Europa Universalis*

It is a problem if scientific concepts lack the grounding in experiences. We should challenge that most students' experience-base in relation to school is more made up of scientific concepts than concrete experiences. A teacher will present the scientific concepts that group together history, geographic or political system. However, in many cases there will be little time for more concrete experiences that lack the abstract, general and orderliness of scientific concepts. For a teacher it is natural to present the scientific concepts (often coupled with spontaneous concepts) as this is the teacher's understanding reached in the field – the cream of the cream. However, without grounding in more concrete experiences whether in school or anywhere else, students will not get a real understanding of a given concept. This is, of course, evermore problematic if school is alienated from students' everyday experiences, which seems to be the natural state of educational systems – school is always accused of trailing behind the real society, which is actually quite natural if built on scientific concepts. Scientific concepts needs time to be built and formulated and there is a natural sluggishness between generations of teachers, each having their canon with them when graduating from teacher's college.

The problem of up-to-date scientific concepts is, however, less important than the overwhelming stream of scientific concepts students are bombarded with. The constant stream of information from lectures, textbooks and talks do not reach students who lack the reason, time and means to invest the necessary energy. The educational experience lacks cracks, roughness, richness, variation, relevance and presence - redundancy and details that may provide the spark for one particular student. The redundancy may provide what is needed for one student to find a part to connect with, although it overall may seem superfluous. The educational system is so pressed to present an ever-increasing curriculum that it disregards the importance of instilling the necessary richness in student's experience-base and ensuring that there actually is a foundation to build on, which is increasingly considered the significant differences between novices and experts (Bransford et al., 1999).

This is ultimately a question of prioritisation in the educational system that is avoided due to its political sensibility. The educational system can't maintain the same breadth in the curriculum if the curriculum actually has to be learned – the breadth requires that some areas are in practice prioritised quite low. The cracks and roughness that language-mediated experiences are deprived of are found in experiences that involve students deeper with seeing, doing, perceiving, feeling and thinking like computer games. These experiences are fuzzier than a well-defined scientific concept, but important, providing the glue and examples for the more abstract concepts. You need to be able to connect abstract utterances with some more concrete experiences. You need a rich amount of experiences to generalize from and experiences that can work as metaphors for larger concepts.

The practical problem is that many of the topics in school are quite hard to get rich experience with: Slave trade, civil wars, national depressions or foreign countries. Especially topics connected to citizenship (social studies) are hard to make relevant within the current physical limitations and financial realities. Inspecting the trenches, in First World War, feeling the depression of the 1930s or even getting a feel for the current political system in your country are not within reach for most schools. Field trips are a popular alternative, but present a lot of practical problems. They are only applicable for a limited number of activities and field trips don't necessarily let the students engage in relevant experiences. In physics and chemistry experimental set-ups are another popular way to give students some concrete experience with the quite abstract scientific concepts that make up these fields. We do, however, not necessarily have to be physically present to explore a given activity. The insistence on concrete experiences is not necessarily tied to first hand experience located in a physical environment, but rather to do one of two things. First you can attempt to put the student's everyday experiences at the centre of the learning process, hereby strengthening the links of scientific concepts with the student's experience with the added benefit of strengthening the transfer of knowledge between school and everyday life. Second, you can engage students in activities that are not approaching a topic top-down, but bottom-up. This can be a role-play of everyday life in a medieval village or an exploration of the role of horses up through story. This is a concrete experience less abstract than traditional teaching. The point I have been aiming at is that a game universe can often provide such concrete experiences. This is later studied in the empirical study and unfolded in the theory on educational use of computer games. A crucial factor in the more concrete experiences is the framing of such experiences through scientific concepts insisted on by the instructor. It seems obvious that we can't have concrete experiences with the plague, world wars or depressions. However, the context of play allows for us to explore such experiences in a safe environment.

Playful learning: the relationship between playing and learning

Until now I have presented a framework for understanding teaching, education and learning, but have yet to discuss the significance of play. Engaging with a computer game is a type of play and this lends it certain advantages compared to other activities (Egenfeldt-Nielsen & Smith, 2000). The focus in the following is on play as a safe environment for exploration and the possibility of paraphrasing actions. This ability makes it possible to gain experiences that would otherwise be hard to obtain. The idea of using play for learning has a long tradition, resting on theorists conceiving play as important for especially children's development. These theorists are paralleled by an evolutionary perspective that takes animal play as its starting point, extending it to humans.

The basic assumption in evolutionary play theory is that through play we have a chance of exploring and training in areas that are relevant in our everyday life. Through framing something as make-believe we can engage in activities that are normally not acceptable, potentially dangerous or completely unknown. In this way animals (and humans) adapt to the surrounding environment and through play ultimately get a better chance of survival (Fagen, 1995). The evolutionary perspective does not see animal and human play as qualitatively different, but as lying on continuum. Most basic human play forms mirror animal play but humans are capable of performing more complex forms of play. The same rationale that works for animals applies to humans and from this perspective play is well suited to engage in new activities and learn about these (Fagen, 1995; Sutton-Smith, 1997). The developmental perspective on play in humans has been the object of study during especially the 20th century. It has roots in the age of enlightenment with its somewhat romantic perception of childhood represented by for example Jean-Jacques Rousseau in his book *Emile* (1762/1993). Play continues to be an important element of pedagogy theories with significant theoretical work picking up in the 1960s. The development perspective has also strong roots in psychology and education championed by Jean Piaget, Lev Vygotsky, Donald W. Winnicot and Erik E. Eriksson. They all see play as a central part of development stressing different functions of play (Bruner, Jolly, & Sylva, 1976; Corbeil, 1999; Makedon, 1984).

The overall idea of play as a safe area for exploration is central for the above perspective, but we have yet to explore the ability of play to paraphrase certain actions. We will, therefore, take a closer look at Gregory Bateson's (1972) theory on meta-communication that describes the characteristics of play as the framing of a context. He convincingly argues for how play is capable of framing a situation differently in that participants negotiate how actions within a certain context should be understood. Huizinga (1986) calls this the magic circle that shelters play from outside interferences and repercussions. Bateson calls the skill, necessary for play, meta-communication and stresses that this ability is widely used in all encounters in society, but is first developed in play.

In this perspective, play can be seen as the basis for engaging in social encounters, where we have different expectations and conventions in different settings. It is through play we learn to appreciate that actions within different contexts do not hold the same meaning. The following situation illustrates the communication in a play situation: Two boys are engaged in rough-and-tumble play. On one level the boys communicate to each other that they are fighting in imitating the movement, noises, thoughts and feelings of a fight. On the other hand, they are communicating that it is not really a fight. When they throw a punch, it is a punch, but still not really a punch. They communicate that this is a play frame and that special rules apply. This makes it an obvious place for exploring new ideas and concepts that may otherwise be threatening or beyond immediate reach of students.

The real significance of the above discussion is perceiving play as one of the first areas, where we are able to construct a fitting context around our actions. We can do something without meaning it or do something so it means something else. Play is important for the development of communication and especially meta-communication. But play is also the place, where we can actually engage in new, strange or dangerous activities with different consequences than usual, as the evolutionary perspective argues. In play we are allowed to change rules and consequences within a given frame to explore different alternatives in a safe environment. The safe environment is even truer of computer games, where you explore through representations that are more flexible and open to our manipulations. You can set-up more realistic situations than would normally be possible in play, for example mountain-climbing, racing, martial arts games or huge battles through the use of a number of props at your disposal with computer games. "All of the power none of the responsibility" as the commercial for the computer game *Red Alert* reads.

The important takeaway is that play has been related to learning primarily as a setting, where it is possible to safely explore ideas, concepts, experiences and sceneries. As discussed computer games provide play with a number of unique capabilities in terms of representing a safe environment and the props available. This will be discussed in the following.

Building blocks for a theory on educational use of computer games

When approaching educational use of computer games one should be careful not to confuse the merits belonging to the domain of respectively computer, game and playing. It is obvious that playing a computer game will share some similarities with the activity of playing - as the framing of the experience, the computer platform as the tool used and the game as the representational form. Here the aim is to understand the manifestation of the latent potentials that in combination make up a computer game and how this connects with educational use. A first natural step is to start with the characteristics of the computer medium, which we have so far neglected.

The charateristics of the computer medium

> Computers can 'only do what they are programmed to do,' but the same is true of a fertilized egg trying to become a baby.

> Alan Kay (1999: 46)

Drawing on Alan Kay (1999) and Niels Ole Finnemann (1999) we can approach the computer as consisting of an infinite number of 'atoms' or a new alphabet that we can use to make different forms of representation. In a computer the manifestations of atoms into different forms can be chosen freely compared to the limitations of traditional artefacts. What is really interesting is what form or architecture we use for shaping the atoms and what implications the exact form of computer programs may have for the actual use.

Finnemann (1999) provides a thorough attempt at describing the computer in terms with little preference for a specific use of computers. He outlines three constraints for use of computers:

- **Informational alphabet**: This refers to the computer as relying on a notation system consisting of units emptied of semantic value that are layered into a sequence. It is possible to manipulate the physical operative unit, which provides us with a high degree of freedom.

- **Set of rules**: Any computer process is controlled by a set of rules, which are systematic. We are capable of manipulating these rules in any way as long as the syntax remains consistent.

- **Interface**: We determine the content of the processes controlled by the rules on the semantic and the rule level through an interface.

This overall implies that we can manipulate the computer on the lowest level – below the semantic content and below the rules level – we can in principal change any process in any way, when it can initially be represented in the computer.

> The notation system (and the presence of the computer) represents the only invariant constraints for any computer process. If something can be represented in this system it can be processed in a computer and thus we can say that the computer is basically defined by a new kind of alphabet.

Finnemann goes on to argue that the computer with its new alphabet is capable of representing a multitude of semantic regimes (i.e. linguistic, auditory, pictorial and logical). The informational alphabet can represent an infinite number of linguistic alphabets while a linguistic alphabet only works within its own limits. Finnemann points out that it is possible to use different semantic regimes for controlling the machine although you will inherit the restrictions of the semantic regime in your interfacing with the computer. The important point is, however, that the computer is a "multisemantic machine", which makes it capable of combining a number of previously unrelated representation forms. Finnemann (1999:146) ends up with what he calls "a whole range of 'first-time-in-history' features". These features imply that the computer provides a new way to represent knowledge by integrating a variety of previously separate knowledge areas. The computer is characterised by:

- Medium for producing, editing, processing, storing, copying, distributing and retrieving knowledge integrating processes earlier separated like writing a book, publishing it and selling it.

- Medium for representing linguistically, formally, pictorially and auditory knowledge while integrating these in the same system.

- Medium for communication making it possible to integrate earlier communication forms.

You can manipulate the information in ways very different from other representations and you can combine these different areas because you have direct access to the underlying alphabet. This also entails a rearrangement of the sender and receiver relation, where they become interchangeable, when the receiver can gain access at the level of the alphabet at any time. The representation of knowledge is not hardwired into the book, picture, artefacts or environment. You can make changes and this is the constituent of what has often been labelled interactivity, which I will return to more specifically in relation to computer games. It should be stressed that interactivity is not a exclusive feature of computer games (Jensen, 1999), although often used to describe the uniqueness of computer games.

Understanding the nature of computer games

When we look to computer games there have, of course, been several attempts at describing what characterised these as implied in the dissertation's introduction. In general, theorists have a hard time defining games as such, including a distinction between traditional games and computer games. It is argued that the form of games is quite suitable for the computer platform due to the focus on rules that is a basic trait of both computers and games, which makes it possible for games to make different kinds of representations than most other media forms. This ability is further enhanced by the computer platform as described above (Juul, 2003; Salen & Zimmerman, 2003).

When discussing computer games in the introduction I ended up dissatisfied with Juul's initial somewhat formal definition,. A game was defined as a rule-based system with variable outcomes that the player is attached to. This definition of games does not grant full justice to Juul's (2003) work that includes a discussion on the importance of the fictional world in computer games, which is really the semantic content of the computer game in Finnemann's terminology. Juul (2003) sees the fictional world as important for the player's actual game experience, although the fictional world slowly recedes into the background in favour of the rules. The fictional world provides the setting for understanding the game rules, making the outcomes meaningful and attaching the player to the outcome. A computer game cannot allow itself to assume a lot of previous experiences concerning a topic, but usually uses a well-established setting and genre. The design of computer games is built on a fictional world and rules that are introduced to the player who can then manipulate the rules to gain different outcomes. A computer game can become complex, but it is in principle always possible to deduce back to some rules that guide the outcome and an overall setting – things don't just happen although a random factor is often built in. You as a player make things happen in a very concrete sense – you will do something and see the consequences in the game universe. Engaging the student in manipulation of the rules is combined with strong audiovisual cues that surpass most textbooks.

The basic definition of computer games does not demand a fictional world as we can have almost entirely abstract computer games like *Pong* or *Tetris* with no fictional world. However, the fictional world makes it easier to play the computer game and proves an important ingredient in creating rich game experiences. The fictional world provides a meaningful coherence and progression in the game. In providing a fictional world the player gets a handle on the computer game. The advantage of using a fictional world is obvious when we are talking about stereotypical universes that most players will have knowledge of and can use as a handle on the game experience. It provides a variation of starting points for different players clearing the way for understanding the game universe. The most popular computer games will initially be those, which can set up an interesting fictional world that players can recognize and understand. The success of *The Sims* and *SimCity* fits nicely into that argument. Also the continuing success of dragons, goblins and trolls in computer games is understandable, providing a strong fictional world for the teenage-minded game population.

However, the actual balance between rules, outcomes and consequences is critical for going beyond the initial interest in the fictional world. We can refer to the diffuse balance as the gameplay that in combination with the fictional world facilitates the game experience. Gameplay is the important ingredient for creating engagement in computer games as it provides the set of rules for interacting with the fictional world and the outcomes from the interaction. The design of the gameplay drawing on other computer games can also serve as a handle for the player. Until now computer games have been described as a combination of rules and fictional world (in combination referred to as the game universe) that the player interacts with. The interaction has often been called interactivity.

Interactivity is often used like a magic wand that can clarify the very nature of computer games. However, we need to get past the vague concept of interactivity as Espen Aarseth has argued and find a more precise definition that differentiates computer games from other media. According to Aarseth (1997:1) a more appropriate description is "non-trivial effort is required to allow the reader to traverse the text". This description testifies to the engagement of the player in computer games and the ability of the game to appreciate the engagement. The player makes a difference as the scenario is changed in accordance to the relation between player and game. Interpretation of the fictional world is not only latent in the player's mind, but manifests itself on the screen. This is not to say that computer games are capable of expressing all feelings, desires and needs of the player, but it comes further down that road than most other media. You interpret the game universe differently depending on your mood, which will lead to a different game experience unfolding. You may also interpret a movie differently depending on your mood, but the same movie still unfolds on the screen (Egenfeldt-Nielsen, 2003c).

Students are having very concrete experience interacting with the computer, where the game universe responds immediately to the manipulations. This is quite different from traditional teaching, where you are told about other people's interaction with a universe – their experiences. You think about these experiences and may connect them with existing concepts and experiences, but you lack the richness and variation that is part of any concrete experience. This richness is supported by the engagement, but also the modal expressions of computers, particularly computer games have a preference for audiovisual orgies. In computer games the combination of different modalities is among the most powerful with computer games pushing the limits of the computer in terms of graphics, sounds, animation and artificial intelligence.

In line with Finnemann's theory the computer as a medium is especially capable of bringing to bear a number of different modal expressions. On a computer the visual appearance, audio use and actions performed open up for different learning experience. The classroom has, of course, always involved other modes than language – gestures, models, movement and gaze, but increasingly other modes are finding their way into school (Jewitt, 2003). It has been found that combining different representation forms (audio, visuals and text) results in better learning outcome - especially if these are presented simultaneously, supplementing each other. When we are involved in learning about a topic we benefit from pictures or animations in combination with hearing. These multimedia effects are especially strong for students with less prior knowledge of a topic and other individual differences like spatial ability may also apply (Mayer & Moreno, 1999).[18]

Next, I present an integrated theory of computer games aimed at educational use of computer games and a number of relevant optics to approach the empirical study. The theory draws on the discussions above, but also links back to previous discussions in the dissertation.

An integrated theory of computer games

To understand computer games we can approach them at three levels: Player, representation and system (Figure 13). On the system level we have the computer that consists of a notational system that we can manipulate in a number of ways. This notational system is used to create a set of rules and a fictional world providing a representation (the game universe). We can create a shed with a hammer (semantic content) and a rule saying that the hammer will change colour when clicked on (algorithm). This representation can ultimately be described as information marking relevant differences. Thus, a computer game is a fictional world with rules represented by marking the important difference through semantic content (fictional world) and algorithms (rules). The player level addresses how we actually approach the computer game, stressing the necessity of the player's interpretation of the differences that make up a game. Through interpretation we can come to understand the information in the game universe and construct knowledge based on this process. The knowledge is the player's active transformation of information attaching it to previous experiences and concepts with or without instruction. The uniqueness of computer games lies in the ability to combine interesting fictional worlds with rules that make the player's process of understanding active rather than passive. This engagement is crucial for understanding the educational potential of computer games.

You can say that computer games differ from other media in offering a new way to appreciate students' ability to understand what differences make a difference. The ability to *appreciate* and *create* differences that make a difference is ultimately what constitutes knowledge. When I learn to read a map I learn to appreciate the differences that make a difference – I will not look at the quality of the paper, the colours used or the aesthetics in general (Bateson, 1972). Rather the borders or terrain are the differences that make a difference. The interesting difference between the paper map and the map on a computer is that you are capable of not only appreciating the differences that make a difference, but creating differences that make a difference. You can move the borders or change the terrain, but only if you appreciate the differences that make a difference. This results in a reinforcing loop driving the student towards understanding and mastering the game universe. The appreciation involves a process of exploring and linking concepts as described by Kolb's cycle.

---

[18] Many game companies are supported by makers of graphic cards to ensure that the development moves forward (i.e. BioWare, 2004). Computer games are the first place were a new generation of graphics cards will make a difference.

An example is useful for showing the important implications from the above perspective that has repercussions for the educational use of computer games. In *Europa Universalis II* you start with a historical map, where you notice a number of borders (see appendix for description of game). This map is constructed through the notational system complete with semantic content and rules for engaging with the map. Students will initially try to get an understanding of the map based on previous experiences and concepts eventually moving on to actually challenge these borders. Students change the borders by for example invading other countries experiencing the implications of such a change – which again reinforces the understanding of the initial difference in borders. In this sense the game process is one of constantly appreciating, exploring and linking differences - setting new differences while understanding the implications of these. This means that the fictional world is necessary for building the differences that make a difference and the rules make it possible to challenge these differences while the rules are also a part of the fictional world. The chance to conquer a French province, explore America, colonize West-Africa or convert Poland to a Protestant country in *Europa Universalis II* is not really meaningful without the fictional world, nor interesting.

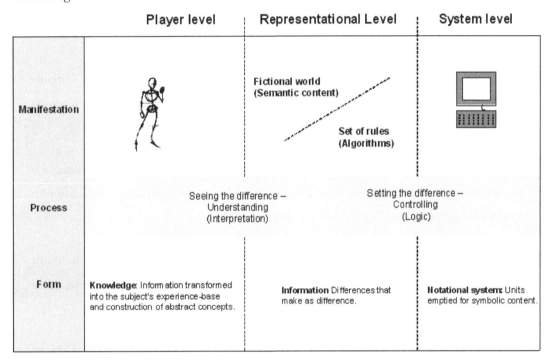

Figure 13: The model shows how to conceive computer games incorporating both a player and system perspective tracking the different forms of knowing, the process to make this transformation and the manifestation of the knowing.

A number of important implications for the educational use of computer games emerge from the discussions above. These points will all play a role in the analysis of the empirical results and later the theory on educational use of computer games.

- Students are actively engaged in constructing the differences that they find meaningful with a clear purpose in mind, and these are laid out for all to see and comment on.

- Students' understanding of the differences is crucial to move the game forward and the understanding has a direct bearing on the following representations. Misinterpretations are explicit rather than implicit.

- Students do not start from scratch with computer games as they will use previous experiences connected to the computer game for playing.

- Students playing can continuously be tracked as any student action is represented in the notational system and these actions can be transformed into any representation during and after playing.

- Students can always question the validity of the representations as it is constantly possible to manipulate the representations, in principle for any user.

- A computer game can represent anything you want it to as long as you can formally describe it and any representation should in theory be able to make up an interesting computer game.

- The representations can draw on all semantic regimes providing experiences catering for all modalities. This ability provides richer and fuller concrete experiences with different handles for different students

- The same semantic content can be re-used with the same underlying rules or minor adjustments. This implies plasticity in adjusting the educational experience compared to the majority of other educational material.

- Students can safely explore the fictional world with few real life repercussions, sheltered by the magic circle.

Reading, hearing, seeing or playing are all equally valid concrete experiences, but as described above differing in their form. The computer game lets you hear, see, observe, do, perceive and feel in a richer universe than most other media while letting you build and test your own concepts to understand the game universe. These concepts will without instruction become spontaneous concepts, but with guidance the experiences can be transformed to scientific concepts. With the right balanced instruction the introduction of scientific concepts can be grounded through experiences in a game universe. This differs from when a student hears a lecture or reads a textbook. Here the scientific concepts are introduced without any explicit grounding in experience unless the student by chance has some experience to bring into the equation – something that can serve as an example, a metaphor – an experience that can crack a hole in the scientific concept to let the student invest something of himself.

Conclusion: Experiential learning an alternative to edutainment

Overall I have argued for an approach to learning, education and teaching that extends from the previous chapter's dissatisfaction with previous generations' approach to educational use of computer games manifested in edutainment. To provide an inclusive perspective of player, computer game and context I took experience as a starting point. This led me to stress the importance of concrete experience for building abstract concepts while maintaining that our concepts will also form our future concrete experience. I found computer games to be a potentially valuable tool for providing such concrete experiences as they present a rich, engaging universe, where students are performing actions - gaining concrete experiences that are self-sustaining and can be used to build concepts. This concludes the second part of the dissertation.

Next I will explore the actual use of educational computer games in a school focusing on what experiences computer games provides. The empirical study provides the last piece to the final puzzle – a theory on educational use of computer games.

Part 3: Main empirical study

This part presents the empirical study and the findings that emerged. The study served to inform and explore general themes in educational use of using computer games to identify problems, limits and potentials. The most important contribution of the empirical study may escape the reader. I strongly believe that the personal experience with educational use of computer games as a researcher made me capable of avoiding classic pitfalls and construct a theory that does not only apply in theory but also describe practice.

Chapter VI: Method Considerations Concerning Main Empirical Study

Though this be madness, yet there is method in't.

William Shakespeare

Part 2 revolved around identifying the key areas in the research field, and building an educational approach that is useful for educational use of computer games. This chapter presents and discusses the formal aspects concerning the collection of both qualitative and quantitative empirical data from this dissertation's main empirical study. The actual findings will be presented in chapter 7, 8 and 9.

The research design can be described as a field experiment using randomised two-group design. Three high-school classes participated in a 2½ month long history course with computer games. Two of the classes were assigned to an experimental group, and the last class was control group. The didactic set-up was that the computer game provided the concrete experiences about history whereas the teacher talks used the concrete experiences to build concepts about history. It was an explicit goal not to change the teaching situation beyond recognition, which meant that the two participating teachers were given quite free hands to implement the course in terms of didactic approach. They were advised to use examples from the computer game to make historical concepts richer and more concrete, although this never really materialized in practice - teaching practice remained unchanged.

It quickly became clear to me that only with great difficulty could the findings be grasped within a strictly empiricist framework. Therefore, it was initially decided that the mix of qualitative and quantitative measures required both the empiricist and the constructivist perspective. This chapter starts out with a description of the empirical study from an empiricist perspective, but then challenges this approach by looking at a constructivist alternative. The challenge is to present different methods for exposing the method problems in both qualitative and quantitative perspective. In conclusion, the empiricist principles are the ideal I was striving for in the quantitative area, whereas the constructivist perspective is the approach used to understand the qualitative area in the following three chapters.

The empiricist perspective

Below the study is described within an empiricist context with purpose, participants, procedure, research design, measurements, and method problems.

Purpose

The empirical study has two different tracks. The first track is to examine the *characteristics of educational use of computer games*, which implies that I am not using edutainment as a self-sustaining game application. Instead I am extending from a 3rd generation perspective, where I see player, computer game and context as equally important.

The second track examines whether *computer games can play a part in fulfilling the purpose of history teaching in secondary school* (age 15-19 years). The focus is on computer games within the current educational setting, the existing teaching practice and the traditional understanding of learning.

Procedure

The study examines students who recently started the first year in the secondary school's three year track. The study ranges over a period of 2½ months, where the students participated in an 8-week long teaching theme on European medieval history (1419-1719). The computer game *Europa*

Universalis II is a part of the teaching experience as a simulation of the historical dynamics at play at those times. There was one empirical study where the three classes participated, but it is split into a qualitative and quantitative part described below (see figure 14 for an overview).

The teacher is initially instructed that a primary didactic principle behind using the computer game is to set history in motion. Computer game is intended to show the underlying dynamics and let the students interact, experience and discuss these dynamics in history through different outcomes. The computer game provides examples for teaching more abstract concepts, while the talks held by the teacher should address key topics and earlier historical knowledge, using the game experiences.

It is stressed that all the students are given the same talks by the teacher and textbook material. The only difference between the experimental group and the control group is the time spent on historical strategy computer games (experimental group) and historical case material (control group). The experimental group works with computer games in groups and the control group works with case studies in groups.

Both groups are initially given a briefcase[19] with the teaching course structure, readings, guides, logbook and surveys. In the first lesson both groups complete a background questionnaire, a motivation test and a personality test in order to obtain basic data about the students.

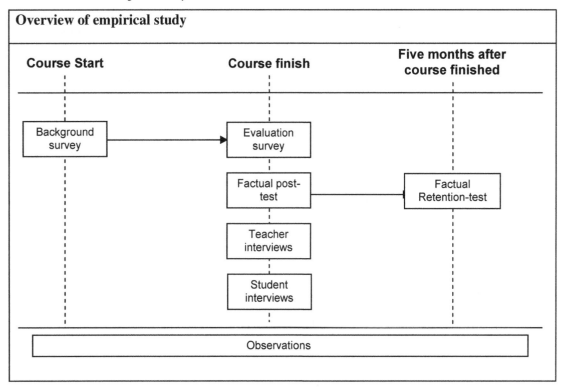

Figure 14: Shows the progression through the course in terms of tools used for gathering data.

Experimental group

The experimental group starts the first lesson with a general introduction to the theme supplemented with the role the computer game will play in the course and the setting up of groups. It is emphasized that this computer game is not similar to other commercial computer games, but is more advanced and complicated. It is also stated that although students may find the game

---

[19] See appendix for the briefcase in Danish.

entertaining this is not necessarily the goal. This is an educational experience, and all are expected to participate. The experimental group is introduced to the computer game by the researcher through a 2 hour introduction starting with a presentation of the game on a video projector, and afterwards the students play the game in groups of 2-3 each. The introduction contains some examples of historical chains of reasoning in the computer game to encourage student thinking along these lines. This is attempted throughout the course by the teachers in the computer room and group discussions when circling around. After the first lessons that serve as introduction, the teaching alters between three states:

- Playing the computer game and parallel with this jotting down notes.

- Reflecting and discussing the game experiences in groups based on questions.

- Teacher talks on a related topic based on the history text book.

The students are given homework each week, either to play the computer game or read a specific chapter in the textbook. The group discussions were guided through questions in the briefcase. The guide consisted of 3-4 specific questions concerning a specific scenario and 6 general questions to start discussions. Each of the scenarios had a theme with a certain style of play that the students are encouraged to pursue. The groups consisted of two groups that played the computer games in pairs (in total 4). It was expected that each pair should describe at least one interesting observation or discussion in connection to the game. The other pair was to asking at least two critical questions. The scenarios below give an idea of the background for the group discussions (Figure 15).

Guide for group discussions

Scenario 1: Military

Which countries are important in Europe and why?

What basic conflicts are present?

How was war conducted at those times?

How do the events in the computer game match that period?

Scenario 2: Religion, culture, diplomacy and unrest

What role do religion and culture play?

Why did one talk about the new and old world?

Why is society marked by unrest and war?

Scenario 3: Economy and politics

What is the normal social order?

How does the production work in society and how does it change?

What importance does trade have and how does it work?

Scenario 4: Expansion/Colonies/Exploration

What areas are discovered?

What consequences do the discoveries have?

What role does shipping/navigation play?

General Questions to the players

What was your game experience about?

How does it compare with reality?

What did you do in the game?

How do your game actions fit with what really happened in history

What did you get out of the game?

What was interesting in the game?

Figure 15: Shows the scenarios during the course for the experimental group and the questions handed out to students in the group discussions as the course progressed through the different scenarios.

Control group

The control group is also introduced to the course, introduced to the casework and split into groups. They are told that they are participating in a study to examine new teaching styles in history. This was plausible as a new reform of the education is due in 2005. After the introduction the control group repeated the following schedule.

- Reading the case material in groups.

- Reflecting and discussing the case material based on questions.

- Teacher talk on related topic in the history text book.

The case material consisted of historical sources like the independence declaration that gave the students concrete experiences with historical material that was then extended in the teaching with historical concepts. The students were given homework each week, either to read a specific chapter in the textbook or finish a case.

Participants

The general characteristics of the full sample of 72 students are as follows: Danish students located outside Copenhagen in a suburban area, predominately white middle-class with a tendency towards upper class background. Their age ranges from 15 to 19 years with a mean of 16.3 and a standard deviation of 0.83.

Quantitative sample

The quantitative part of the study used two high school classes in total 55 students with the same female teacher. The class assigned experimental group consisted of 27 whereas the class assigned control group had 28 students.

The two classes were chosen, because they had the same teacher, had recently started secondary school (academic track) and were both on the mathematical line. In that sense the sample can be said to have been *randomly* drawn from the population of more academically oriented students as students are randomly assigned a class, when starting the academic track[20].

---

[20] See appendix for a description of Danish educational system, and how the sample was randomly drawn.

Qualitative sample

The qualitative sample used the entire sample described above, which included the quantitative sample above, and additionally one extra older class with a male teacher. The 17 cases from the older class added to the qualitative sample only differed on the parameters: teacher and age.

Playing the game

The students played *Europa Universalis II* in a computer room in pairs each week for 47-94 minutes (47 minutes equals a lesson). The first two weeks they played 94 minutes to get an impression of the computer game and the rest of the time only 47 minutes. The students were also playing at home, but it varied considerably between students how much playing this involved; furthermore, some students did not get the computer game installed at home. The course was structured along the below plan, but was not carefully followed as some of the countries you could play were altered at the request of students and teachers (see appendix for detailed description of the computer game).

- Introduction: Denmark or other *small manageable* country – to learn the game (1 hour homework).

- Follow up: Continue playing Denmark – follow up on *technical problem* and installing game at home.

- Scenario 1: Play Denmark with an *aggressive* approach (2 hours homework).

- Scenario 2: Play England/France/Spain with a *careful* approach (2 hours homework).

- Scenario 3: Play England/France/Spain with a *balanced* approach (2 hours homework).

- Scenario 4: Play a country of your *own choice* with any strategy (2 hours homework).

These scenarios were intended to introduce the students to different aspects of the computer game, but it proved hard to control their playing styles. Students tried to adopt the suggested approaches to the game, but only players with some control of the game really understood the differences.

Teaching style

> Using Civilization III as a simulation tool changes the method of studying history from one of memorizing facts and mastering sanctioned narratives to one of defining the terms and rules of the system (either similar to or contradictory with those thought to describe events in real life) and then exploring its emergent properties.

> (Squire, 2004:74)

The purpose of the teaching was not to teach students factual history, but rather to use the computer game to explore historical events, dynamics and narratives. In the computer games the students had the opportunity to play with the underlying dynamics of the events and to appreciate some of the historical factors that consistently played a role through European history from the 15th to the 19th century. Appreciation, exploration and linking through reflection and discussion of historical material were central in the course description extending from experiential learning described in previous chapter.

This educational style also draws on current understanding of history both described in the Danish national curriculum (Uddannelsesstyrelsen, 1999) and the increasing research interest in counter-factual history (Ferguson, 1997). The counter-factual approach sees a potential in exploring alternative paths in history in order to see how certain factors and key events influenced history. It has most strongly been advocated by Niall Ferguson (1997), his work presents a number of scenarios for alternative developments in history. Such active exploration can spark more interest among students, but it seems that it demands some background information on history. Without a certain amount of background information you can't appreciate the consequences and scope of the counter-factual accounts. It, therefore, seems to be more applicable towards the end of a given topic to crystallize and play with some of the key factors in history.

I have in earlier chapters argued that the variety of learning perspectives stress different areas of learning, each appropriate for different learning experiences. The role selected for the computer game in my course favours culturalism, while the computational view on learning is retained in the course through the textbook, teacher talks and factual test which understand history as a more fixed size. From this perspective learning involves the construction of knowledge through the learner's interaction with the world. The computer game expected the player to actively construct an understanding of history based on a number of games played out. The history text books on the other hand favoured the computational approach, telling the students the facts of history.

History teaching

Danish history teaching is described in the following way, which also was behind the overall design of the empirical study's history approach and the educational style above:

> Students continue the development and qualification of their historical awareness. This implies that they come to realize that they and other constantly interpret their surrounding world in interplay between understanding now, understanding past and looking to the future. In this way they gain a perception of themselves as created by their cultural background and history and the opportunity to both understand their current time and create their own and the society's future. This also provides them with a background to participate in the democratic process in society.

(Uddannelsesstyrelsen, 1999)

Based on this overall description three explicit goals are further outlined that can be identified as the goals for the history course:

- Knowledge about political, economical, social and cultural conditions in a historical perspective.

- Skills in defining and explaining historical problems.

- Historical awareness as an indistinct term for appreciating the historical situatedness of things.

The history course with *Europa Universalis II* was designed to fulfil these goals by using existing textbook material, choosing a relevant time period, encouraging reflection of history in groups and the existence of historical dynamics in the computer games (see appendix for a description).

Quantitative research set-up

The set-up can be described as a field experiment randomised two-group design with two groups who received a post-test[21] (Coolican, 1994; Judd, Smith, & Kidder, 1991). Some pre-tests are administered to verify that the randomisation is successful on basic criteria like age, gender, motivation, academic achievement, personality and school attitude.

A pre-test on factual historical knowledge is not initially administered. This decision is based on the potential adverse affect such a test would have on the course promoting factual knowledge, as this is what a pre-test would suggest. The administering of a pre-test should not be necessary in an experimental design of this type (Campbell & Stanley, 1969; Judd et al., 1991; Wolfe & Crookall, 1998). One other argument for the lack of pre-test is that I wanted to construct the test based on actual topics brought up in the case studies, teaching and playing of the computer game. I didn't want to base the test prematurely on the content in the computer game, case studies or text book as these were static representations. Instead, I wanted to make sure the questions addressed relevant areas which the students had gained some experience of through the concrete teaching. This was also to avoid that the test only measured who had read the text book, as that was not my intention. I will return to a more thorough description of the post-test. A retention test, identical to the post-test, was also performed approximately 5 months after the course finished.

In general, the field experiment is said to have a higher external validity than for example a experimental study in a laboratory setting, making it easier to generalize from the findings to a real setting. After all, a field experiment closely adheres to real settings. On the other hand, the lack of tight control with the confounding variables in the experiment makes it hard to access whether your dependent variable is exclusively affected by the independent variables (Coolican, 1994). The uncertainty surrounding confounding variables was a chief concern in this study. The statistical methods used for the data was descriptive statistics and parametric tests, which will be discussed in chapter 9. Results were interpreted, drawing on qualitative data and earlier research in the field.

Qualitative research set-up

The qualitative data has been gathered through observations, written evaluations, interviews, logbooks and field notes[22] to ensure the different angles of the experience is covered. Each of these data forms has strengths and weaknesses. The observations are not recorded beyond field notes, as this was not technically possible. This is problematic as field notes are contaminated by the researcher's selection and often somewhat interpreted before jotted down. To counter this lack of direct data I used logbooks where students weekly wrote down thoughts, reflections and game experiences. The interviews with pairs of students are also selected to represent different types of experiences with the game.

To analyse the qualitative data the software package N-Vivo was used, which is designed to help order, organize and code qualitative data. The procedure used involved coding the relevant parts in

---

[21] The question of attitude towards history teaching, attitudes towards school, history preparation time, school preparation time, actual history grade and own suggested history grade (all variables had pre-test and post-test).

[22] All the qualitative data is attached in appendix. The field notes are attached in an English version as appendix whereas the logbook and interviews are in Danish.

interviews, field notes, evaluations and logbooks. The codes both emerged out of the initial key topics identified in chapter 4 and 5, the two tracks described earlier in this chapter and themes that emerged from the material. All the material was read through until no new themes emerged. This was done to ensure that different parts of data did not fall victim to one theme being discovered late in the process. This was also possible as the data was limited in size. It consisted of 5 interviews, 7 pages of field notes, 23 logbook entries and 9 written group evaluations. I did far from receive a complete logbook from all participants, but the number of students represented in the logbooks is considerably larger than 23, as several students indicated that during group discussions they had filled out the logbook together. On the other hand, a number of these logbook entries are very thin consisting of no more than a few sentences. Finally, the themes were written out separately and central points examined. The data was compared and discussed in relation to earlier findings in order to examine the theme.

Coding

The participants in the study were coded randomly and all material handed out was coded. The code key was kept during the study to identify students who were observed or interviewed, but after the study the key code was destroyed. When drawing on empirical data the codes are used (see figure 16). The codes were to ensure that the students are anonymous and they had no need to fear any subsequent consequences of their statements. The students were informed of this procedure at the beginning of the course.

Code	Class	Description
21x-48x	Class 1X	Primary experimental group
1-28z	Class 1Z	Control group
1x-20x	Class 2X	Secondary experimental group (only qualitative analysis)

Figure 16: Shows the coding using for the different groups.

Description of approach to gathering data and the tools used

Below I describe the tools used in the study. This is not done in detail, but the appendix has copies of the material.

- **Background questionnaire**: This was initially distributed to students to gather information on demographics, course preferences, course expectations, computer games experience, peer assessment and academic achievement.

- **Debrief questionnaire**: The questionnaire was administered to access the students' subjective experience of the course in respects to motivation, peer assessment, learning outcome and learning process.

- **Personality test**: The personality test IPIP-Neo by Dr. Lewis R. Goldberg[23] was used to access whether there were differences in the two samples. The personality tests available

---

[23] This test is freely available to all at http://ipip.ori.org/. The short version with 120 items was used here.

in Danish were not suited for the purpose of this study and therefore an English test was translated.

- **Motivation test**: The motivation test was based on an English test called Academic Self-Regulation Questionnaire (SRQ-A)[24] translated through the procedure described below. It has four outcomes: External Regulation, introjected regulation, identified Regulation and intrinsic motivation. It was used to test whether the two samples initially differed on motivation.

- **Weekly logbook**: The students wrote a diary over the process to give information on problems, successes and experience with the process in general. This was also an integrated part of the discussion, reflection and works with the computer game.

- **Observation/Field notes**: During teaching the students and teachers were observed to identify the learning environments and involvement of the computer games. The observer acted as a part of the learning environment, helping with game specific questions, but did not involve in reflecting the game experiences from a historical perspective as this could bias the results.

It was expected that I could serve as a technical assistant with the computer game, and that my assistance would decrease as the students became more competent. This decrease didn't occur, and the field notes are, therefore, very scattered and jotted down a few hours after the observations were made.

- **Teacher and student interviews**: The interviews were conducted in the end to identify differences between the teachers in respect to experiences with computer games, teaching style and course expectations. During the teaching process, informal talks with the teachers were common every week concerning experiences, problems and the learning environment.

One interview guide was constructed for teachers and one for students based on the two overall tracks identified concerning computer games in history teaching and computer games in general. The weight was mostly on the first track which refers to the concrete

---

[24] Test described at http://www.psych.rochester.edu/SDT/measures/selfreg_acad.html

use of Europa Universalis II in the history course which students and teachers participated in[25].

- **Factual post-test**: In collaboration with the teachers, a questionnaire was constructed to test the issues and dynamics that the students should acquire during the one-month theme. This test was administered after the course.

- **Factual retention-test**: After 5 months the factual test was re-administered to see whether there were differences between experimental group and control group in terms of retention.

- **Task evaluation questionnaire**: It was based on the questionnaire Intrinsic Motivation Inventory (IMI)[26]. It was translated from English by the procedure described below. It had the following scales: Interest/enjoyment, perceived competence, perceived choice and pressure/tension. It was used to evaluate different aspects of the teaching experience.

Building the factual post-test and retention test

It was not possible to obtain an existing test in the area of European history in this period, as this is not usually carried out in Danish schools and certainly not standardized if it is. One of the teachers did, however, have some earlier tests of own design which were used as inspiration for constructing the factual test. The teacher's tests only contained open-ended questions, but these were used to guide the level of difficulty and the content of the open-ended questions.

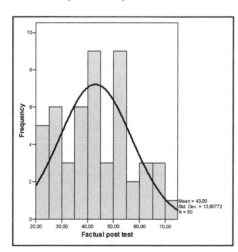

Figure 17: The graph shows the distribution of scores on factual test, which approach a normal distribution slightly negative skewed.

The factual test and retention test had the same items and were constructed in collaboration between researcher and teacher. They were based on notes taken during teacher talks, textbook material, case studies and computer game content. It was important that any question appeared in at least two of these sources. Initially, 50 questions were constructed, and the 28 perceived as most precise were chosen in collaboration with the teachers. The final test consisted of 8 open-ended questions, 2 questions by drawing the answer on a map, 1 question linking pairs of statements, 2 questions ranking three statements and 15 multiple choice questions with four options. The final test was discussed with teachers and other researchers, examined for normal distribution and checked for internal consistency. The results were normally distributed with a very slight negative skew (Figure 17). This indicates that the test

---

[25] The Danish interview guides for both students and teachers can be found in the appendix.

[26] Questionnaire described: http://www.psych.rochester.edu/SDT/measures/intrins_scl.html

118

was probably a bit too hard (Kaplan & Saccuzzo, 1997), which was also commented on by the students.

To ensure internal consistency among the different items in the questionnaire Cronbach's Alpha was calculated to 0.75 (Cases=102, Items=28). There were no obvious items that could be removed to get the internal consistency reliability above 0.8, which is usually recommended if possible. However, in general 0.75 is also considered in the good end (Garson, Unknown).

Overall, the factual test seemed to be understood by the students, although some questions did lead to questions, when the test was administered. These were handled by the researcher who was present at the administering. The number of questions not answered was very low for the multiple choice questions, whereas the last five open-ended questions were left unanswered by quite a few students.

scoring the factual post-test and retention test

The scoring of the factual tests was carried out as described below. All multiple choice questions gave a maximum of 3 points. Questions where you were to rank a statement gave 1 point if you had the first one correct, but not if you only had the second or third one correct. The question with graphical plotting of countries gave 3 points for all countries and one point if you missed one country. The graphical drawing on religious border was evaluated with points from 0-3, based on evaluating whether the answer included all four religions plotted in and the degree of resembling borders especially between England, Germany, Poland, France, Italy, Turkey, Russia and Africa, where the major divides run.

The open-ended question was evaluated with 0-5 points, depending on how detailed the answer was, and whether they mentioned the different aspects expected from a correct answer. A long detailed answer on the importance of Spanish weapons for defeating the Aztecs and Incas would be awarded 2 points, whereas a short answer basically saying weapons would be awarded 1 point. However, for more points to be awarded they had to name other factors like horses, internal strife or religious beliefs. A five point score was only rewarded for a detailed answer, integrating the majority of important factors. The test was only scored by the researcher due to lack of resources, but this was done three times to ensure that any changes in scoring practice would be equally distributed.

Translation of the tests

The translation of the tests was all performed by the same procedure, which serves to minimize translation problems, but does not formally test whether the test is still valid and reliable after translation. A translation should normally be followed by a complete re-examination, including reassessing norms and validating questions to ensure that the translation is correct and do not jeopardize reliability and validity, but this required too many resources (Kaplan & Saccuzzo, 1997). The procedure chosen was to use two different persons, who taken together had knowledge of translation, education, psychology and testing. Differences in the translation were resolved through discussion. The most significant problems concerned an item, which asked the political standpoint of students. This was hard to translate into a Danish context. This precise question also triggered questions from the students when filling out the test.

Building the questionnaire

The construction of the questionnaire was based on experiences with earlier questionnaires in terms of socio-demographic variables, computer games habits and computer use.[27] It was hoped

---

[27] Especially Danish studies were used (Drotner, 2001; Egenfeldt-Nielsen & Smith, 2000; Egenfeldt-Nielsen & Smith, 2002; Fridberg, 1999).

that this would limit the problems with the questionnaire. In general, the 11-point model by Judd, Smith & Kidder (1991) was followed, although it was not possible to pre-test the questionnaire. Other rules for constructing the questionnaire suggested by Judd, Smith, & Kidder were also followed: The general questions came first, bias caused by earlier questions was avoided, questions were split in topics and more revealing items came last. Other basic questions like leading questions, sentence length, full category span, biased questions and difficult questions were also considered. It was kept in mind that the target group was quite young.

The questionnaires mostly had closed questions, as logbook and interviews were used to gather data more appropriately addressed in open questions. These were also chosen because the questionnaire primarily gathered data in relatively well known areas, where we would expect to know the full response range.

Deciding on observation optics

It is usually recommended to consider tools for supporting your observations for both awareness and documentation purposes. These take very different forms depending on your research questions. Judd, Smith, & Kidder (1991) find that you should be very explicit in the actions that will be accepted as leading to recording a particular item. This is in reality quite hard to live up to especially when your research questions are quite open. It is also in opposition to Guba & Lincoln's (1989) hermeneutic approach, which I will return to later.

I chose a 'soft' approach where I prior to starting the empirical study identified a number of optics in the existing research on educational use of computer games in order to guide the gathering of qualitative data. It was the intention to be especially alert to the following optics:

- The role of motivation in computer games and the learning impact of computer games

- Different student groups benefit from computer games (personality, academic standing, subject interest, age, gender, computer experience, game experience, attitude to using games and attitude to games)

- The possibility of changing perspective in computer games and their bearing on learning

- The role and importance of reflection in relation to computer games

- The learning form and approach in computer games

- The characteristics of computer games in learning environments

- Social interaction around computer games during educational use

- How was the computer game received and perceived.

- References to game culture in general

- The role of conflict and competition during the course

- Barriers including technical, structural and other difficulties

- Balance between playing the game and learning

- Interaction around computer games – discussion, reflection, talk, comments

- Different roles occupied by different students

The optics were meant more as perspectives, events and actions to look for during the study than closed, concrete items that could be observed under specific circumstances.

Analysing the qualitative findings

It is always hard to analyse qualitative results as they are weaved into each other. Where does one start and how does one give a balanced presentation that shows both the limited scope of the observations in some places where little data is accessible and brings forth other findings stronger supported by multiple voices among the participants in the course? The number of participants was more than 70, and trying to convey their separate experiences by referring to their names would most likely confuse matters. I also find that to see each respondent as providing an isolated piece of data runs contrary to the knowledge we have of communities, developmental psychology and language as expressed by Bakhtin, Wertsch, Wenger and Vygotsky.

I wish to stress that I see the classroom as a community where each respondent is never alone on an intra-personal plane. A respondent's utterance whether in a logbook, action, interview or game world is situated in a socio-cultural context. For example, the classroom is historically situated in an institutional setting with certain expectations of the teaching, the classroom size, student-teacher relation and often less than good experiences with computers. The classroom context is both the tool for doing and saying something and at the same time a part of the action. The classroom context is the most immediate, but each respondent is also using and influencing a number of others' situation. The situatedness implies that our analysis should, of course, look for the strength of a given voice, but remember that a voice is never just representing one person. A voice is not just saying something by virtue of its content. Rather, a voice has implicit meaning and reflections referring to the broader classroom context, discussions and groups: To whom is a student saying something, why is it important and is the timing random? Why did the student bother to say something and what other voices is the student mirroring, reflecting, subverting or using to support the case (Vygotsky, 1986; Wenger, 1999; Wertsch, 1991, 1998)?

The findings presented throughout the following chapters will therefore have a generalized approach drawing on all qualitative data and presenting some of the most typical examples from the data material. In general, I operate with three different levels of labels, indicating the strength of an expression, when talking about qualitative data. Voices can speak generally about atmosphere or purely about their own experiences, which also influences the interpretation.

- *One voice*: A single participant voices an interpretation, observation or conclusion regarding the course.

- *Few voices*: Refers to 1-3 participants in the course supporting their interpretation, observation or conclusion.

- *Some voices*: More than 4-8 participants support an interpretation, observation or conclusion, directly or indirectly.

It should be stressed again that even one voice as explained above is not seen as one voice, but as mirroring the classroom context and other voices. The degree of strength in a voice can be supported by my general observations or stand in contrast. Differences will be noted, and the differences analysed and discussed. From the basic statements, observations, interviews and descriptive statistics I will further discuss and analyse the implications for educational use of computer games, drawing on earlier research mostly presented in the preceding chapters. The analysis and discussions are to some degree echoed in the post-interviews with teachers and students, where I tried to present my impressions to have them evaluated, sophisticated, improved and expanded in line with the constructivist method perspective presented at the end of chapter 5.

Method problems

The study in general suffers from a compressed time schedule, a small sample, limited access to classes and the researcher's role in the teaching. The most important problem in all the computer game classes was the major part the researcher had to play by assisting with technical and gameplay related questions. This clearly influenced to what degree the results can be generalized, as teachers will not usually have an assistant resulting in increased bias.

Another general, unexpected problem was getting access to other classes for pre-testing questionnaires, interview guides, tests, log-books and observational optics. It was hard to get enough classes to participate in the study and, therefore, no pilot was conducted. The time pressure that ensued from problems in finding classes also resulted in less time for properly pre-testing different tools used for gathering data. This did lead to problems with the different methods used for gathering data. Problems were on the surface mostly spelling, repeated words and unclear sentences. These problems were minimized by first running most tests on the older experimental group and then list the corrections for the next class on the blackboard. This is also the reason why the older group is not used so extensively and not included at all in the quantitative analysis. The results obtained in general were threatened in all classic areas, usually identified in empirical studies: External validity, internal validity and reliability. The impact of this on the qualitative measures is harder to access but may also lead to problems. Before turning to look at the method problems associated with qualitative and quantitative designs we will look at the problems with the overall research design for this study.

Problems with implementing the research design

Some students in the control group class didn't buy the rationale for the study. They heard that another class was playing computer games and some were quite unhappy about not being in that class. Still, much was done to avoid the Hawthorne effect, for example providing a copy of the game to the control group at the end of the course (promised at the start of the course). The plausible reason for the study was further supplemented by the researcher being equally present in both classes, although slightly differently engaged in the two groups. In the control group the researcher was more a passive observer, taking notes, as there was not the same need to introduce the computer game and take care of technical difficulties related to the game. In the experimental group the researcher was consulted on all games-related questions.

The procedure planned for the course does not completely work for the experimental group throughout the entire study. Some of the teaching time is converted to computer game time so the students learn to play the computer game. These changes result in the control group receiving more teacher talks on key historical topics. It also seems that the experimental group spent considerable time just learning the most basic actions in the computer game and spent less time on the actual historical questions and content.

Another unforeseen development is that all the students in the experimental group are not able to get working computers in the dedicated computer room. This means that an average of 2-3 students spent the first 15 min. of each lesson trying to find an available computer. The alternative computers are usually located in an open media room, but access to this room is in competition with other students. We tried to cope with this by installing the computer game on other machines in the school, but these couldn't be booked in advance, and therefore the students couldn't always get hold of a computer. This results in some students gathering around a computer in groups of four students instead of the intended two. Even more problematic is it that this gives the weak students in computer games a chance to hide and legitimise a withdrawal from the game, which is quite apparent in the groups taking to the open media room. Comments from these groups were often that it is too hard, they would rather watch, they are unsure of what to do and they don't fancy computer games.

This stigmatisation is further enhanced outside the school and the computer room. First of all the weak students simply didn't install the computer game at home and played it as homework. This is not due to a lack of computer access or technical problems as all students had access to a computer, most even had their own (see appendix for computer access). They just didn't prioritise it very high compared to other school work and their paid jobs parallel with school. Second, there were more inexperienced computer gamers than expected. We were ready for some inexperienced students with little to no experience with computer games, but the number turned out to be quite high. Within the current system it is difficult to give such a big group the extra help needed.

Qualitative method problems

As to the observations, logbooks and interviews we should be concerned mostly with, what we could call the degree of naturalness and the sampling issue. Judd, Smith & Kidder (1991) talk about different levels of naturalness that is important when we talk about observation, but I believe it can be extended to include logbooks and interviews. The first issue concerns the *natural setting*, which refers to whether observations were made in a setting that would also be present without the experimental set-up. The setting in this study at a school had a high degree of naturalness, although the presence of an assisting researcher partly challenged it. The students definitely saw this as a course in history that was part of their schooling. The second issue concerns *natural behaviours* which refer to whether behaviours were only performed as a consequence of the experimental set-up. The student and teacher behaviour that were observed or written down as field notes could be considered natural behaviour, but not those obtained from interviews. The logbooks documented natural behaviours by virtue of being a place to write down answers and reflections on historical questions posed during group work. The third issue is the *natural experimental* which refers to whether the outcome observed would also have been present without the experimental set-up. In this case, the outcome covered a wide range and some of the outcomes were natural. In relation to observations made this held true when observing interaction between students and teachers, but interviews and logbooks were not natural in that sense. Neither was the entire range of quantitative tools used.

The logbook is potentially the richest source of information due to the problems with the overlap between observation role and assistant role. But the interviews are also important. However, the interviews are a retrospective approach to the course and are as such not first-hand data. However, there is a sampling problem with the logbook. We could expect the logbooks to be written by the more interested students and this also seemed to be the case. The students who expressed the most scepticism and experienced most problems with the computer games wrote very short accounts in the logbook. The accounts from the weak students mostly evaluated the problems and limits of the study. Most of the elaborate accounts in the logbook were from male students with history interest and/or computer games interest. This is kept in mind when interpreting this data.

In respect to the observations it proved hard to use the optics described earlier for focusing the observer's attention. The observations mostly take place during the hectic lessons where the observer is also acting as technical assistant. The list of optics also turned out to be too long and lacked specific criteria for assessing what counted as evidence of certain behaviour. It was not defined when for example an observation was labelled as showing more or less motivation in relation to educational use of computer games.

In general, the field notes were based on my impressions while helping students with the computer games. This led to an overweight of observations concerning the problems with the computer games and less observations of the places, where students actually used the computer games smoothly. Looking at the field notes the empirical study looked like a catastrophe, but this mostly reflected the weak students, looking at the logbooks a different picture emerged.

The interviews with the teachers did not yield any specific method problems although the interview with the female teacher was delayed to a week after the course was finished, whereas the other teacher interview took place on the day when the teaching finished. It was noticeable that the interviews did give the researcher a chance to explore issues further and adjust questions that arose during the study.

The group interviews with the students proved to be a bit more problematic. Class roles, expectations and political correctness showed up and were handled by the researcher. It was clear that some of the students were afraid to criticize the study when the researcher was sitting in front of them. I went to great trouble to emphasize the importance of honesty and detaching myself from the results. I stressed that I was not convinced of the role of computer games in education, but wanted to find out more about both the advantages and disadvantages. It seemed to work as through the interviews the students became more calm, relaxed and free in their responses.

Quantitative method problems

The different tools used for collecting quantitative data had some flaws. Especially the factual test was weak, and the questionnaire could also have been pre-tested with great advantage to ensure better validity and reliability.

As described earlier the factual test was carefully constructed and did also live up to some of the criteria for a well-constructed test. However, there were not resources and time to check the factual test properly in terms of reliability by retesting or split-testing and the external validity is also unclear: To what degree the constructs did really measure what they were supposed to measure? There were no trials to test whether they linked with for example grades, history grades or peer-evaluation of students' academic level. Overall, the factual test is quite problematic, and the results from it should be treated with care.

The factual test measured to what extent the students learned factual history, but during the study it was clear - both in observations made and comments in the logbooks - that factual history was not linked to the computer game (see chapter 7). This meant that the control group had a far higher exposure to historical facts on several levels (increased time-on-task). This was through the case studies, but also more teacher talks and the reading of their textbook as homework, which was neglected by the experimental group as they used the time for playing the computer game.

The construction of the questionnaire was done quite carefully, but lacked iterations to pick up weaknesses. This was not too problematic as most of the questions and topics were adopted from other questionnaires; however, the sequence may have been problematic. The threat to validity and reliability is in general found to be small for the questionnaires. The task evaluation test and motivation test are exceptions. As they are adopted in full it hasn't got the sequence problem. However, the translation poses a problem as the phrasing and norms may have been inappropriate for Danish students. As described earlier this was partly avoided, but it is uncertain to what degree this was successful. The translation poses overall minor threats to both reliability and validity (Judd et al., 1991; Kaplan & Saccuzzo, 1997).

Summing up method problems and moving on

The study has two tracks which are examined through triangulating qualitative and quantitative methods. The sample was a small randomly drawn group of students from a secondary school. Some differences were discovered between the experimental group and control group in terms of procedure and background, which should be kept in mind when analysing the data.

The study was conducted over a 2½ months period with control group and experimental group reading the text book, hearing the same teacher talk and being expected to spend the same amount of time on history. The only difference was that the experimental group played computer games while the control group worked with case studies.

A number of tools were used to gather data with different strengths and weaknesses. In the table below the different tools are presented in relation to the most important method criteria.

	Sampling	Reliability	Validity			Naturalness		
			Internal	External	Construct	Setting	Behaviour	Treatment
Field notes	++	+++	+	++	+++	++	+	++
Logbook	++	+++	++	+	++	+	+	++
Teacher/student interviews	++	+++	++	+	++	+++	++	+++
Background questionnaire	+	++	+	+	++	+++	+++	+++
Debrief questionnaire	+	++	+	++	++	+++	+++	+++
Factual post-test	+	+++	+++	+++	+++	+++	+++	+++
Factual retention-test	+	+++	+++	+++	+++	+++	+++	+++
Task evaluation Questionnaire	+	+	+	++	+	+++	+++	+++
Personality test	+	+	+	++	+	+++	+++	+++
Motivation test	+	+	+	++	+	+++	+++	+++

+ :	Few/No problems
++ :	Minor problems
+++ :	Serious problems

Sampling:	The degree that the sample can be said to be biased. This is in relation to overall sample in the study.
Reliability:	Will the tools produce consistent results over time and context
Validity:	Does the tool measure what it is intended to measure.
Naturalness:	Is the tool able to gather data that is real and can be generalized to normal teaching situations.

Table 1: It shows how the basic threats reliability, validity, sampling and naturalness spread out on the different tools used to gather data.

It can be concluded that the above method problems result in many threats to the data collection (Table 1) and hence endanger the foundation for analysing both quantitative and qualitative methods. This was also initially expected, which was one of the reasons for adapting a broad spectrum of methods to triangulate data. It should be mentioned that a low reliability does not have the same impact on different tools for example logbooks have low reliability, but that is not really the point with this tool. On the other hand, low reliability on the factual test is quite problematic as we expect the test to stay constant over time, in principal only measuring changes from the experimental condition.

The most pertinent problem was the lack of resources and time to rule out confounding variables. This means that the results presented can only to a limited degree be generalized to other teaching situations, as we may not have accounted for all influencing variables. This does not mean that we can conclude that the results for educational computer games were better or worse than could be expected. There are tendencies in both directions, for example the experimental group may have been older, but less strong academically. It also seems that the experimental set-up with a researcher benefited the final result, but it may also have hindered the teachers in engaging fully with the material, hindering closer links between computer game and teaching. We can, however, conclude that we cannot know whether the same results would have been reached with different teachers, students, settings, tools and researchers. We will go closer into this in the analysis in the next chapter as some of the results are in line with earlier findings and may, therefore, indirectly support generalizations. Direct generalizations should at least limit themselves to social studies, more complex computer games and academic settings with youngsters. Before looking closer at the data, I have to make one more little detour, as the discussion of method is from the still dominating empiricist perspective, which may not be the most appropriate for studying computer games – especially not the qualitative findings. The problems with a quantitative approach to computer games were discussed earlier in the dissertation with reference to Wolfe & Crookall (1998). They find that computer games are too dynamic to be measured by quantitative tools and that the knowledge in computer games does not fit in the current teaching practice in most schools.

A constructivist method perspective

> Certainly proponents of more conventional forms of evaluations are likely to consider
> a shift to responsive constructivist evaluation as unfortunate, incurring many losses.
> For one thing, there is the implicit admission that there can be no certainty about states
> of affairs; there is no objective truth on which inquiries can converge. One cannot find
> out how things really are or how they really work. That level of ambiguity is almost too
> much to tolerate.

(Guba & Lincoln, 1989:46)

One thing that emerges from the discussion above is that I really do not know what variables influenced the study and I have a feeling that despite alterations to the research design many of these problems would persist. Indeed this was expected given the warnings of Wolfe & Crookall (1998). Until now the discussions about method problems and research design have been from an empiricist perspective heavily problematising the findings. However, there is a certain unsatisfactory quality to this, as I strongly feel that the empirical study has tremendously improved my understanding of educational potential. In informal discussions with colleagues, friends and teachers the findings have sparked interesting discussions and recognition. It, therefore, doesn't quite seem reasonable to leave the impression that these results are so flawed that they loose relevance. Especially the qualitative findings seem too constrained by the empiricist perspective.

From a constructivist perspective it should be stressed that the findings are very closely tied to my background as researcher which have been presented in rich detail for the last almost 200 pages. I speak from a certain position and may on the surface be unable to draw strong conclusions, observations and categorizations. This is, however, what I have constantly done in informal talks with the teachers, students and colleagues before, during and after the empirical study. These discussions have to some degree been reflected in the field notes, but far from completely, and on a micro-level they most certainly have influenced the concrete implementations of the research design and the technical help with the computer game through the study.

I have tried to find a way to reflect this approach and find support for a method approach that does not reject the important guidelines inherent in the empiricist paradigm, but have at the same time acknowledged that these guidelines can never be followed completely especially in relation to qualitative findings. When they appear to be following it completely, it is often due to a reductionist presentation of the research design, a glancing over method problems or researchers with a tremendous discipline and almost machine-like approach to conducting experiments (which I believe entails other problems). Through this study it has become increasingly clear that below the surface of all empirical studies is omissions, estimates, opinions, subjectivity or in one word: social interaction between humans. To explain this interaction in objective ways would mean a detailed description and a layered analytical approach that would be painstakingly cumbersome. The Hawthorne effect points to the influence of human presence on performance and behaviour, shows how subtle, but also strong an effect human interaction can have on research results (Asplund, 1997). Any attempt at generalizing from the current empirical study with the method problem presented above becomes problematic from an empiricist perspective. This is not just related to my help with the teaching preparation, participation during the course or mere presence. It would be enough to look at the teacher as an uncertain variable and the interaction with specific students. Clearly what seemed as insignificant events during the study may have resulted in strong effects. The simple choice of combining computer game competent students with less competent students seemed a good idea, but it resulted in exclusion of a large group of girls. In another situation this might not have been the case due to different group dynamics. The break-down of one computer resulted in three students being excluded from the first hours and more or less giving up on the computer game. The fact that I first presented the computer game for one experimental group, and unconsciously changed some minor points and stressed some aspects for the next class, is also hard to grasp the scope of. We could also discuss the importance of the teacher's teaching style and attitude towards respectively the experimental group and control group. I could probably go on with smaller and larger examples that in subtle ways could influence the results obtained.

In my opinion you benefit from setting up a qualitative research study in line with empiricist guidelines to measure the educational effect, but this should not entail the reduction of the course to an artificial setting that makes it impossible to transfer to a normal teaching situation. Here a closer adherence to the qualitative nature of the findings is warranted. This doesn't imply that the empiricist criteria do not point to important issues. I find that they are important as guidelines and keep us alert to different threats to the interpretations and conclusions we draw. We should, of course, try to minimize these threats, but in reality it seems to be unrealistic when we examine social relations. We should, therefore, not despair when we bang our heads into a wall of problems that threaten to render our results useless.

This criticism is supported by Guba and Lincoln (1989) both strong proponents of the so-called Fourth Generation Evaluation, which attempts to give empiricist principles what you might call a human face. They do acknowledge the well known principles of reliability, validity, sampling and generalization. They are not as such opposed to these principles, but find that they have to acknowledge that the specific researcher and participants play an important role in what findings are discovered. Especially the interaction between what they call stakeholders in the process (coming from an evaluation perspective) cannot be reduced to fit within operationalisable and neat variables. Instead, the interaction between in my case researcher, teachers and students is the core of the findings. It is in this interaction the educational experience with computer games is made meaningful. They stress that findings should be seen as a construction not without bearing on reality, but produced as a result of the people involved in the study. These results may have smaller or larger bearing on other context and people, depending on the amount and quality of information included. The construction can be built on idiosyncratic concepts, few artefacts and little interaction between participants, which may result in a construction with little relevance to the field of educational computer games in general. My analysis might for example completely ignore the earlier discussions of the problems as to the balance between playing and learning or neglect the problems involved in transferring knowledge from the computer game to other teaching practice. The findings would rightfully be considered limited and problematic by most researchers, although they might still use parts of it connecting it with other knowledge, assuming it didn't run contrary to the discussions omitted.

With this in mind, Guba and Lincoln's (1989) support for rich descriptions of the material is understandable. Through rich descriptions it is possible for other researchers, colleagues and interested parties to draw their own conclusions. The concept of rich descriptions is for good reasons vague as it inherently depends on perspective. One might find certain connections and assumptions reasonable, while others will not have a similar perspective, demanding that all observations leading to the connections are fleshed out. The fourth generation evaluation suggests to some degree that it is hard to make general conclusions based on studies due to the findings being local and bound to context. I find this a bit vague, and feel that one should be careful to leave it at presenting and analysing results. You should have the courage to draw some conclusions, extending your findings to the entire research field. These conclusions may not hold up when scrutinised, but they are necessary to position the findings and move the understanding of the field forward. They are not problematic as long as you are explicit about the foundation of your generalisations.

Alternative criteria for research design

In an attempt to lend the constructivist perspective credibility and scientific rigor Guba and Lincoln (1989:228-252) describe principles for assessing the *quality of goodness* of a fourth generation evaluation. The advantage of these principles is that they do not presume quantitative or qualitative methods to be superior, but apply to both, whereas the principles above are originally constructed in a quantitative perspective. They do, however, on the basic ontological and epistemological premises differ as the constructivist perspective sees everything as more or less strong constructions depending on the context. Guba & Lincoln (1989) have an example with a psychological personality test. The constructivist will see the test result as a *construction* of personality located in this context, whereas empiricist perspective will see the test result as *the* personality of the tested that may vary with the degree of reliability.[28]

The presentation below is built on Guba & Lincoln's (1989) work, but somewhat adjusted as their book focuses on evaluation.

- **Trustworthiness**: This is the foundation for conducting the study, drawing on empiricist principles like objectivity, reliability and validity but insisting that we cannot refer to any real world, but have to acknowledge that our findings are constructed in a specific context. The important criterion is in some sense to document this context so others can 'access' our context, and our analysis and conclusions are transparent.

- **Nature of the hermeneutic process**: This refers to the researcher's internal process of constantly testing assumptions, findings and data in general with participants. The hermeneutic process implies that you revisit your data and findings from different perspectives with still more sophisticated explanations for the phenomenon.

---

[28] It seems there is a compromise between these two, but I will keep this presentation simple by stressing the pure form of the constructivist and empiricist perspectives.

- **Authenticity**: This concept goes beyond methods and deals with ensuring that the participants' constructions are present in the findings (fairness). Furthermore, it refers to how the researchers and participants may gain more information and utilize it more sophisticatedly.

Especially the concept of trustworthiness is worth spending a bit more time on, as it outlines some interesting alternatives to the basic foundation for conducting research. Trustworthiness operates with four sub-concepts: Credibility, transferability, dependability and confirmability.

Credibility parallels internal validity, but is concerned with securing the connection between constructed realities and the participants' understanding of the reality. This is done by incorporation of certain characteristics in your research design like pro-longed engagement, persistent engagement, peer debriefings, negative case analysis, progressive subjectivity, triangulation and member checks. Most of these are self-explanatory; however, negative case analysis and member checks require some explanation. Negative case analysis refers to the constant exploration of data, so all cases are included in the final analysis. The member check stresses that the findings should be tested with the participants, as I did in the post-interviews with teachers and students.

These different characteristics outline how continuing interaction with participants and constant reflection of own assumptions, findings and data with or without participants increases a study's credibility. The researcher must constantly be critical and alert to own constructions and constantly document, reflect and check these with participants.

Transferability is similar to generalisation, but moves the responsibility for generalizing from the sender to the receiver. The researcher is to describe the empirical study in such a way that the receiver is able to access whether the results can be generalized to his/her specific purpose. In that sense, findings in a study may in some cases be transferable, while not in others.

Dependability is comparable to reliability and is concerned with keeping measurement stable over time. In a constructivist perspective this is not ensured by keeping measurement stable over time, but rather by making the necessary adjustment to the measurements when conditions change. Inquiry may very well lead to changes in design and this is seen as the result of successful inquiry. It is stressed that these changes must be closely documented as they show findings and insights.

Confirmability is parallel to objectivity and tries to ensure that the findings are not a result of the researcher's imagination. This is not secured by a detached researcher but rather through total accountability for data collected and the process of collecting. It is compared to auditing where you must show everything you do and how you do it. All findings can be tracked back to the source, so others can make their own conclusions and the data can be revisited.

Conclusion: Revisiting my research design with a constructivist perspective

The choice to include two quite different method perspectives does far from solve all my problems, but it does support some of my unorthodox, continuing informal discussions with teachers and colleagues and partly adjusting the teaching process to take the newly discovered problems into account. One example is when one teacher suggested that playing a bigger country was more appropriate in the next lesson as this related better to the teacher talks. This was implemented instead of staying with the schedule, where a smaller country was originally chosen to keep the playing simpler. I did not simply observe the educational process unfold, but intervened, questioned, probed and drew on a number of sources to gather data from different perspectives. In this sense, I tried to improve the credibility and dependability of the data. I constantly engaged with the participants to verify the data gathered and adjusted the gathering of data so it matched my current knowledge of using educational computer games. The question of confirmability is attained to by clearly describing how data was gathered and the problems with gathering the data. Furthermore, data is available in the appendix.

Overall, I find the basic constructivist notion of constructing findings more in line with the empirical study performed especially the qualitative part. I doubt the results could ever be duplicated, although some of the descriptions and findings may be transferable. I see the concept of transferability compared to generalization as important. In my analysis I will argue for different interpretations and conclusions, but it will be up to other researchers to judge whether they have the necessary information to transfer the findings to their research area. In this decision they will hopefully be alert to the method problems I have mentioned but also appreciate that I have at least pointed out areas that deserve attention and potentially point beyond the context it is gathered in. After all, I didn't conduct the research in a vacuum, but drew heavily on earlier research within the field of educational use of computer games, educational psychology and computer games studies.

In my mind the most pertinent problem that remains as to the above is the lack of documentation of large parts of the empirical data. Here different criteria colluded, as I found it highly problematic to constantly have a tape recorder for recording data. From a practical viewpoint this concerned the amount of data that would be gathered, the naturalness perspective as the participants would be influenced by me switching on a tape recorder and an ethical perspective that stopped me from recording them without telling them.

The following three chapters will look at the actual findings from the empirical data relating these to the previous chapter on educational theory and point forward to chapter 10, where a theory on educational use of computer games is presented.

Chapter VII: Practical Barriers and Perception of History

> He looked for truth in facts and not in stories, that history for him was no more than the pretext for rueful fatalism about the present, that a man with such hair was prone to a shallow nostalgia that would inevitably give way to a sense that life was as mundane as he was himself.

> (Flanagan, 2003:20)

As we have seen in earlier chapters, the educational use of computer games is still quite limited, often caught up in a limited perception of what we can expect from the use of educational computer games. We have already looked into the barriers on an overall level in chapter 3, whereas this chapter will look at how barriers and structures manifest themselves in the actual educational computer games use in classrooms.

This chapter starts by outlining the significant groups that emerged from the empirical study, pointing to expectations, problems and potentials in different student groups. The groups are by no means characterized by fixed and clear borders, but are rather guiding groups to illustrate the positions that students occupied during the course. The main findings presented relates to the actual practical barriers in the use of educational use of computer like preparation time, learning to play the game, lesson plans, physical space and teacher resources. One unexpected finding was the discussions the use of computer games led to concerning history and learning. Lastly the strong resistance from some student groups both in relation to the alternative learning approach and history understanding is examined, which also was surprising given previous research into the area.

It is concluded that introducing computer games in an educational setting is quite hard due to the variation in student background, practical barriers, the challenge to student's naïve history understanding and the resistance from the students that gained to lose from using computer games.

Different groups' use of and approach to computer games

In earlier chapters, we touched on the exposed position of computer games when used for educational purposes. We have stressed that the structural setting and the teacher is decisive factors, which was also clear in the educational framework presented in chapter 5. Instruction was seen as necessary to evolve scientific concepts. However, in this empirical study another important factor surfaced: the reluctance to use computer games in education among the students.

The students are not a homogenous group but differ on a number of parameters with critical implications for educational use of computer games. The first obvious split is between those who played computer games and those who didn't. This is, however, too imprecise to account for the students who experienced problems during the course. Practically all students in the experimental group did play computer games, but this meant very different things. The students, who were what we might call casual gamers, were on uncharted waters concerning the complex strategy game. The term casual gamer does not come with a fixed definition, but with the term I refer to students who usually play simple, easy accessible, traditionally inspired computer games for a limited amount of time each week. They do not really consider themselves gamers any more than most would identify themselves as movie goers.

Distinct demarcation lines between students, furthermore, evolved around historical interest, gender, academic ability and school interest. Initially all students were positive towards using a computer game for teaching history, which was evident from the questionnaire completed at the onset of the course. However, in the same vein, less than half found that you can in general learn from computer games. This is in opposition to the earlier results presented by VanDeventer (1997) concerning adults' belief that you can learn from computer games. Interestingly it might actually be the case that students are more sceptical towards using computer games for educational purposes than adults, which is also evidenced by the problems edutainment experiences as students grow older and gain more control of the titles bought. Despite the small sample in my study it is interesting that only a small part initially find that you can learn from computer games. This challenges the popular belief that teachers are the primary barrier for using computer games for educational purposes. Despite the general scepticism of students towards educational use of computer games the students in the current study could best be described as curious, confused, sceptic and interested in the course. As one girl states in her logbook after the first week, echoing many students:

> I don't think I have learned anything on the subject. But there are many who are
> normally not engaged in the teachings who now seem interested. It is also fun with a
> bit of alternative teaching but I don't really see it as teaching. Hopefully it will come
> (Student 5x, logbook).

This quote echoes the general trend, especially among those struggling with learning the computer game, who was mostly those with less varied experience with computer games. They had continuously a hard time figuring out what the purpose was both in the computer game and the course, and getting anything out of it. The result was that weak students gave up. Those who were hard pressed for time and had trouble keeping up in general, downgraded the course in their overall school efforts. They quickly decided that the course was not worth their efforts and could not be taken seriously. They had other more important homework to do. The evidence of this retraction was more indirect than direct as few students themselves admitted to withdrawing from the course. However, it was touched on in all the post-interviews and was observed during the course. Clearly, a rather large group had given up on different accounts.

An overview of different groups

Before looking closer at the barriers I set up groups that outline differences in barriers, but also serve to point forward to the next chapter's discussion of the actual teaching with *Europa Universalis II*. Clearly, some students have a harder time approaching the computer game, because they have few concrete experiences to draw on and lack concepts to group experiences. Weak links to both previous game and history experience becomes quite explicit in the empirical data among some students, because students do not naturally accept the computer game as an educational experience. A warning that we should not expect that computer games can by magic be an activity that all students can approach equally. There seems to be some consistency in factors that contribute to forming different student groups. The '+' indicates how important the factor is considered to be for a successful educational experience with the computer game, and is a compression of all the findings described in this and the following chapter.

Factor	Influence	Critical stage
Gender	+	Start-up
General academic ability	+	Start-up + underway + late stage
General energy in school	+	Start-up
Historical general interest	++	Start-up + underway + late stage
Computer game literacy	+++	Start-up + late stage
Historical knowledge	+	Underway + late stage

Table 2: Informally points to the factors that were found to be significant for the students' success throughout the course.

You can identify different categories based on these characteristics (Table 2). Each category denotes a different approach to the computer game, and 'fights' about how the course should be understood was a returning theme, engaged in by the individuals representing different positions: Was it irrelevant, waste of time or did it have some serious merits? I will about each of these categories as a group of students.

Give-up: Within the first two weeks this group gave up on the computer game and hence the course. All in this group had little experience with computer games. Some had less overall surplus of energy in relation to school and limited interest in history, adding to the inclination to give up. In this group were also a large number of students who simply didn't see the relevance of investing time in this course, due to the nature of computer games. It seemed that their critique of the computer games was also a defence of their own position in the higher end of the hierarchy in the history course, which is later discussed further.

Upwardly mobile: These were mostly boys who knew and liked computer games but who rarely excelled in school. They liked history in general, but had less liking for history as it was taught in a school context. Through their competence and interest in computer games they managed decently in the course, but lacked the historical background information and academic ability to really engage with the computer game from a historical perspective. There were few connections of the concrete game experiences with scientific concepts in other parts of the course. They were, however, keen to try on the historical perspective and were interested in connecting the interest in computer games with schoolwork. They saw the introduction of computer games to their advantage. This group was somewhat unobtrusive, as it did not really use the logbooks and seldom asked for help with the computer game.

Runners-up: This group was able to learn the computer game through a lot of homework, observing other play and persistence in general. This group was positive towards the computer game but never really got beyond the focus of seeing it as lacking in historical facts. Although, they learned to play the game satisfactorily they lacked the energy and historical awareness to engage with it more reflectively and historically. There were some girls in this group, especially those that ended up playing in pairs with an experienced player that mastered tutoring.

High achievers: These were generally boys who knew computer games, liked history and had a surplus of energy in relation to school. They were able to approach the computer game from a more abstract perspective, not limiting themselves to the lack of facts and the diversions from factual history quite acutely present in the computer game. They seemed to be able to achieve the best of both worlds although in general quite critical towards the implementation of the course, they believed it had potential. In the oldest experimental class a group of boys was especially clear representatives of this group.

The categories described above captures the majority of the students, with the high achievers being the smallest groups, whereas the group that gave up was probably among the largest, including up to ¼ of the students. Next, we will look more closely at the barriers present in this study and how they had different bearings on the groups described.

Practical barriers of using computer games

> Teachers often spent more time learning about the game and solving technical problems, than they initially allowed for or found acceptable.

> (Kirriemuir & McFarlane, 2003:3)

In general, the discussion on educational use of computer games still remains on a quite abstract level. There is very little room for research criticizing educational potential of computer games and clarifying limits and potentials. This is also due to the limited everyday use of computer games in educational settings and the continuing experimental status of computer games for education. It is hardly by chance that most sceptical studies mentioned in the earlier research overview have originated in Australia, a country that has made substantial attempts to integrate computer games into the national curriculum. Nor is it by chance that the few other sceptics have centred on edutainment as this genre has for several years been successful in the home learning market with a rich experience base to draw on (and criticize). To launch an adequate criticism beyond technophobia there has to be a rich experience base to criticize. It is also quite hard to really criticize experimental use because it will never claim to generalize beyond an experimental setting. However, limiting a research field to experimental use is problematic as it hinders the field from moving forward.

In the following, I will describe how you can benefit from a more critical stance towards educational computer games use. I draw on the limited amount of earlier literature on the subject covered in earlier chapters to identify classic areas of difficulty. The earlier identified barriers, especially in chapter 2, are gender, time schedule, physical setting, class expectations, teacher background, genre knowledge, technical problems, group work experience, teacher preparation, priority issues, class size and attitude towards games.

Gender differences

Those who struggled with accepting the educational experience with computer games were to a higher degree girls rather than boys. There were several reasons for this. First of all, it was generally agreed that boys had an advantage over girls in approaching the computer game, because the boys knew strategy games. A girl observed that, "Boys often play such games and therefore have a great advantage" (Student 15x, logbook). This impression was also supported by the teachers. The gender differences would be strong throughout the entire course, surfacing in students' approaches to computer games, learning outcome, motivation and perception of learning history.

Gender distinctions may partly have been an indirect consequence of less experience with playing computer games, as descriptive statistics showed that girls do play less. However, it was clear that this was only part of the explanation. More importantly, from quite early on, the girls felt some degree of stigmatisation in the course. This was not limited to computer games habits in general but seemed to rest on more specific characteristics of this course. The specifics are hard to outline, but other contributing factors than game experience were the genre strategy, the specific game universe and the subject history. Already at the introduction to the computer game many girls voiced their concerns about the suitability of the computer game:

> When the question of how to wage war appeared the boys were clearly excited and wanted to go to war straight away. The girls were quieter. After class some girls had commented to the teacher that it seemed to be all about war, with the underlying meaning that this was not good. (Field notes, week 1).

The computer game was a strategy game which did not seem to sit well with the girls and they perceived it to be a too abstract depiction of history and too focused on the war aspects. The focus on war partly subsided through the course, but it contributed to initially alienating some girls from the course. The approach to playing the computer game also supported this compared to the boys the girls were more interested in building colonies and in exploring the world rather than wage wars. Also, despite an overall high use of computers the girls, when it came down to it, seemed less interested in computers and had more technical problems with installing the computer game at home.

Other important gender variations were apparent in the pairing and access to the computers. The pairing of a girl with a boy who excelled in the computer game often resulted in exclusion of the girl. The boy forgot the less competent girl, which is also an all too common event found in learning with other multimedia in pairs (Littleton & Light, 1999). However, some of the experienced male players were capable of sharing knowledge. The lack of computers also resulted in some students being marginalized, mostly girls who were too slow to get to the available computers in the computer room. They, therefore, had to go to the general computer room, where less help was available, and where you couldn't be sure to get computers. The girls who succeeded usually did quite well in history in school and had at least some experience with computer games.

The educational setting

In chapter 2, I discussed the educational setting, which was found to influence the use of games. In an educational setting the day is split in small segments with each subject having its own allocated time slot. To learn a computer game, get it started and get into it requires more than an hour, which also caused problem in this empirical study. It proved very hard to introduce a computer game and then continue the introduction two days later. Most of the students had little recollection of the initial introduction and in the next hour started more or less with the game tutorials from scratch. This was not limited to the first steps with the game, but continued to be a problem in the following weeks. The students played the game on Tuesdays and were then supposed to connect it with teacher talks on Thursdays. This time gap was not feasible, as the game experience was too far away to connect with the teacher talks and also in opposition to traditional game culture (Jessen, 2001).

The physical frame also caused problems, as the school was not adapted to group work, the computers didn't work and there were too few of them. This was despite months of preparations in advance, where the computer game had been installed and tested. The limited number of computers later proved to become a problem that was not solved by simply putting 2-4 students in front of the same computer. The students did not find the set-up with 2-4 students pr. computer to be acceptable, due to computer games' emphasis on an active student role, which is also a central part in my educational perspective presented earlier.

During the first weeks most students were for the first 10 minutes of a lesson (47 minutes) tied up with login problems, bad cd-rom drives, incorrectly wired computers, video driver problems, choosing the right scenario, locating a saved game and starting the computer game. These problems could be viewed as temporary and of little relevance if we contribute them to the current limited knowledge and use of information technology in general and computer games in particular in the educational system. It could also be pinched on this specific school. However, the situation found at this school is consistent with earlier research on use of information technology in schools and this suggests that the school's problems are representative. The lack of computer equipment is commonly reported as a problem in research, and it doesn't seem to be about to disappear. To see the lack of equipment as a temporary problem is dangerous thinking as this may continue to be the situation for many years onwards. Indeed, it may be argued that use of information technology including computer games will always create obstacles, when you have to coordinate 30 people's simultaneous use.

The lack of computers was just one problem. Perhaps the most severe problem was really that computer support was too weak and that some students vandalised the computers by for example rewiring monitors, mouse and keyboards during recess. It should, therefore, not be underestimated that the technical problems will be an important challenge, when using computer games in most schools. However, there are some indications that this may change in the future. A year after this study was performed the Swedish secondary school Västerås, specializing in information technology, experienced few technical problems when using the same computer game in history teaching. Such a school may point to a future more tech-savvy educational system (Markgren, 2004).

Preparation phase

From the beginning the success of this teaching course was hampered by the lack of deep knowledge of the computer game among the teachers, which was also found to be a general problem for teachers in chapter 3. It was not that the teachers didn't play the game (*Europa Universalis II*) because they played it for several hours. But they didn't achieve a deep enough knowledge about the game to help the students later nor did they acquire enough concrete game experience to use as fuel for more traditional teaching. The teachers didn't really get into the computer game and failed to acquire the necessary knowledge to integrate computer game, group work and teacher talks. This was very much against the original plan, but the teachers were under hard pressure from other temporary assignments and illness, hence preparation was constantly behind schedule. This is problematic because the educational perspective I presented maintains that teachers require quite deep knowledge about the computer game to use the concrete experiences from the computer game in their own teaching, introducing scientific concepts.

The male teacher did have quite a great deal of experience with strategy games and was more capable of adapting, but still he wasn't really able to fit the game, group work and teacher talk into a coherent whole. The teachers' approach to the game was reactive rather than proactive - playing and learning the computer game parallel with the students and it was ,therefore, hard to plan the teaching in connection with the game. This was in the post-interviews recognized by both teachers as a significant problem.

It is also a clear example of the experimental set-up obscuring the realities. My role as technical assistant could, of course, be filled out by more competent teachers or technical competence. However, it is highly unlikely that schools (at least in Denmark) could set aside the necessary resources, especially if this is expanded to include all classes. It also seems that the current upgrading of teacher competences in information technology has, if not failed, then missed the target, mostly focusing on teachers acquiring more skills instead of changing the teaching practice. It is, of course, necessary to have basic computer skills to use computers for educational purposes. However, you need to consider the concrete challenges in planning the course. This has been attempted with the Danish Pedagogic PC Education, but skills in information technology remain quite detached from concrete school practice. The teachers take a course and are then left to their own devices when they return to the everyday teaching practice (Egenfeldt-Nielsen, 2001; Mortensen & Svenstrup, 1998).

The preparation phase in this study was also impeded by a general lack of time on the teacher's part for preparing classes, problems with installing the computer games and allocating computer rooms. The install took longer than necessary as a server install did not work for this particular game. Instead the game had to be installed on each computer separately. In general, many subjects in the Danish educational system experience cuts in preparation time, which is extremely problematic if you want to support new teaching styles for example cross-curricular teaching styles where computer games would be particularly constructive.

Also the coordination between the two history teachers and researcher concerning the content in the teaching was not easily solved. Here the challenge was primarily to find cases, relevant parts of the history book and match these with the computer game. This was far from a trivial task, and it might have been easier to take the computer game universe as a closer starting point than was attempted in this course. As explained earlier, instead, it was attempted to fit the computer game with the existing content in history teaching. The attempt to fit existing material may in hindsight seem naïve, especially given the educational perspective outlined previously as you should be very explicit in identifying the important experiences, and how these can be linked to students' previous experiences and historical concepts usually taught in school. On the other hand, it was found that if you could fit computer games with the existing material it would have a much better chance of actually being used beyond experimental use in actual history teaching.

Learning to play the computer game

Computer games were a new tool which students needed to learn how to use and connecting it with history turned out to be anything but a trivial task. As discussed in chapter 5, using a new tool entails both potentials and limitations, and this became quite obvious during the study. During the selection process of a relevant computer game for the course (see appendix) I feared that the computer game would be too hard to learn and according to many students this later proved to be warranted. One male student said,

> It went well, I think the game is a little hard, but it will probably become better in time
> (Student 37X, logbook, week 1).

The game was as complex as strategy games come, but this was also the strength of the game. This made it possible to have a richer representation of the historical universe and give the students more options for exploring history dynamics. The teachers could also appreciate that this was not a superficial action game or a war game only. As the teaching progressed the teachers pointed to this as important and in the final evaluation they also found the game to present the historical dynamics in a fruitful way. The delicate balance between presenting complex problems and making these accessible wasn't found with this computer game.

> We didn't really get very much out of the course. You spend too much time learning
> and controlling the game, to also remember the data that some times suddenly surfaced
> in a split second (Students, Group evaluation).

In hindsight one should have chosen a less complex computer game, but looking back on the short list of computer games to select from, none of the alternatives seemed to strike a better balance (see appendix). Most of these computer games involve fewer variables, dynamics and tend to have a more narrow focus on the parts of history concerned with war. The real alternatives were actually more complex, and it seems strategy games are far from becoming simpler. One avenue that might prove interesting is to look at older strategy games, where the complexity is smaller as players tend to demand still more complex computer games (Egenfeldt-Nielsen, 2003e; Gee, 2004a).

To alleviate some of the problems with learning *Europa Universalis II*, the tutorials (Picture 11) included in the game were used. With the tutorial the first problems with the nature of computer games arose. First, there was a large difference in how fast the students learned the game. Clearly the students with computer game experience learned the computer game much faster and especially those with prior experience with the strategy genre. Not surprisingly, most of these were boys. Some students finished the tutorials within the first hour, whereas 3-4 weeks later others were still struggling with basic concepts from the tutorial and, indeed, some hadn't completed all the tutorials satisfactorily. According to the interviewed students up to 1/4 in the class fell into this group. This group never really got involved with the computer game and didn't get the game to work at home. The students were expected to play at home to increase their skills and reduce the time span between playing sessions. When the weakest students didn't play at home the discrepancy between strong and weak students quickly accelerated.

Picture 12: Shows the tutorial for religion. The green arrow points you to different key actions and options.

Second, a lot of students, especially the less knowledgeable about strategy games, didn't find the tutorials necessary. Contrary to the teachers' advice they quickly jumped into the scenarios in the game and were quite overwhelmed. This was not like other games they knew, where they could quickly overview the possibilities. A lot of time was wasted, and many students experienced a lot of frustration and thought they would never master the game. Hardly the best start for a course. It was clear that experiences of success were too few at first compared to student expectations with computer games. At a later point one student noted that "It has been one of the most amusing lessons because it went well" (Student 43X: Week 4). This was one of the first successful game experiences for that student. For the students success was an important part of the game experience, and it was vital for them to continue playing even though it was difficult.

Third, the first scenario was constructed in a way that went contrary to normal game experience. The first scenario was intended to show the students that mindless war wouldn't work and, of course, they threw themselves into fierce battles instead of careful diplomacy, trade and development of their nation. Therefore, most of the students lost with a big bang. This made them very frustrated and unsure of the game. Normally, a game is constructed so the difficulty slowly increases to match the player's increasing skills (Rollings & Morris, 2000). In this case, however the players (student) did not experience a slow increase in difficulty, but a very steep learning curve. The position the students were put in was a rather difficult historical period for Denmark, chosen for its familiarity, relatively low number of national provinces and bad fit with war-mongering[29].

---

[29] The first scenario started in 1492 when Denmark is quite strong and in a position to expand. However, if depending too much on loans and war taxes, the country will destabilise.

We wished to make the students go through a historical learning process where they learned to appreciate other important historical factors than war. This was done through some initial scenarios where they would experience the limits of war. This was somewhat naive and counter-intuitive to the computer game. In the game you would normally start to learn how to wage war, and as the challenges grow you learn to take other factors into account to overcome even greater challenges. This is sometimes called a layered approach and is a characteristic way for computer games to present information to the player. In a layered approach the player is presented with the necessary information, and the game gives the player more options as his skills increases (Egenfeldt-Nielsen, 2003e). In this course you started with a challenge which was too tough, and you never really learned to wage war. The course tried to place students on too high a level of playing too fast - showing how learning can obscure natural exploration that is inherent in computer games.

From the perspective of the teachers this was the natural way to go as you could control what experiences the students had with the game. After the first hours we knew they had tried to play a small nation and had experienced defeat in war. This fitted best with the weekly teacher talks which were to match the game scenario. If the students were in completely different places in the game and had experienced completely different things, then how would the teacher be able to make a meaningful and relevant talk? That was the assumption anyway; looking back it would have been more appropriate to stress playing the computer games first and then slowly increasing the reflection, discussion and teacher talks. Especially considering we wanted to let students hook up with the computer game and find their own handles to ground the game experiences in previous experiences and extend the scientific history concepts from this. After the initial failure with war the students instead of turning to more subtle features in the computer game and becoming interested in what the teacher could offer concentrated on understanding how to wage war and the dynamics in this process. It is highly likely that teacher talks on the particulars of waging war in medieval Europe would have drawn the students as this related to playing the game. As the waging of war was mastered by the best students towards the end of the course more layers were added in the playing of game. This could have been a natural way to extend with other teacher talks. Quite naturally, students find an interesting part of the computer game which they see as relevant, can engage with and invest in, although this was criticized by other students as an illegitimate way to learn history, which we will return to.

The problems with teachers and students learning the game parallel to each other is also stressed by Kirriemuir & McFarlane (2003) as a common problem. The immediate access to computer games is quite important and they also suggest that support material could ease this and some of the problems described. An interesting recent example of this is the two teacher packages produced as an extension of Kurt Squire's PhD dissertation. They both use *Civilization III*, but with different historical periods and focus (Squire, 2003a, 2003b). I am doubtful that this will do the trick. In fact, my empirical study did include a sheet with hot tips, hints and breaks to encourage students helping each other, but mostly it wasn't used and it didn't seem to make a difference. The material by Kurt Squire is somewhat broader than just providing support material for students and the general idea of teaching material is definitely an important step to help teachers appreciate the difficulties, challenges and possibilities with computer games in educational settings.

Teachers

The teachers did play a large role in overcoming the practical barriers as the number of students that gave up was quite different between the two teachers. The male teacher had students who came back from the dark side. A girl in week 4 developed from being frustrated with the computer game and unsure of the purpose to altogether more positive. She writes:

> In general, I think the game has been much more fun and with more substantial
> content this week. Earlier we just waged war on the other countries, without

considering strategy. I also think we put more emphasis on other things, like trade, technology, points and stability. This makes the game more meaningful and you can do more things. […] As you learn the game and its features better, you have more energy to notice the historical facts. I have especially learnt something about religion, but I still think I get more out of a normal history lesson. (Student 5x, logbook)

The older class in general had few who completely gave up and this was probably due to characteristics of the teacher in the class. The teacher had a closer integration between computer game and teaching. In general, he also stressed the role of the computer game more and somewhat adjusted the teaching to match it. He was also more capable of helping the students due to his experience with strategy games. Also the smaller number of students somewhat decreased the risk of becoming completely lost. It was clear that in the older class some of the initial misgivings were resolved, although the scepticism towards what history you learned remained a problem. None of the teachers were really able to get the students to feel comfortable with the tools *Europa Universalis II* offered for supporting the educational experience.

Tools for reflecting on the game

One of the strengths of the computer game as a tool is the option to report and monitor the progression for later discussion and comparison. Too little attention was paid to, how students' game experience could be 'moved' between different contexts by using the reporting system in the computer game. It was for instance, very hard for the students to sit down in groups and discuss the computer game, because it took place in a different physical location than the computers. Group discussions in connection with the computers were not possible due to the size of the computer room and a strong demand for using the computer resources. This gave the students a bad framework for working with the computer compared to the control group which worked with the cases in front of them. Even without access to the computer games more could have been done to facilitate the students' discussions, for example maps of the game world to support the discussions.

The students were encouraged to use log books to facilitate these discussions, but this didn't really spark interest and discussion. The best functionality would be to have the computer game record and represent play actions, events and outcomes. There was actually a reporting mechanism in *Europa Universalis II* (Picture 12), but the students never really used it despite some encouragements. It was too abstract and hard for them with their limited knowledge of the computer game.

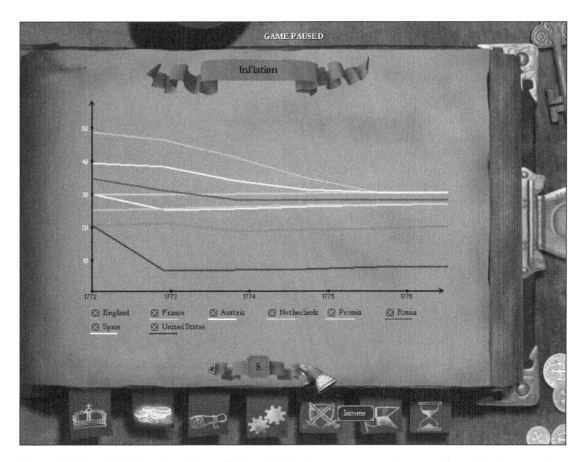

Picture 13: Shows the ledger from Europa Universalis II where you can overview a number of developments in key variables. Here it is inflation.

Reporting mechanism, saved games and possible options for reviewing a game have been suggested by several researchers (i.e. Kirriemuir & McFarlane, 2003; Squire, 2003c; Squire, 2004). It also seemed to be appropriate in this context. Computer games like *Europa Universalis II*, *Civilization III* and *Age of Empires II* actually have these functionalities implemented to different extents. In the Civilization-series you can play an overall movie of how the civilizations spread in your game. This could be very useful for teachers to review and see different students' experiences and present game experiences to each other. However, currently it is not possible to save these overall replays. This is possible in *Age of Empires II* where it is actively used by players to learn the game, discuss strategies and document game outcomes[30].

Next, I will take a closer look at a more abstract, cultural barrier to using and thinking about computer games in an educational setting. I have earlier hinted that the students were reluctant to accept the computer game, but how exactly did this take place?

The fight over what it means to learn history with computer games

Discussions with friends whether we learned anything (Student 33x, logbook, boy)

Before really engaging with the computer game from an educational perspective students discussed whether this was a valid history approach. This was a serious barrier that arose early while continuing to influence the students' learning experience throughout the course. The discussions

---

[30] The web-site with these saved games can be found several places among the biggest are http://aok.heavengames.com and www.mrfixitonline.com

among students about what constituted learning and history basically took as starting point history as concerned with facts and events since ancient times. This quite conservative approach to history among students has also been observed by other researchers. Stearns (2000) finds that students brings in quite naïve understandings of history influenced from a rich number of sources, school do far from have the monopoly on history.

In this study most students constantly stressed how computer games did not live up to the standards of traditional teaching despite the continuously stressing of the interaction between computer game, group discussions and teacher talks, as the important element in the experience. The intention of the course was not to replace teaching with computer games. Rather, the computer game was to supplement teaching. Neither was it the plan to replace one learning understanding with another, but to promote a balanced approach. This was probably partly misunderstood due to the computer game standing out as the experimental part. Thereby, attracting most student attention. When students in post-interviews were confronted with the underlining course set-up more than one looked puzzled and surprised.

The question of the merits of a more counter-factual approach to history was much discussed and commented on by the students who were constantly questioning and evaluating the educational use of computer games. In that sense, they were extremely critical and reflective, however, seldom this reflection and critical sense was used to discuss the experiences in the computer games and compare them with the teacher talks, readings or previous historical knowledge.

Few students really appreciated history as something else from facts. Those who did see some merits to a more counter-factual approach didn't really think it worked in the course. Still, they had great sympathy for the idea when discussing it. The discussions on learning with computer games are reflected in a number of comments by students and were also constantly experienced during the course. Notice in the quotes below how the new approach to history is constantly devaluated or actually denied (marked with bold). This was typical of most students' attitude.

> Regarding learning I **only** think you learned the consequences of what happened when you did different things, but historical facts were in short supply, you only acquired this knowledge from the book (Student 21x, logbook, boy)

> The outcome of the game and group work **limits itself** to a general understanding of the time period. Which is also fine, but there are not enough facts (Student 27x, logbook, boy).

> It was exciting to play the computer game, this is not something I do that often. But I think I had **less benefit** from it regarding history than expected (Student 38x, logbook, girl).

> It was good that we were allowed to learn in a different way. But we had too hard a time getting started with the game. We are not many who think you learn **anything** from playing (Student 40x, logbook, girl).

There existed an invisible schism between the objective and subjective world in students' approach to history. Apparently, it provoked a lot of students that the computer game obviously disregarded historical facts and changed the events of history, presenting a subjective view on history. This discussion mirrors the battle fought between counter-factual historians and more traditional historians (Ferguson, 1997). They found this to be completely inconsistent with history teaching and rejected that they could learn anything. There was a constant call for more historical facts, especially supported by the students who had limited success with the computer game.[31] The scepticism towards the history the computer represented was aggravated by the cultural standing of computer games, and a general resistance from students as newcomers to the community of high-school.

Resistance to educational use of computer games from the emerging community of students

Computer games have links to popular culture, gender roles and violence discussions, which currently seems stronger than for other media forms. It is rare to see a newspaper dedicate entire columns even front pages describing violent television, problematic board games or excessive outings to the cinemas. When other media problems are described it is certainly with less explosive material and reactions. You will not have worried parents, psychologist and politicians engaging in discussions through the public press (Beavis, 1999b; Egenfeldt-Nielsen & Smith, 2004).

In other media forms the low and high culture parts have successfully been split into separate spheres. We have great movies accepted as art, but also popular movies that still venture poorly in educational settings. One can argue that the split between movies of low and high culture have given television and video an easier way into education. This has still not happened with computer games despite attempts of elevating them to art.

In that sense it may be challenged if it even makes sense to treat computer games as a neutral medium, as it frequently has been (i.e. Wolf, 2002). A medium does not imply neutrality for example camera angles, cuts and voice-overs influence the impression a program leaves. Content in documentaries is influenced in the way it is presented and what is presented. For the majority of media the critical awareness of the platforms' impact on users' perception is still neglected. In this dissertation's perspective I will maintain that there is a degree of 'mediumness' to computer games as we want to use computer games as a platform for delivering educational content. This platform is, however, not neutral in terms of values, props, culture and teaching (Buckingham, 2003; Newman, 2004).

The cultural position of computer games makes it hard to draw directly on findings from the introduction of other media in school. Television, radio, video and computers may in general have fought hard to be integrated in schools as we saw in chapter 1. However, compared to computer games they have a strong push from governmental authorities, and these media are to a lesser extent perceived as leisure, fun, popular, teenage-like, dangerous and a waste of time (at least it has improved over the years) (Buckingham, 2003). From a teacher perspective computer games are strongly culturally loaded and completely alien.

However, it was not only the teachers who opposed computer games in an educational setting. It has not earlier been suggested that students would be a barrier with their understanding of computer games, learning, and history, but this was certainly the case in this empirical study. This lack of reference to student misgivings about computer games for education may be a consequence of a somewhat optimistic approach to computer games, resembling some of the early experiences with computers and subsequently the internet. Computers, internet and computer games are seen as the true learning form of the new generation, forcefully claimed by Prensky (2001a), Tapscott (1998) and to a lesser extent Gee (2003).

Some of the unexpected strong resistance might also be found in the students' newly begun road towards an academic carrier. The students' approach could overall be described as conventional and Wenger (1999:154-157) would characterize the students as being in an inbound trajectory. He points out how newcomers are often less progressive than established members of a community, due to the general uncertainty of how to act in the community. In an inbound trajectory members

---

[31] The focus on facts in history was despite not having an initial factual test, which would probably further have supported a traditional understanding of learning by showing what was important in the course, namely historical facts.

are struggling to find their place in the community and invest a large part of their identity in the enterprise. Unsure of their position and the boundaries, they are inclined to seek continuity and security rather than discontinuity. This may become even more marked as the engagement of students with the academic community is quite unequal, artificial and detached as they are split off from old-timers. They have a distant contact with teachers who present material to them and hardly explore the more subtle and tacit assumptions inherent in the academic community.

This is supported by the youngest class, which is just entering the academic community, being most critical, although the tendency was also clear in the older class. The emerging consciousness as serious academics may have led to a stronger rejection of the computer game. The initial interest and motivation was calmed when the students experienced that this did not involve the usual kind of history that they knew and for many in fact neither the computer games they expected. They couldn't really connect the experience with any relevant area in their current practice.

In Gee's (2003) perspective identity is inherently linked with learning and people cannot learn without being able to see learning as relevant and desirable for their identity, which extends well from my educational theory. Gee (2003) finds identification to be present in computer games both on a structural level and in the domain of computer games. He states that deep learning,

> [...] is inextricable caught up with identity in a variety of different ways. People cannot learn in a deep way within a semiotic domain if they are not willing to commit themselves fully to the learning in terms of time, efforts and active engagement, Such a commitment requires that they are willing to see themselves in terms of a new identity, that is, to see themselves as the *kind of person* who can learn, use and value the new semiotics domain. In turn they need to believe that, if they are successful learners in the domain, they will be valued and accepted by others committed to that domain.

(Gee, 2003:59)

Clearly these factors were not present in this course on computer games for students in the group who gave up. The student prioritised other school areas higher and didn't really see the computer games as worthy of academic attention. This poses a considerable problem, remembering Dewey's description of the quality of an educational experience, where relevance is very important. You might also see it as a clash between adults' tendency to rationalize play in a progress rhetoric opposed to a frivolous rhetoric as they are described in chapter 5. Many students did not buy the rationale: play being potentially developing and being able to teach them about history. Convincing them of this took the rocky road over changing their entire notion of, what history meant to them, but also challenging their perception of what the academic track was. The alternative to the safe, mundane world of history as facts seemed too exotic and uncertain - in opposition to the general school culture. Looking back, it is hardly surprising that the students resisted being caught in this limbo. A computer game that tells me about history that really isn't history - but rather stories about history – surely this must be a joke.

It is somewhat absurd that one of the most important entry points for using computer games becomes its main Achilles' heel: Namely, a closer relation to students' identity and a different approach to history. The students were supposed to appreciate a well-known media for exploring a more modern version of history, but this clashed with their in-bound trajectory to academia. These findings has critical implications for how and when to introduce computer games as it tends to challenge existing notions of learning, teaching and student identity, which requires some self-confidence and risk-taking on the part of the students. It would probably have proved easier to introduce computer games towards the end of primary school, where students are well-established and looking for new ways to explore a subject. The use of computer games should probably also be presented more forcefully as a real alternative instead of a shaky, uncertain, experimental teaching style, which was the impression students were given, especially as the teachers and researcher were quite uncertain of where the course was going. The facilitation of change and new thinking again stresses the role of the teacher as a facilitator of computer games as an acceptable academic tool. This also explains why the teacher who was more competent in computer games had less students who completely rejected the computer games as historically relevant.

Bermuda triangle of incompetence, conservatism and no ressources

This chapter has highlighted the particular problems with introducing a highly successful leisure activity into the educational system, where it becomes caught between heaven and hell. Not really able to live up to the expectations normally entertained towards leisure computer games experience and not really able to present itself as a trustworthy addition to the life of a student. This is aggravated by a range of practical barriers.

We have examined the problems that computer games trigger by looking at how the course was marked by different groups' very different resources for participating in the course. All these groups were affected by the numerous practical barriers experienced in the course, but with very different outcomes. Interestingly, it seems that although some of these problems were partly triggered by the complex computer games, none of them were qualitatively different from what you would generally experience in a course using computer games in a 3rd generation perspective. Instead the problems were aggravated and presented themselves more clearly. The barriers described above fall in three categories.

- **Practical/structural**: The technical limitations, the limited space, the time slots for lessons etc.

- **Game-related**: Learning how to play the game, the complexity of the game, the balance between playing/learning and integration of computer games with teaching.

- **Expectations**: The students' and the teachers' initial way of thinking about computer games, history, learning and teaching.

The confusing start with technical problems and a steep learning curve alienated some students who were normally doing well in school. They were inclined to take the bite out of the computer game as relevant to history. Furthermore, the position of the students as newcomers to the community of academia may also have led to stronger reactions. Computer games could not be seen as acceptable in academic work on the road to university. The normally high-ranking students who fared less well were not inclined to accept the computer game course as reasonable for accessing and hence undermining their position in the hierarchy in the subject history.

The course also ran into a variety of problems that made it very hard to get to the point, where the computer game proved itself different than traditional teaching. The practical barriers were overwhelming, and this was clearly also a warranted reason for the criticism. It is hard to settle on just how large a role the barriers played, but they definitely didn't account for all the scepticism. Finally, the computer game represented history in a way unknown to most and they were unsure of how to treat conflicting views. History teaching is despite good intentions still mostly taught from a textbook which hands down the 'undeniable truth'.

Chapter VIII: Issues in Teaching with Computer Games

> To understand clay is not to understand the pot. What a pot is all about can be
> appreciated better by understanding the creators and users of the pot and their needs
> both to inform the material with meaning and to extract meaning from the form.

Alan Kay (1984: 41)

Until now, we have covered a variety of the factors influencing educational use of computer games without looking specifically at the teaching. Still, it is in the actual teaching that we can see, whether computer games have a role to play in the educational system.

This chapter's goal is to examine the teaching that manifested in the empirical study, and examine why it turned out to be less than successful. This is done by examining the critical properties of the teaching style including student autonomy, playful learning, student-centred teaching and the problematic linking of different learning sites in the educational setting. After introducing the teaching style follows three examples of lost learning opportunities and one example of a strong learning experience, which are used to examine the factors in teaching that hindered the facilitation of learning. The factors influencing the educational experiences that are examined extend from the research overviewed in part 1 and 2. These are, especially play vs. learning, superficiality vs. depth and instruction vs. no-instruction.

It is concluded that the critical problem lies in the linking of students' concrete experiences, gained when playing the computer games, with historical concepts. This linking requires an active change of teaching practice coupled with extensive knowledge of the computer game, which will not automatically emerge in most educational settings.

Teaching style when using computer games

> I still think it is a very frivolous teaching style where you of course get some historical
> facts on the way, but if you were told them you could have learned them in 5 minutes
> in a history class. I think the game should rather be used as a supplement to the
> teaching than as the teaching (Student 5x, logbook, girl)

A different approach to history was facilitated by using a computer game in this empirical study. As we saw in the last chapter the course was initially well received. From a cynical perspective it could be argued, mostly because it stood out from normal teaching. The conventional approach to history among students was not mirrored in an equally conservative approach to the new teaching style. Any teaching style not resembling traditional classroom teaching was welcomed by most students. However, the honeymoon period didn't last long.

The teaching overall centred on playing the game, discussing the game in groups and hearing the teachers' talks. Students appreciated this variation in learning sites, and especially one-way teaching was not missed. All students also felt they had more autonomy, a higher degree of choice, and were more interested in the teaching. The teaching style suggested a course, where teaching evolved around students' experience with the computer game, but such an approach never really materialized. Instead, the teachers continued their normal teaching practice in the teacher talks, only to a very limited degree connecting computer game and teacher talks. The largest problem was that the teachers failed to make any links between these different sites for learning. This meant that there was no red thread in the course, and that the concrete experiences from the computer games were not extended beyond merely being relevant in a game context.

A key characteristic of teaching with computer games were previously identified as depth vs. superficiality and play vs. learning. The teaching aimed to use the computer game's ability to present a number of connections that students could explore in a safe, playful environment. Students could save and load games, make mistakes without any problems, and most were more engaged than normally. The safe and playful environment was certainly in place during the teaching, although we will see that this was not exclusively a didactic blessing.

The balance between play and learning

> There should maybe have been somewhat firmer settings around the whole project. People have been committed, but at the same time frivolous. It is just a game (Student 5x, logbook, girl).

Fundamentally most researchers in educational computer games expect that learning and playing can enrich each other, but in this empirical study it became quite clear that the enrichment may turn out to be more accurately described as a conflict. This is not necessarily due to an inherent conflict between learning and playing, but more likely a consequence of the existing approach to learning practiced in the educational system. Education and learning are seen as work, which is opposed to play in modernity (Mouritsen, 2003).

Education and play are two modes that we may want to combine, but to some degree we also feel guilty about combining them. More than one student questioned whether playing the computer game was schoolwork based on the simple premise that it was play. Even though habits and expectations may give some explanation of the resistance to combine play and education, the resistance also displays fundamental differences relating to learning and play. Play differs from learning as it abides less to specific rules; it has a more voluntary nature than learning. The student engaging in playing a computer game will expect more autonomy, although it may later be criticized when the learning part of the experience is evaluated. Earlier research points out the advantages of supporting features for educational use of computer games like guiding, supporting, scaffolding, introducing and debriefing the experience, all of which are partly in opposition to play. All of these interventions present demands to the game experience constraining the perceived freedom in play. However, opposition against such interventions relates more to an idealized understanding of play rather than play per se.

There are other more fundamental differences between play and learning, which Andersen & Kampmann's (1996) account of play can help clarify. They distinguish between deep play and social aspects of play. Deep play is described as the complete absorption with play, where you forget about time and place. On the other hand the social play is the surrounding activities that support and facilitate the deep play. The scope and importance of social play is according to Andersen & Kampmann (1996) often underestimated although it actually seems to be one of the main elements in play. Social play is the place where you learn about power relations, social conduct and develop your identity. What I find worth noting in both play culture and from research on fan culture in computer games, is that the social play is necessary to frame and reflect the game experience. Deep play is the player engaged in the computer games, whereas social play represents everything around this gaming experience. When students play *Europa Universalis II* they are engaged in deep play. This deep play is framed, broken, nurtured and changed by group discussions, teacher talks and other students. This gets at the quite engaging nature of most computer games, where the concentration and required attention are similar to deep play. You lose sense of time and place totally absorbed in the game universe[32]. You constantly play a computer game and in most genres do not have time for actually reflecting and evaluating your efforts. It

---

[32] This argument gain support from the theory on flow (Csikszentmihalyi, 1992).

happens very much in a continuous state drawing quite automatically on previous experiences. There is little time to stop, reconsider and reflect – indeed observations of game players will show almost complete absorption (Jones, 1998).

In this empirical study the balance between playing and learning seemed to be somewhat individual and it was not possible to dispense the same verdicts for different student groups. The supporting features were positioned differently for the groups participating in the course, but in general most students had problems stepping out of the deep play mode. The high achievers wanted little introduction and scaffolding concerning the computer game and history in general. They played around and were able to learn the computer game without formal help. After the initial learning of the basics of the game they were quite interested in extra material, linking the computer game with teaching and working on their own. They did not see the great benefit of group discussions, as they often found these to be irrelevant and a waste of their time. The give-up group was, of course, in extra need of introduction to the computer game, but also basically in need of appreciating the relevance of the course. Perhaps even to conceive the rationale for spending time on history in general. The students in the give-up group had a much harder time finding the line between play and learning compared to the high achievers. The runners-up were somewhat strong in all areas and benefited from most of the supporting features introduced in the course. The upwardly mobile did not need help with the computer game and were eager to go off on their own. They did, however, need guidance to engage with the learning perspective.

The different groups were more or less in balance concerning the play and learning. For most groups teacher interventions were needed to actually turn the course from a play experience to an educational experience. In general, the students used either play or learning as their handle on the course. For the students missing historical awareness, play became a way into the computer game, but it remained hard to expand the play interest to history. For the students, with less interest in the play part, history could be a way in. The give-up group had no handles and therefore did not really engage the course whereas the high achievers were able to connect the two experiences based on previous experiences with both playing computer games and learning history.

An unfortunate consequence of the course conceived as play was the frivolous approach taken often by some students, and by most students at some point. Although, the teaching with computer games was by most perceived as characterized by high engagement this was not the whole story. The engagement was mostly linked with the deep playing of the computer game and the rubbing off on the learning part was for most students limited. Furthermore, the playing part led some students to take a laid-back approach to the course. The laid-back approach did not seem to be a constant phenomenon, but rather varied. Students were more inclined to drift for their desire; in one lesson quite interested while in another marginally interested. This seems natural from a play perspective, but of course problematic from a teaching perspective, where you expect more continuity. There was no stabilizing factor called - this is schoolwork and one should work seriously with it. This is not necessarily a reaction that will persist if computer games are integrated more into the educational system and obtain more legitimacy.

The supremacy of playing over educational experience was also apparent in the cases where history set some gameplay limits in the computer game. The criticism of the computer game's failure to adhere to historical facts and events did not stop students from heavily criticizing these limitations in the next instant. In fact, the student who saw the link to real history in the in-game exploration of the world criticized it in the next breath for limiting the gameplay. On one hand, students found that the computer game should reflect history and that in a number of areas it did. On the other hand they criticized the limits this historical reality imposes on their gameplay. "We don't want it to be that rigid" was the formulation many used.

Although, play and learning did not blend perfectly it did give the course a progression with more student engagement, although this engagement was not always educationally relevant. Next, three examples follows that show learning experiences at different critical points in the teaching with *Europa Universalis II*: appreciation, exploration, and linking. The focus is on the actual transformation of the concrete experiences into abstract concepts through the experiential learning cycle (see chapter 5). You start by appreciating the differences that make a difference. You then explore and reflect on these differences found in the concrete experiences, ultimately linking it to other experiences. In this process you will revisit your concepts, and through instruction construct scientific concepts[33].

First example of a lost learning opportunity: No Appreciation of historical information

The example shows the *lack of appreciating* simple historical information that student yearned for. When historical principles and limits were at play in the game universe the students were mostly ignorant of these sound limits.

For example, in an interview one student complained that it didn't make sense that in one province you could raise a meagre 1,000 men while another province could boast 8,000 men. He didn't explore the reasons behind this limit and failed to recognize the historical information in the experience. However, there are perfectly good historical relevant reasons for the differences that are mirrored in this student's game experience. Not all provinces have the same capacity for raising troops, for example due to population size, loyalty to the crown, cultural background, religious beliefs and the infrastructure. Furthermore, you can't continue to raise troops from a country, only so many men are capable of bearing arms in a country.

Students didn't seem to understand that the game's historical universe made up a lot of the important actions that you can say history has at its disposal, and that the computer game was built on quite a detailed model of history. Many students couldn't really appreciate the historical correct factual information, background, dynamics and events even when it was right under their nose. This was not related to scepticism towards the entire enterprise described in the previous chapter, but rather a missing historical and game awareness. Clearly, most students lacked the historical awareness and game insight to appreciate the detailed model, and the historical information at play.

Second example of a lost learning opportunity: Appreciation of historical facts but no further exploration

This example shows the *lack of exploration* although the opportunity exists as students have already appreciated the presence of historical information, dynamics and events. The students recognized the historical information but failed to engage further with it.

The students were playing Denmark, and were in a war against Sweden. After at series of wars they managed to get the upper hand over Sweden, which they knew was against the historical realities. This did not result in the students asking questions to the effect of why is that – they were busy enough playing the game, and one might add digesting the facts. The students found the non-historical victories over Sweden rejuvenating, but they failed to ask what accomplished the victory and neglected to engage with game's history representations as more than subjective descriptions of history with little relevance. The students simply noted that winning over Sweden were not in agreement with history as taught by the teacher and the textbook and dismissed the game as relevant for teaching history.

Third example of a lost learning opportunity: exploring historical connections but no linking

The *incapability of extending* the game experiences beyond merely exploring the game is demonstrated quite well in the following example. There is potentially a connection between game universe and

---

[33] Kolb uses another terminology: Appreciation is referred to as grasping via apprehension, exploration as transformation via intention, linking as transformation via extension (Kolb, 1984).

historical thinking but it is left hanging in two boys' description of the proper strategy for Napoleon to bring England to its knees.

> Napoleon's ambition: Recipe for beating England. 1). Secure the borders against Spain with a peace treaty to disengage troops. In this case it is done by conquering a province in North America and then making peace. 2). Destroy the British fleet by attacking small groups of ships with superior forces. 3). Leave a considerable force to fight off sporadic attacks from Austria. 4). Collect all troops from France and send them over the English Channel 5). The British will face a force 5 time their size 6). Therefore, it can't go wrong. It was surprisingly easy to beat England. It was impossible to defend the [newly conquered English] provinces.

> It was surprising that England had so few men in England. The reason for this might be that they felt secure against invasions as long as they controlled the British Channel. They didn't have resources after the Independence War (Student 21x, logbook, boy).

In the plan there are elements of historical relevance although not consciously exposed. They are aware of the geographic elements, the threats from Spain/Austria, the importance of outmanoeuvring the enemy, the importance of the British fleet, Spain's vulnerability in the colonies, the British ability to intervene at their discretion on the continent through their superior navy and the importance of gaining the upper hand through sheer size (see map from game picture 14).

Picture 14: Shows the political overview of the countries bordering up to the UK in the early 17th century.

The problem is that nobody really exposes potential concepts and connects the experiences to history teaching in general. The students end up with the conclusion that this is merely part of playing the computer game with no bearing on history in general. Indeed, most of their thinking and historical knowledge is quite relevant, when looking at European history.

The students' main comment is how they find it surprisingly easy to pull off their plan, beating history. But in fact a number of things could go wrong with their plan reflecting historical dynamics. A new enemy might show up or internal rebellions break out. France was in the late 18th century also strong, so gameplay-wise it actually resembles the historical situation quite well. The two boys are surprised at the resilience of the rebellions in the newly conquered British provinces, but this is also historical relevant as one of Napoleon's greatest problems was indeed to keep peace in his new conquests especially triggered by differences in culture and religious turmoil. The problems they experienced could be explored by discussing the problems of occupation in history and relating their strategies to Napoleon's problems with occupying Spain and Italy. However, this wasn't pursued from the teacher side, and neither did the students take up the challenge themselves.

These boys who had quite elaborate reflections and discussions about the game experiences, found they achieved a good general insight into the historical period, but they did not obtain what they really desired, namely historical facts. They were able to draw some of the historical connections above, but others escaped them, because they lacked the options for exploring them further in the course, and they were not given much support for further exploration from the teacher. This example shows that the computer game can certainly provide relevant concrete experiences, thinking, student engagement, and investment, but without the teacher to facilitate it more than anything remains a game experience – with low educational quality.

An example of a strong learning experience: Linking

There were few examples of learning experiences that arose from the game experiences, even when the exploration of the game was quite deep. The few successful learning experiences support the claim for using concrete game experiences as a starting point for building concepts about history, and that deep explorations of the game can lead to interesting learning opportunities. Students were interested and engaged when history could be tied into their specific game experiences especially when links could be made from the game to history.

In one example, a student constantly experienced problems in southern France due to religious turmoil between the Protestant subgroup the Huguenots and the state religion Catholicism. The historical reasons for this conflict were perceived as most interesting by the student. Especially, when suggested that the downfall of the heretics was paramount to France's success and showed the student how he could send missionaries to the infected provinces, change their state religion or the tolerance towards different religious groups. The student remembered the importance of religion in other games, and was interested in exploring the reasons behind the turmoil in his beloved France both game and history wise. He engaged with the computer game, and invested in it. He was more than ready to expand on his knowledge, when he got the chance with the teacher. The student could actually recognize the relevance of some of the material from teacher talks and the textbook on the religious unrest during this historical period. In a very concrete sense he could see that religious differences led to rebellion, financial losses and domestic problems.

Why the teaching with computer games failed

In their study of the area Kirriemuir & McFarlane (2003) are disappointed that educational use of computer games does not seem to expand beyond short experimental periods. In that sense they find that educational use of computer games remains experimental rather than pilots for broader use in the future. Disappointment will probably not get us far. To see computer games as 'merely' a neutral medium we can use for delivering content, skills and attitudes is lulling ourselves into dreamland. We can shape the teaching with computer games but they also bring baggage. Changes in teaching practice are far from unproblematic and not without cost. Whereas small changes and adjustments are a constant part of a community of practice, major chances on both an individual and a group level require an extra effort (Wenger, 1999). Several challenges to the teaching practice are apparent from the examples above. Basically, there are three apparent problematic areas from the examples above, indicating that educational use of computer games can work well, but it requires that you find the right balance on a number of axes:

- **Appreciation of historical elements**: Students are not capable of appreciating relevant historical information, events and dynamics.

- **Exploration of historical elements**: When historical elements are identified, students are not exploring the historical implications. When they do, they tend to focus on the factual information.

- **Linking of game experience**: Students are not capable of connecting the concrete experiences in the computer game with teacher talks, history in the textbook or other spheres of life.

It is worth noting that most students did not have a problem with the engagement and motivation. They invested in the computer game, and were interested in learning more if relevant to playing the game, although this wasn't true for all the student groups (see chapter 7).

Appreciating the historical significance in the computer game

The ability to distinguish the relevant from the irrelevant is recognized by Wenger (1999) as one of the important characteristics of being a member of a community of practice. From Wenger's perspective this would imply the teacher teaching students what differences make a difference in the community of playing historical computer games in school. This includes the ability to recognize the relevant elements in a computer game history course, both historical information and computer game representations. These were indeed the characteristics which most of the high achievers demonstrated. There is a quite thin line between what counts as relevant history information, and what features are merely part of the game universe. In *Europa Universalis II*, interpreting the game experience demanded more intimate knowledge of history and the computer game than was initially the impression.

In chapter 4 this was discussed as an area still vastly overlooked. When the information is appreciated in the game universe it is often taken at face value or simply dismissed. Grundy (1991) finds that many students have an almost blind trust in the computer game's ability to tell the truth, despite other opposing sources. In my study this is supplemented with an almost automatic rejection by some students, when the trust in the game is broken. My study paints a more fine-grained picture of what students relied uncritically on in the computer game and why this was the case sketched in group descriptions in chapter 7. There is an automatic rejection in the give-up groups whereas the upwardly mobile took the history at face value. The runner-up students were struggling to find the balance, whereas the high achievers were actually able to find the right balance, appreciating the right elements.

Despite the outspoken criticism of the historical facts and inconsistencies concerning the game the concrete criticism was not very elaborate, and appreciation of historical elements quite superficial. The problems that did get mentioned were the most obvious, but also least interesting, for example winning a war, declaring marriage, shift in ownership of provinces or outcome of battles. The criticism was often also quite misguided and lacked appreciation of finer details in history. It took as starting point contemporary borders and other historical periods. For example, Denmark's continuing struggle in the game to overtake Schleswig-Holstein in the 16th century, which was sometimes successful, but not permanent. Denmark conquering Schleswig-Holstein was by students seen as completely non-historical, because students tended to see Germany as a unified country, even though this process only begun during the mid-18th century. For most students it became quite apparent that marriages and wars did not reflect real history, as they changed when they replayed the scenario. This led to the critique that the computer didn't teach them any history – they wanted facts and the real events.

Usually, the girls were more sceptical towards the different learning form of computer games and more prone to see history as learning about facts and events. They were the strongest critics as to the lack of correct facts and events, whereas it seems the boys were more capable of abstracting from this and identifying the relevant areas. This was probably also a consequence of the boys' more extensive experience with computer games. They knew how computer games worked and did not expect them to be just like traditional history teaching, which were more often the girls' expectations. You may say that the girls appeared more conservative, but in reality the difference related to weak versus strong students in the course. The better you did on the axis history interest, history knowledge, computer games and academic ability the more you could appreciate the alternative form of history teaching - to a large degree this matched gender.

You might say that the problem is really to believe rather than disbelieve. One does not read a historical novel, play a computer game or watch a historical movie with the expectation of it being accurate. The hard part is to strike the balance and appreciate that some parts are relevant, while others in a sense mock history. In novels and movies the production team often goes through great trouble to ensure historical accurateness. In *Pirates of the Caribbean* the pirate ship is built from scratch in a real size model, consulting experts and old drawings of Spanish ships (Verbinski, 2003). The pirate ship was the setting for the movie, and in that way mirrors history and the same desire is obvious in most historical strategy computer games. In movies, novels and computer games you want to provide the setting but the actions and outcomes are not necessarily accurate. If the Pirate captain should be required to climb the ship's mast with a wooden leg in a hurricane for dramatic effect it is not a problem. Even though, historically this was highly problematic.

In the computer game the drama or narrative is not necessarily the main force and the instructor is not in command. Here the setting is at the player's hand and should one be compelled to take France out of its neutral policy in the late 16th century and declare an all out war on the major powers, so be it. It comes down to being able to think abstractly and see the larger perspective in an action. You may argue that this seems intuitively easier in a computer game, where the player is aware that he/she is actually choosing an action between different alternatives. This freedom of choice must entail that the outcome from your choices is not necessarily in keeping with history text books, but most important it opens up for an appreciation of history as more open-ended than factual accounts set the scene for. And, indeed, most students did realize the openness of the game, but they stopped there and did not so to speak get back on the horse. Instead they focused on what they perceived as the computer game's shortcomings historically.

Just the facts, please

It was clear from the empirical study that students have a conservative approach to anything else than history as facts. Clearly, students felt bombarded with historical facts and events, especially, during the teacher talks, not really engaging with the historical information, but snatching as much they could. Similarly, students felt overwhelmed by the computer game, but on closer examination it wasn't due to the amount of facts. Rather, the computer game's complexity was in the connections *between* the information rather than *in* the information. However, these connections couldn't really be appreciated without a proper grounding in history – most students lacked this grounding, and were therefore not capable of appreciating these connections and especially not exploring these connections. There are good reasons for students' narrow focus on the historical facts.

In the introduction to this dissertation I presented six levels of educational objectives, which may serve as an introduction to why a deeper appreciation, exploration and linking of history had a hard time. The six levels are knowledge, comprehension, application, analysis, synthesis and evaluation. It was stressed that the first levels are necessary for the following levels to make sense and that might have been the real problem for the students in this study. Students were still grappling with constructing a basic knowledge foundation and a comprehension of the massive amount of facts and events that they were bombarded with during history teaching. They felt they needed more facts and events to get a picture of what history was and were not comfortable with seeing or doing something more beyond facts. To apply the knowledge in a game setting, adopt an analytic stance and evaluate this process was way beyond most student groups' capability.

In the perspective presented in chapter 5 you can say that the students lacked a sound experience base for beginning to construct scientific concepts, but for students the concrete experience in the game wasn't feasible for constructing the concepts – they wanted facts straight out of the textbook. They were somewhat stuck between these two positions. Resulting in historical information staying in the textbook and teacher talks, while concrete experiences stayed in the game room as the student indicates in the quote above. In both learning sites students felt like drowning, and retorted to defensive manoeuvres evident in the previous chapter's uncovering of barriers.

In the case of *Europa Universalis II* the computer game delivered more complexity than the students could cope with, although the students found the historical facts too limited. The broader approach to history as a dynamic process with underlying variables that lead to events was here premature considering student level. In the teaching students were primarily concerned with digesting facts and had little initiative for going beyond these facts – the very thought of linking these contexts was an abomination for all but a few high achievers.

Edutainment pop-ups in the search for facts

The inclination to prefer facts was also most apparent, when students talked about what parts of the computer game actually worked. Students looked for the computer game to provide facts, and thereby link better with other history teaching and their history understanding – unifying the learning sites in the course. Given edutainment's dominance in the current market it is interesting that characteristics from edutainment surfaced as a solution – a way to unification.

Edutainment's characteristics centre on pop-up boxes - the one element in the computer game that most students consistently connected with history teaching. Pop-ups boxes were consistently seen as the most educational part of playing the game and by students suggested as a way forward for a more educational game experience.

The pop-ups in *Europa Universalis II* actually spanned a variety of types (see picture 15). In some of the pop-ups you did get necessary information for making an informed choice in the game. Some students did also consider these pop-ups interesting. Still, most students were not impressed with the pop-ups, even though they actually provided the facts and events from history they accused the computer game of not delivering. When students had the chance to acquire historical facts in the computer game setting they didn't find it fitting, as the quote below attests to:

> Well, when you are playing, then suddenly one of these windows pops up. When there
> is something about a historical event, for example the French revolution or another
> famous person who pops up and then dies. For example, this guy Ove Guldberg, I
> think that was his name, when I played Denmark. Then he popped up and then there
> was a long description of him. How it happened, and that was okay but I mean... I just

> think it was suddenly a bit dry… It might be educational, but I think it was kind of, dah. (Students, Interview 2, boy).

The paradox of pop-ups being attractive, although failing, points to the perceived strength of edutainment. Although, pop-ups extended from an edutainment formula intuitively attracting students' educational 'instinct' they in reality had little teaching capacity. Pop-ups are scorned as irrelevant to the game and usually quickly clicked through.

> When you are sitting there and playing then you are playing the game. I don't think you really want to take the time to read the pop-ups. There are many, I know we also did, who clicked away from these pop-ups. We didn't have time to read them. We were sitting in the middle of the game and then suddenly came that pop-up. It was kind of an intrusion towards the end that they kept popping up (Students, Interview 2, girl).

Picture 15: The popup describes the consequences of the Welsh act when you play England.

On the other hand, exactly these pop-ups are suggested as a basis for more historically correct computer games. By expanding on the pop-ups with movies, sound and more historical information students believe a higher educational impact could be achieved. On closer examination students recognized the limits of pop-ups, but were still tempted by the promise of pop-up boxes as a simple way to get historical facts and events – not changing students' practice of learning, where facts were in the driver's seat.

Pop-ups are basically going down the path of edutainment's sugar-coating of content in picture and sound, introducing information of little relevance to the computer game and changing the game experience to live up to premises opposing its own. The demand for factual information is as strong with students as any parent buying an edutainment title or publisher living up to the national curriculum. At least, it seemed so when students were asked in this study, however, it also reflected their struggle with fitting the computer game into an educational setting. We should be alert to this tendency in educational settings for preferring edutainment that reflects underlying propositions in education and history. Indeed, edutainment would seem more in line with the history perception found among students in this study. Students preferred the approach to history as facts both on a didactic level, and a more personal level. History was facts – not much else. This was challenged during the study causing great discussion among different students groups. Next, we will look at the challenge of the facts, when students were expected to explore the game experiences beyond their face value.

Exploring the game beyond facts

In general, the exploration of different implications of game actions was not something present in students just starting to familiarize themselves with the game's interface, a new approach to history, and drowning in facts from the teaching. Rather, the exploration slowly evolved as students learned to appreciate the finer details of the game universe. Whether the teaching can be described as deep or superficial is a harder question.

A deeper exploration was critical for teaching with *Europa Universalis II* to extend beyond unreflective playing, and to offer something else than learning the facts of history. Exploration in depth implies a more complex representation of a topic, however this is somewhat inaccurate. It doesn't fit with the discussions the students had in this course, the observations made during playing and it is at odds with the structure in most computer games. Looking at the rule-based universe of *Europa Universalis II* students were far from struck by the complex information delivered. The information represented by historical facts and events was not overwhelming compared to the textbook and teacher talks, which as documented in the previous chapter led to scepticism from students. The rules in *Europa Universalis II* are the most important and interesting elements from the given historical universe it represents – simple rules were at the centre of the game experience not detailed information.

The confusion related to complexity arises because we tend to think of complexity as a function of the amount of information. However, any computer game's complexity arises from the interconnections of simple rules - the dynamic relationship and parallel interaction of variables (see chapter 5). When the students read their textbooks things happened in a particular order and a more or less linear narrative was presented. Not so in *Europa Universalis II*, where students' game actions spread in different directions and students were expected to willingly explore the different connections.

In this study the complexity was evident several times as students paused or slowed down the game to examine the exact implications of a game event. The complexity was clearest when students in *Europa Universalis II* experienced historical events, declarations of wars, offers of alliances, political crisis or discovery of new regions. These experiences forced the students to make important choices balancing a number of possible outcomes against each other exploring different alternatives. In these cases, students take a pause in the game or at least changed the speed to very slow. Especially the high achievers commented on the role of speed in the computer game. To some degree the use of speed was a demarcation line between high achievers and the other groups who didn't use the manipulation of time very often.[34] Some students did explore the game in depth, although most perceived the game experience as superficial due to its lack of historical facts.

The exploration did not only depend on students' computer game ability, like pausing the game, but also their historical background information and general historical awareness. Only a few high

---

[34] The use of game speed is also a well-known playing style in SimCity where you will regulate the game speed according to the complexity you have to survey.

achievers became capable of seeing the potential from exploring the game experience from a historical perspective beyond facts:

> It is also that even though the history [in the game] doesn't follow what the history textbook says then you are still learning something. What makes a society like it is and what consequences your actions have and likewise. (Students, Interview 3, boy).

> Good – interesting, but you don't learn that much about events, on the other hand, you learn about the underlying reasons for the events (Logbook, 39x, boy)

Exploration really began to show up among the high achievers and partly the runners-up towards the end of the course. However, the students were unsure of what to make of these explorations and they were not sufficiently encouraged during the course. It did not mean that the strong students thought the course had been excellent, but they criticized it for not facilitating a better, different explorative learning experience and focused less on the lack of facts. In the following quote from a post-interview you clearly sense uncertainty and vagueness as to the nature of this alternative approach to history. It is hard for the students to formulate the meaning of history beyond facts and events, but high achievers in the end sensed something more than facts were out there in the last evaluations.

> I think that this was also something that the game did. I mean it gave a general understanding of the period and that was it. There were some dates, events and similar things but it wasn't something you learned in the games. It was something you knew before, I think. The game gives a general understanding of how it worked. And that was good; it was really good in the way it did it. But I am not sure whether we learned it because of the game or the parallel teaching. I don't know if the game could work by itself (Student, Interview 1, boy).

There seems to be an appreciation of the computer game's potential, if only it had been done a bit differently. Although this holds some truth, as there were technical problems, it seems that the problems stem more from the general problems in teaching with computer games, which we will continue to examine in the following. One initial hope was that the inaccurate historical events could spark such exploration, however, in this study it didn't seem to happen.

Linking concrete experience in the game with scientific concepts

The missing links between the different learning sites were constantly noted by students. According to some students the computer game playing might as well have been a separate subject with no connection to teacher talks on history. This, quite naturally, led to a lack of appreciation of historical elements in the computer games, especially the facts.

> When you sit and receive teaching from the teacher then it is primarily facts that are hurled at you. I mean she really tells what happened in these periods, right. When you sit and play the game then it is not like it happened in reality. So, it is not completely correct how it [the game] follows history. So I don't think you can draw any parallels to the teacher talks, I really don't (Student, Interview 2, boy).

The lack of connection is demonstrated in a teacher's quite elaborate description of mercantilism not being accessible in the computer game. Few students if any used the knowledge of mercantilism in playing the computer game although this was central in the teacher talks and the textbook used. Mercantilism was more or less the basic economic model the computer game used. In an interview with a girl she indicated that she couldn't really use the teacher's description of mercantilism for anything because as she said about the computer game:

> It's not as if you notice it when you obtain a bank loan and then you have some money. Then you use some money to create armies, to build a navy and go to war and then suddenly you don't have any more money. (Student interview 2).

It is interesting that in that short sentence she has - although not very eloquently - described central elements for most monarchs before trade became prominent as a way to bolster the revenues. When you add trade to her description, which she did later, you have some important elements of mercantilism. The reason why she doesn't use mercantilism as support for the game-playing, points to interesting problems when teaching with computer games. The way the concept of mercantilism is constructed in the teaching was by the teacher showing a model of mercantilism, which the students were then to more or less memorize. There wasn't really made any attempts at linking this to student experiences in general or the game experiences in particular. This meant that the concept of mercantilism didn't really link with students' experiences beyond the history lesson. There are no handles other than external tools like the teacher or model presented, which will usually not be available to the student when playing. Most of the students would probably have been able to explain the model when confronted with it, but students did not internalise it. You can say that mercantilism floated in thin air.

What I have argued in chapter 5 is that mercantilism should have been approached the other way around by using concrete game experiences to build the richness of the concept. This was also what was demonstrated in the example of a strong learning experience earlier in this chapter. The students would have a number of self-sustaining concrete (game) experiences that could be drawn on in using and understanding the concept of mercantilism. In addition to giving a strong understanding of mercantilism it would also imply that the core of mercantilism could be recognized, in later similar experiences. The next time the student played the computer games she would be able to recognize that this related to mercantilism, which would again expand the strength and richness of the concept of mercantilism.

A reason why this approach didn't manifest was as previously discussed partly due to teachers' reluctance to change teaching practice, but also because it wasn't made explicit during the course preparation. The initial idea of the study was to examine how far teachers on their own could get with computer games in an educational setting - on the schools premises. Therefore, the course used normal textbook and traditional teacher talks, which were only partly adapted to the computer game experience. Teachers didn't really change their teaching practice despite encouragement, which indirectly led to the teacher talks and textbook having a less than perfect fit with the playing of the computer game. The less than perfect fit led students to reject computer game as having a bearing on history as no connections were made. Students just like the teacher took as a starting point what they knew, and that was the facts in the history textbook. For the students there was little meaningful transfer of knowledge between the two contexts. This was hardly a conscious choice on their part or the teachers, but more a consequence of little resemblance between the computer games and the more traditional teaching.

It is worth noticing that the lack of connecting the game experiences with the teaching does not necessarily mean that the experiences with the computer game or mercantilism would not be activated in other contexts. The dominating feeling among students that the playing had little to do with learning history in school may paradoxically make it more transferable to other everyday contexts because the students construct other handles (Schank, 1999) for these experiences through spontaneous concepts. For example some students said that the playing of the history game had led to discussions with parents and some of the male students even played it with their fathers. Such experiences provide quite different handles than normal school experiences, transferring the game experiences to a home environment.

The teacher's role

We saw in chapter 3 that the teacher has been identified as a significant resource when information technology is integrated in schools and this seems to hold true for computer games as well. However, teachers have also been considered one of the main barriers, which was also the case here as seen in chapter 3 and 7. Indeed the findings from this study concerning teachers and computer games mirror previous findings on educational use of information technology, although technical challenges on the surface seem to play a larger role. The continuing prevalence of edutainment stuck in a 1st generation perspective shows that teachers so far have not been able to change their teaching practice to accompany the use of computer games. The resilience to change in the teaching practice is well known from educational use of information technology in general, and was also apparent in this study.

Veen (1995) finds that the teacher's belief about teaching in general steered the way information technology was used. Important elements were whether the content was perceived as relevant, preferred teaching style, teacher's role in the class and the teacher's broader conception of education. The teacher's skills were also a strong indicator especially their pedagogical skills and to lesser degree computer skills. It is interesting that the computer skills did play a role but is outperformed by the pedagogy challenges, which also seemed to be the real challenge in this empirical study.

On closer examination the resilience in teaching practice makes good sense though, as the change of teaching practice is closer to the identity and practice of being a teacher. Changing teaching practice is putting you as a teacher at risk, and it will be easier to stay with the normal classroom teaching. The teachers in this study used the computer game in ways that fitted with their practice and there is no reason to believe this should be different for computer games. Changes in teaching practice cannot be expected to arise by themselves.

Looking closer at the challenges the teacher faced with *Europa Universalis II*, the variation in student experiences emerges. There is not one solution, and the students may be able to win the game through problematic assertions and decisions. One player experienced that military expansion is the dominant strategy in *Europa Universalis*, basing this on 2-3 games, whereas another player sees diplomacy as superior. This calls for changed teaching practice where you engage more closely with students' interpretations and assertions from their learning experiences. The large difference between the different student groups (see chapter 7) in playing the computer game give extra support to the importance of the teacher intervention. The teacher needs to facilitate an approach to history including historical information, events, and dynamics while balancing learning versus playing. Additionally, the challenge of facilitating appreciation, exploration and linking lies with the teacher. The teacher must solve computer problems and help students playing the game. In general, the amount of new challenges meant that teachers stayed with what they knew, and this meant staying with a traditional teaching practice. The fact that teaching practice didn't change was not due to lack of will among the teachers. Considering the expected reluctance among teachers in engaging with information technology the teachers in this study were quite positive. Their frustration and scepticism was not based on a rejection of the learning approach tried with computer games, the content in the computer games or the general perspective on history in the computer game. It was rather a quite expected and logical consequence of resource prioritisation. Both teachers were interested in alternative ways of approaching history and the students were faster than the teachers to reject the new learning approach inherent in the course's use of a computer game. Despite interest in changing teaching practice, the teachers in the end found it overwhelming to actually adjust their teaching to include the computer games.

Interestingly, the teachers differed in how far they came down the road of changing their teaching practice – or perhaps more precise, to what degree their existing teaching practice and background fitted with using the computer game in teaching.

Teacher differences

The two teachers were quite different on several parameters (table 7) and this proved to have bearing on the approach to teaching the course. It is interesting to take a closer look at the two teachers who participated in the study to assess advantages and disadvantages of different teaching styles.

	Teacher A	Teacher B
Gender	Male	Female
Age	Middle-aged	Middle-aged
IT experience	High	Low
Game experience	High	Low
Expectations	Optimistic	Wait-and-see
Teaching style	Overall, general	Detailed, thorough
Ambitions for students	Moderate	High

Table 7: The key parameters for the participating teachers.

Teacher A was on a technical level much better equipped to approach the game and integrate it in the teaching. He learned the computer game relatively quickly and found it interesting to play the computer game for long stretches at a time. Teacher B took 5 weeks into the course before saying that: "Ah – I am finally beginning to see, how this game can be used in teaching history". This was when she was familiar enough with the game. This is believed to be the development most teachers will run through. The first time around they will tend to learn the computer game parallel with the students, unless they beforehand have a private interest in the computer game.

The teachers didn't prepare examples from the computer game that could be used in the teaching. Consequently, teacher talks had little use of events and experiences from the computer game. For this to happen teachers should have played through some scenarios and picked up interesting examples for the teaching, which was, however, too overwhelming a task. This point is supported by Squire (2004) that had some success with just-in-time lectures but also considerable problems. On one hand just-in-time lectures seemed to be the only relevant approach to connect computer games with teaching. But on the other hand the students weren't that interested in engaging with the teacher when playing the computer games. They had civilizations to destroy and wonders to build. Students were only really paying attention, when it was directly relevant for playing the computer game.

Teacher B was significantly more worried whether the students received the historical material on a level which was detailed enough. Her ambitions were higher and her approach more sceptical. This was not in a negative way, but rather a healthy approach to a new teaching style. She was very much caught up in a prioritisation problem, where she constantly felt that more time was needed to teach students the necessary history. She also had several problems with overviewing the class as she had 28 students compared to 19 in teacher A's class. Teacher interventions were clearly hard to manage when the students played the game. Some students became somewhat stuck in the game and here the degree of familiarity with computer games became apparent between the teachers. The game-experienced teacher could easier identify problems and pick up on interesting discussions. One of the things that students clearly found very worthwhile was such interactions with the teacher. However, much of this interaction for the female teacher centred on concerns.

The female teacher worried that the students might actually conceive all game experiences as factual accounts. In the post-interview she mentioned how interventions were important to highlight, when history was incorrectly presented in the game universe. Her wording was interesting as it seemed she didn't extend history from the game experiences, but questioned their validity. This was perhaps relevant for the less experienced gamers and weak history students, but it also facilitated the 'obsession' with facts that were more evident in her class.

When interaction worked the students would encounter a problem and discuss it with the teacher. The teacher would explain the background and challenge students' assumptions, for example the reasons behind religious unrest in southern France during the beginning of the 17th century. Here the interest and motivation of the students were driven by a concrete experience in the computer game. These intermezzos were, unfortunately, quite rare for both teachers, although the male teacher A had more instances of intervention. The limited number of intermezzos was probably due to class size and more practical problems that arose while learning to play the computer game demanding the teacher's time. Furthermore, successful learning experiences required that the teachers had knowledge of the computer game and of the historically relevant knowledge. This was easier to live up to for teacher A, because he connected history more with the computer game compared to teacher B due to more experience with playing computer games in general.

The teaching style of the two teachers differed in how well they fitted with educational use of computer games. The more general and overall approach of teacher A was closer to the game, and, therefore, to some degree this supported better what was happening in the game. On the other hand the more detailed approach from teacher B was a good supplement to the game that presented the larger picture, but it lacked the building of scientific concepts and finer details of a scientific concept. The more detailed account of history in teacher B's talks seemed to make it harder for the students. Instead of using concrete experiences, more details were added, not really helping students identify the overall important concepts. It is hard to judge one approach as being better than the other, but the students presented with the detailed approach struggled more with the clash between history as facts and history as a process. Students exposed to the general approach were also somewhat more capable of using the teaching in relation to the computer game. The male teacher's focus on providing an overview did not bury the obsession with facts among students, but it did limit it somewhat.

Other sites of learning support appreciation, exploration and linking

Until now the student and teacher have been the primary focus for facilitating the transformation of concrete experience to scientific concepts, making students gain knowledge of high educational quality. Squire (2004) suggests that the school setting may overall be described as quite impoverished for learning to play computer games referring to *Civilization III* and this also seems to holds true for *Europa Universalis II*. The characteristics of the game culture normally surrounding the playing of computer games are lacking, although it is hard to specify closer it will be attempted below. There were few examples of distribution of learning and the students couldn't figure out what approach to take in learning the game.

The exploration and linking of the game experience could have been explored further in the social setting around the computer game, namely the group discussions, teacher talks, teacher interventions and informal peer discussions concerning the game - but there was little surplus of energy for such endeavours as we will see in the following. Indeed, other sites did support educational use of *Europa Universalis II* in this empirical study:

- **Class collaboration**: This includes interactions between the two players in front of the computer game, between different pairs playing the computer game, and in groups discussing the different experiences with playing the computer game.

- **Spark of interest outside school**: This relates to situations and contexts outside school, where students' appreciation, exploration and linking of the game experiences were supported.

Students did little to cooperate beyond the pairs they worked in and the group discussions didn't work. Many students mentioned that discussions played a role outside school but many students also stated the opposite. Even the collaboration between two players was far from unproblematic. This challenges some of the popular held beliefs about the importance of social dynamics around computer games that are increasingly becoming popular (Jessen, 1998; Newman, 2004; Sørensen, 2000). I far from reject the importance of the social setting and its potential for facilitating a richer learning experience with computer games, rather I challenge the idea that collaboration will by magic appear around computer games in an educational setting leading to a stronger educational experience.

Class collaboration

Class collaboration happened between the pairs working together around the computer and to a lesser degree by students walking around the computer room. The earlier example with the recipe for Napoleon to defeat the British is actually based on quite close collaboration between two students but another girl highlights the imbalance often present.

> So, then I just actually sit and try to follow what happens. It is someone else who is playing. It has actually been like that most of the time (Student interview 1, girl).

In some pairs it worked well with novice and experts together, while in others it was problematic. Despite efforts to match those with computer games experience with those less experienced, this was not easy. It was hard to know who the good players were and the students wanted to be together with someone they knew - both experienced and inexperienced players took this approach, resulting in groups with very different combinations. It seemed that often it actually worked better by splitting the experienced and inexperienced, because the in-experienced couldn't keep up the pace. They gave up, and the experienced players were far too absorbed in playing and raced ahead.

The work by Littleton and Light (1999) on group interaction around computers seems to shed some light on the problems. They find that boys are not good at helping other students, and that they tend to dominate around the computer especially if their skills are better than those of girls. This was also mostly the case in this study, although a few boys were quite excellent in teaching the girls to play the computer game. However, in general the boys were the most experienced gamers, and that may explain the less than collaborative atmosphere.

Broader collaboration among students in general in the computer room didn't really happen. The following snippet from an interview highlights the students' perception of the missing collaboration in the class which is quite interesting. In the quote the students struggle to explain why collaboration didn't really work with computer games.

> Boy: Well. You can't [help], it is kind of hard to go and help. If you are sitting and playing, then well, of course, you can, but it is different when you are in a computer game. It is something different with homework. You know, you calculate this by doing so and so.

Boy: The, others are sitting in another situation, right. It is not similar to other subjects. It is a different situation and then it is hard to go and help them. You can, of course, try but… First, you have to understand their situation and then try to help them and then back to your own. You can't expect that the solution will be optimal when they are in another situation.

Interviewer: So it is really hard to cross between each others' games because you are in different places?

Girl: The only thing you could help them with was to tell them what different icons were.

Boy: Yes, what the different things did, that's the only help you can offer. You can't just say that you have to build up your country or make it stronger, here you go. There the help percentage was quite low.

Girl: But how do you do that? But you are France and I am Spain. I have a completely different situation here than you have. You just have to do it (Students, Interview 2).

Clearly these two students didn't find the help between students very useful, and it was not prevalent in the class. This is also discussed by Squire (2004), supporting the notion that social collaboration around computer games is quite hard. Although socializing between students were stronger in Squire's study this did not necessarily facilitate learning history and only partly supported learning to play *Civilization III*.

The boy in the interview is among the high achievers and was actually often in a role, where he was asked for help. Although normally used to this role, he found it harder to accomplish with computer games. Of course there was some interaction but it was limited and unfocused. Thus, the burden on the teacher for helping out with even the smallest problems was not lessened by experienced players slowly being able to step in. Both students are really circling around the student autonomy when playing computer games, the openness computer games allow for. It is hard both for students and teachers to relate to each others' experiences. This was a continuing problem throughout this course with computer games.

The appreciation, exploration and linking was not supported by the group discussions. In these the intention was for the students to discuss in pairs to reflect on difference in their game experience and challenge each others' decisions and assumptions. These group discussions were by the high achievers seen as superfluous and a waste of time, whereas the least capable groups treated the group discussions as a free pass. The complete lack of relevance expressed by some of the students may be over the top. There was a lack of understanding of what the group discussions were any good for and especially the less experienced were not ready to engage with harder questions concerning the game. They hardly knew how to raise an army, let alone how to discuss the game in relation to history.

The students suggested that the discussions should have been at a much later point and in general they found the introduction to the game too short and limited. It proved extremely hard for the students to think beyond the computer game experience and use the historical information in another context – the group discussions were not the answer. As we have discussed identifying the underlying historical information was cumbersome, and this became painfully obvious in the group discussions. Despite ideas for questions to discuss and game examples from each student, the groups seldom got beyond describing what they had done in the computer game on a very concrete level. Experiences were not reflected beyond the computer game nor linked to history and especially weak students took historical information at face value.

There were, however, indications especially in the last two scenarios that as you get further into the computer game it is possible to discuss, reflect on it and possibly relate it to history teaching in groups. Some students did get a feeling for the different outcomes that the computer game offered, and in that sense became aware of how some of the underlying factors that could lead to quite different historical outcomes. The lack of success in the group discussions may also partly have been related to the setting of the group discussions. It was not possible to hold them within the classroom or computer room and instead they took place in recess areas. This hardly framed the experience for the students as serious and as they were already a bit unsure of the purpose they slipped into talking about topics unrelated to history.

The lack of class collaboration does not necessarily disqualify the notion that educational computer games are strongly supported by the surrounding social context. It rather stresses that this social context does not emerge by itself and that the use of computer games in an educational setting may not automatically offer the qualities we see in leisure game culture. The theories by Jessen (2001), Newman (2004), Buckingham, Carr, Burn, & Schott (Forthcoming) and Gee (2003) point to the rich social life and culture around computer games and this plays a significant role in learning to play computer games and the potential spin-off learning often found in game forums. The game culture has a lot of support for playing a computer game and sharing the different experiences. You have the more formalized representations like forums, magazines, modifications of games, elaborate walkthroughs, strategy guides and game-related art to name some. These representations reflect an underlying game culture that thrives on social interaction and sharing game experiences. This indirectly makes up a quite interesting learning environment that is automatically often associated with the nature of computer games; however as Jessen (2001) stresses computer games are embraced because they live up to the existing play culture among children. The sharing, helping and collaboration is in this perspective more an intrinsic quality of children's play culture than of computer games. It can be argued that the use of computer games in an educational setting is at odds with children's culture and, therefore, the rich social interaction often found around computer games tends to disappear.

In a learning perspective engagement arising from computer games is highly relevant for getting strong concrete experiences but it also has drawbacks. The players are so absorbed that they will not really connect the game-playing beyond the immediate context. Importantly, this shortcoming of computer games in a learning perspective is in game culture remedied by the rich social interaction and fan culture. In this empirical study these cultures weren't really appreciated and built by students as many lacked the necessary game experience. For the most avid gamers such a shared space was naturally constructed but hard to extend to less experienced gamers, especially for the girls, which is parallel to findings on game culture in general. Many girls feel excluded from the strong male game culture (Jessen, 2001)

Spark of interest outside school

There were indications that among some students the context of learning expanded beyond school, especially among male students. Before the course started, it was also hoped that the exploration and linking of the game experiences would expand beyond school, and this partly seemed to happen[35]. It was not possible to observe the exact interactions outside school but an evaluation question covered this area. A survey asked whether the teaching during the course had played a

---

[35] This was based on the extensive historically relevant discussion found in online forums when selecting the game (see appendix)

role outside school for example in discussions in recess, at home, with parents or other. The student responses below indicate the variety of answers:

> Have discussed it a lot with both classmates and parents (Student 39x, logbook, boy).

> My father thinks the game is fun (Student 45x, logbook, boy).

> My parents were interested in the alternative teaching style (Student 21x, logbook, boy).

> It's the only homework (besides French) that I talked about at home. But I have mostly told about the influence I had on the world (Student, 16x, logbook, boy).

> Has been exciting to tell about something at home that they didn't know anything about (Student 40x, logbook, boy).

> I don't think it has played a large role outside of school, but we have discussed it a little at recess (Student 24x, logbook, girl).

> Discussions about the game itself, but it has been very limited. Sure, we have talked about it at recess, but not a lot (Student 27x, logbook, boy).

Overall, most students indicated that they hadn't discussed the computer game outside of the class room, but a few very enthusiastic students said that it was discussed a lot and quite a few boys pointed to an interesting connection with parents. In general, more boys than girls indicated that the computer game played a role for them outside the classroom. This is also in line with earlier findings which find computer game culture as more in line with boys' culture in general and the prevalence of playing computer games among boys (Jessen, 2001).

Conclusion: Students and teachers never really got the idea

In general the teaching with *Europa Universalis II* never really reached a level where it could be considered a success as there was too much uncertainty, resistance and problems related to the course. Still, the course did provide a blueprint for some of the key challenges in using computer games. These were outlined as the progression of students from appreciation over exploration to linking – all of these having their own problems in an educational setting. A major challenge when using computer games lies in the linking of students' concrete experiences, gained when playing the computer games, with historical concepts. This linking requires an active change of teaching practice coupled with extensive knowledge of the computer game, which will not automatically emerge in most educational settings.

The resilience of the teaching practice is interesting as it points to the potential of computer games. We should not believe that by magic computer games will be used differently from traditional classroom teaching. Even though computer games have the potential for facilitating alternative teaching styles and challenge current perceptions of learning with information technology, no guarantees are given. Computer games may have to wait for teachers to change before significant transformations in teaching practice can manifest. As such computer games are caught in a paradox. On one hand, they are championed as possessing new ideas and concepts for teaching and learning. But on the other hand, it may precisely be this innovative approach that makes it so hard to get computer games through the school doors.

Chapter IX: Evaluation of the of Learning Outcome

> It is an interesting way to learn history. But, on the other hand, I do not think you learn that much about the 'real' history.

> (41x, logbook, final evaluation)

Until now the focus has been on the more qualitative experience of using computer games in teaching, the structural limitations and how computer games influence the learning process. However, an important question relates to how computer games measure up in terms of learning outcome when compared to more traditional teaching.

We saw previously that few rigorous studies have been done and few studies have really asked the right questions. Previous studies do not really compare computer games with other teaching styles or activities. Hence, these studies can only convincingly argue that students learn from computer games, but have no way of substantiating a claim for actually expanding use of computer games, as using computer games isn't proven superior to existing teaching practice. The current status is that no study has yet considered whether using computer games in social study subjects is worth the initial efforts of learning the interface, setting up computers and the countless problems discussed in the previous qualitative analysis[36].

The study presented below tries to address some of these problems, but is flawed by problems with the randomisation of the sample, the lack of a pre-test prior to the course and the low strength of the test used for measuring learning outcome. Still, it is worthwhile to look at the results to contribute to the discussion on potential differences in learning outcome. The final conclusion is that there is no significant difference in the actual learning outcome between the experimental and control group but the retention for the experimental group is better. The study also points to the experimental group as significantly more interested, feels less pressure and experiences more autonomy during the course. The students playing computer games evaluate the content in the course more negatively.

The study's findings is in line with previously discussed research, where it has been found that students are more motivated and interested when computer games are used. This lead to better learning outcome especially related to retention, which has previously been found high, when researchers have compared traditional games with other teaching practices. The autonomy has not previously been studied in-depth but extends well from a basic belief that computer games facilitate more active learning.

A number of questions are examined, all aiming at studying the learning outcome from computer games.

- Do the control group and the experimental group differ significantly in learning outcome measured as the difference between factual post-test and factual retention-test?

---

[36] One exception to the lack of rigorous studies is the E-Gems project that has conducted several studies which can be described as a standard experimental set-up (Klawe, 1998).

- Is there a significant difference between the control group and the experimental group in intrinsic motivation measured as general interest, motivation, pressure and perceived competence after the course?

- Is there a difference between control group and experimental group when students' evaluate the course in terms of the content, teaching style and the general engagement in the course?

- Finally, it is examined whether there is a significant difference between control group and experimental group in the perception of history as a subject and interest in history teaching during course?

Method considerations

The analysis is performed by using parametric tests to gain more strength in examining the hypotheses. The significance used is the 5% level as is usually the case in social science (Coolican, 1994). The use of parametric tests requires that the dependent variables are at least interval data, which is achieved here. The sample should also be normally distributed, which is also supported by the sample being randomly drawn. For the factual test we can use t-tests as the variables Factual post-test and Factual retention-test have the same distance between each value. For the rest of the variables we cannot assume the same distance between each value and, therefore, use chi-square tests. The analyses are performed by using the SPSS package v. 12.00. The important variables are described in figure 18 below.

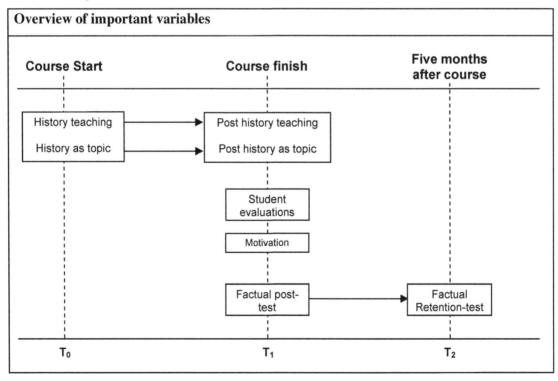

Figure 18: Provides an overview of the important variables pertaining to learning outcome and their development throughout the empirical study.

Results on the learning outcome

Below the results in relation to the questions above are presented split into the four overall questions outlined above. However, the first step is to take a look at the sample.

Checking whether the sample is succesfully randomised

The randomisation failed on some quite important parameters, namely age and playtime, where the experimental group turned out to be older (Table). The experimental group also played computer games more and scored lower on identified regulation pointing, to less intrinsic motivation at the start of the course. These variables could potentially influence the dependent variables, but more importantly point to latent differences between the two samples, which I may not be aware of. There were no differences on external regulation (p=0,598), introjected regulation (p=0,389), intrinsic motivation (p=0,355) (Table), personality variables (p=0,09-0,89) (Table), gender (p=0,22) (Table) and general approach to school (p=0,59) (Table).

Indepedent samples T-Test to check randomization for age and playtime

	What class are the student in	N	Mean	Std. Deviation	Sig. (2-tailed
age	Experimental group	26	16,462	,811	
	control group	28	15,857	,591	,003
Hours playing computer games a week	Experimental group	21	7,762	13,238	
	control group	25	1,760	2,245	,031

Table 8: Mean for age and hours playing at the course's beginning, and that this difference is significant.

Indepedents Samples T-Test for differences in initial motivation

	What class are the student in	N	Mean	Std. Deviation	Sig. (2-tailed)
External Regulation	Experimental Group	20	2,390	,473	
	Control Group	21	2,495	,755	,598
Introjected Regulation	Experimental Group	20	2,665	,492	
	Control Group	22	2,882	1,035	,389
Identified Regulation	Experimental Group	20	3,165	,300	
	Control Group	22	3,564	,672	,019
Intrinsic Motivation	Experimental Group	20	2,790	,691	
	Control Group	21	2,595	,641	,355

Table 9: Mean for the 4 variables for motivation at the course's beginning, which are not significantly different.

Indepedents Samples T-Test for personality differences

	What class are the student in	N	Mean	Std. Deviation	Sign. (2-tailed)
IPIP Extraversion scale	Experimental Group	21	61,571	21,367	
	Control Group	24	55,375	24,142	,370
IPIP Agreeableness scale	Experimental Group	21	59,381	22,353	
	Control Group	24	58,417	23,493	,889
IPIP Consientionsness scale	Experimental Group	21	48,762	22,050	
	Control Group	24	58,417	20,028	,131
IPIP Neurotiscism scale	Experimental Group	21	22,571	11,387	
	Control Group	21	32,000	22,516	,090
IPIP openness to experience scale	Experimental Group	21	29,905	21,658	
	Control Group	24	26,000	20,576	,539

Table 10: Shows the fives variables for personality differences for the two groups. There are no significant differences between the groups.

Chi-Square test to check if sex is different for the two samples

| | | | sex | | |
			female	male	Total
What class are the student in	experimental	Count	10	17	27
		% within What class are the student in	37,0%	63,0%	100,0%
	control	Count	15	13	28
		% within What class are the student in	53,6%	46,4%	100,0%

Table 11: Shows the distribution of male and female students.

Chi-Square test to check if attitude towards highschool is different for the two samples

| | | What is overall attitude to highschool | | | |
		Neither interesting or uninteresting	Quite interesting	Very interesting	Total
experimental	Count	3	15	3	21
	% within What class are the student in	14,3%	71,4%	14,3%	100,0%
control	Count	2	21	2	25
	% within What class are the student in	8,0%	84,0%	8,0%	100,0%

Table 12: Shows the distribution of attitude towards school in the two groups.

The differences observed in age, motivation and playtime have some obvious problems, potentially influencing the dependent variables in different directions. The age can both imply more maturity and longer exposure to history teaching, which should improve the experimental sample's learning outcome. However, it probably also indicates that some of the older students in the experimental group have attended one more year in primary school, which implies that they were not found fit for high-school the first time around because they were academically too weak or in general too immature. Halfway into the study the teacher remarked that more of students in the experimental group seemed to have taken an extra year in primary school, and that they seem more interested in computer games.

The playtime should improve the chances for the students in the experimental group to benefit from the computer games, whereas the higher age indicates less maturity and academic strength – the differences should balance each other somewhat. The lower intrinsic motivation for the experimental group should be less problematic, as the later analysis shows that intrinsic motivation is higher for the experimental group after the course. Hence, the initial motivation differences make it harder to find significant differences in the later analysis on intrinsic motivation.

Was the learning outcome different for control group and experimental group?

The first question analysed is whether the retention differed for control group and experimental group.

Establishing a baseline by looking at score for factual test

In the following it is analysed whether there was a significant difference in the test scores for factual post-test between experimental group and control group. No significant differences are found (Table), and we have, thereby, established a baseline for examining the development in retention score.

Independent Samples Test for Factual Post-test

	N	Mean	Std. Deviation	Sig. (2-tailed)
Experimental group	26	39,885	13,216	
Control group	24	46,375	13,909	,097

Table 13: Shows the mean for the two groups on factual post-test, no significant difference found.

The analysis also indicates, with some reservations, that students learning outcomes were not related to whether they used computer games or not. This could, however, be related to initial differences between the two groups, which we cannot rule out due to the lack of a pre-test. Unfortunately, such a pre-test was not conducted due to the problems outlined in chapter 6 and the problems were aggravated by the failed randomisation of the sample beyond my control.

In a future study, sampling should be better to make sure differences are only an effect of the experimental manipulation and cannot potentially be attributed to differences in the initial baseline and sample. These problems are also the argument for concentrating on the retention of students in the course, as the factual post-test can serve as a baseline for the factual retention test, limiting the problems of the skewed sample. There can, of course, still be some differences between the samples that didn't influence the factual post-test, but kicked in with the factual retention test, which is a weak point.

Checking for linearity to determine method for calculating difference between factual retention score and factual post score

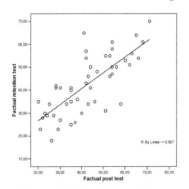

Figure 19: The relationship between factual post-test and factual retention test.

To decide on how to find the differences between factual retention score and factual post score I need to determine the nature of this relationship. The relationship between the two variables can be examined by estimating the inclination and point of intersection through a scatter plot (Figure 19).

The line does not cross in 0 and has an inclination of approximately 1, which means that the difference between the two variables can best be described as Y-X rather than Y/X. We next examine the difference in factual retention score for experimental group and control group as factual retention score (t_2-t_1) by using a paired samples t-test.

Analysing whether there is a significant development from t1 to t2 for experimental group or control group

There is a positive change from the factual post-test to the factual retention test for the experimental group but the change is not significant (Table). The negative change for the control group approaches significance and can be considered level sensitive. However, for now we must conclude that there does not seem to be a significant change in factual score for either group. Looking at the development of the two groups we could expect a significant difference between the two groups as the development in mean for the experimental group is positive and negative for the control group. This is examined by using an independent sample T-Test looking at a new variable Factual test$_{t2-t1}$.

Paired Samples T-Test for Experimental group

	Mean	N	Std. Deviation
Factual post test	38,958	24,000	13,337
Factual retention test	41,917	24,000	12,853

	Paired Differences		
	Mean	Std. Deviation	Sig. (2-tailed)
Factual retention test - Factual post test	2,958	9,702	,149

Paired Samples T-Test for Control group

	Mean	N	Std. Deviation
Factual post test	46,375	24,000	13,909
Factual retention test	42,917	24,000	13,101

	Paired Differences		
	Mean	Std. Deviation	Sig. (2-tailed)
Factual retention test - Factual post test	-3,458	8,267	,052

Table 14: Shows the difference in mean on factual post and retention test for each group, and whether this any difference is significant. The question is whether any of the groups have a significant difference in the scores right after the course (factual post-test) and 5 months after the course (factual retention test).

Analysing whether there is a significant difference in the development of factual score from t1 to t2 between experimental group and control group

There has in fact been found a significant difference between the two groups' development in factual score (table 15). The experimental group learning outcomes develop more positively than the control group's learning outcome in the 5 months after the course has finished. Looking at the means above (table 14) we can see that the scores for control and experimental group approach each other after 5 months, which is interesting for future studies. It would be worth further examining whether students using computer games have smaller learning outcome immediately after the study, but make up for this due to stronger retention. This seems to be the case in the study, but we lack the factual pre-test or a fully randomised sample to really substantiate the claim.

Independent samples T-Test for differences between experimental group and control group in Factual post test and Factual retention test

	N	Mean	Std. Deviation	Sig. (2-tailed)
Experimental Group	24	2,958	9,702	
Control Group	24	-3,458	8,267	,017

Table 15: Shows the statistics on whether there is a difference between the two groups development from factual post-test to factual retention test.

Or to put it another way: Students using computer games seem to learn less, but will remember significantly better what they have learned compared to students using more traditional teaching methods. Next, it is interesting to examine whether the experimental group and control group differed in terms of motivation, as this has often been found to be an indicator for more successful learning experiences.

Is there a difference between the two groups in terms of motivation?

The motivation was measured on a number of variables which together constitute a high intrinsic motivation. Interest/enjoyment, perceived competence and perceived choice load positively on intrinsic motivation, whereas pressure/tension load negatively. I look at each variable separately, because they each relate to classical questions in relation to using computer games in education. The question of more interest and enjoyment from computer games is a returning claim as well as more perceived choice, whereas perceived competence and pressure/tension have not been examined previously in the literature (see chapter 4).

Indepedent sample T-Test for differences in intrinsic motivation between experimental group and control group

		N	Mean	Std. Deviation	Sig. (2-tailed)
Interest/enjoyment	Experimental Group	24	4,167	1,048	
	Control Group	23	3,452	1,353	,048
Perceived competence	Experimental Group	23	4,130	,930	
	Control Group	22	4,462	1,227	,312
Perceived choice	Experimental Group	23	4,374	,911	
	Control Group	23	3,343	1,457	,006
Pressure/tension	Experimental Group	22	2,127	,689	
	Control Group	22	2,764	1,049	,022

Table 16: Shows the development in motivation between the two groups from course start to course end. Three of the variables have significant difference in mean in favour of the experimental group.

From the analysis above, we can conclude that two of the three variables that load positively on intrinsic motivation are significantly higher for the experimental group and pressure/tension that load negatively for intrinsic motivation are, furthermore, significantly higher for the control group. The experimental group can, therefore, be said to have overall a stronger intrinsic motivation. This is in line with previous results within the research field.

It is perhaps surprising that students playing computer games do not perceive themselves as more competent despite the use of computer games. However, given the quite hard and complex computer game used in the course this is understandable. The use of computer games experienced a hard birth as discussed in previous chapters. We can from the analysis above conclude that students playing computer games were significantly more interested in the course, enjoyed it more and felt they had more autonomy, while feeling less pressure and tension compared to the students with the more traditional teaching. Next, the question is whether the increased motivation manifested in the actual evaluation of the course.

Is there a difference between the two groups in terms of evaluation of content, teaching and engagement

In the following the evaluation of content, teaching and engagement is examined, with only the content turning out to be significantly different between the two groups (Table). I switch the method used to Pearson's chi-square, as it is usually used when checking for homogeneity in contingency tables, which means that we want to see whether the count for some cells in the table below falls outside of the expected range. Pearson's chi-square[37] still has the advantages of a parametric test, but looks at the distribution, not the differences between the values, which is a necessary limitation as the variables for evaluation do not have the same interval between the values.

We can see that there is a significant difference between the experimental group and the control group in terms of evaluating the course's content, with the experimental group being more dissatisfied with the content of the course. This is hardly surprising, given the discussion in the previous chapters on students' reluctance to accept the historical strategy game as valid history. Somewhat surprisingly, there is no difference in the engagement which somewhat contradicts the results from the intrinsic motivation. However, we should be careful with this measure of general engagement as it has a quite low cell count of 2, which makes the method somewhat inaccurate. Furthermore, general engagement is an assessment on group level whereas the intrinsic motivation variables are on individual level. One should rely on the measurements on individual level as more precise as students describe their own engagement. Next, I look at whether the differences between the experimental and the control group manifested in the approach to history teaching and history as a topic.

---

[37] The Pearson's chi-square looks at the probability for occurrence of given cell count and calculates a finale value that should be below 0.05% to reject the null-hypothesis (null-hypothesis being that the contingency table is homogeny).

Chi-Square to examine difference in content evaluation between experimental group and control group

		Evaluation of the course's content			
		Somewhat bad	Neither good or bad	Somewhat good	Total
Experimental Group	Count	6	11	7	24
	% of group	25,0%	45,8%	29,2%	100,0%
Control Group	Count	4	5	16	25
	% of group	16,0%	20,0%	64,0%	100,0%
Pearson's Chi-Square Sig. (2-sided)					,046

Chi-Square to examine difference in teaching evaluation between experimental group and control group

		Evaluation of the course's teaching			
		Somewhat bad	Neither good or bad	Somewhat good	Total
Experimental Group	Count	3	10	11	24
	% of group	12,5%	41,7%	45,8%	100,0%
Control Group	Count	10	7	8	25
	% of group	40,0%	28,0%	32,0%	100,0%
Pearson's Chi-Square Sig. (2-sided)					,093

Chi-Square to examine difference in engagement evaluation between experimental group and control group

		Evaluation of the general engagement in the course			
		Somewhat bad	Neither good or bad	Somewhat good	Total
Experimental Group	Count	2	8	14	24
	% of group	8,3%	33,3%	58,3%	100,0%
Control Group	Count	6	11	8	25
	% of group	24,0%	44,0%	32,0%	100,0%
Pearson's Chi-Square Sig. (2-sided)					,129

Table 17: Shows the distribution in the scores between the two groups for the three evaluation variables, and whether any differences in distribution are significant.

Do the two groups change in their approach to history?

The last step is to look at whether the different learning experiences affected students' perception of history. It is not possible to examine as detailed as the analysis of the factual score as I have to use chi-square and the cell count becomes too low for some of the analysis steps. I, therefore, limit myself to looking at two analyses for history as a topic and two analyses for history as teaching: The first analysis tests whether the two groups have the same baseline by looking at whether control equals experimental at t_0 and the second examines whether control equals experimental at t_1.

Do the two groups change in their approach to history as a topic

There is no significant difference between experimental group and control group in terms of attitude towards history as a topic, when the study commences (Table). When the course finished this had not changed significantly (Table). Hence, there is no indication that using computer games changed the attitude towards history as a topic.

Chi Square on difference on attitude towards history as a topic between two groups

		Attitutide towards history as topic			
		neither interesting or uninteresting	Quite interesting	Very interesting	Total
Experimental Group	Count	2	13	6	21
	% of group	9,5%	61,9%	28,6%	100,0%
Control Group	Count	7	13	5	25
	% of group	28,0%	52,0%	20,0%	100,0%
Pearson's Chi-Square Sig. (2-sided)					,281

Table 18: Shows the distribution in attitudes towards history as a topic between the two groups before the course. There is not found any significant difference.

Chi Square on difference on attitude towards history as a topic between two groups after the course

		Attitutide towards history as topic after course				
		somewhat uninteresting	neither interesting or uninteresting	Quite interesting	Very interesting	Total
Experimental Group	Count	1	5	11	7	24
	% of group	4,2%	20,8%	45,8%	29,2%	100,0%
Control Group	Count	4	5	8	8	25
	% of group	16,0%	20,0%	32,0%	32,0%	100,0%
Pearson's Chi-Square Sig. (2-sided)						,509

Table 19: Shows the distribution in attitudes towards history as a topic between the two groups after the course. There is not found any significant difference

Do the two groups change in their approach to history teaching ?

Here the analysis examines whether the attitude towards history teaching differs significantly between the experimental group and control group both at the outset of the course and when it ends (Table). These analyses do not reveal any significant differences between the two groups. Computer games do not influence attitude towards history in this study.

Chi Square on difference on attitude towards history as teaching between two groups

		Attitude towards history as teaching			
		neither interesting or uninteresting	Quite interesting	Very interesting	Total
Experimental Group	Count	1	11	9	21
	% of group	4,8%	52,4%	42,9%	100,0%
Control Group	Count	6	11	8	25
	% of group	24,0%	44,0%	32,0%	100,0%
Pearson's Chi-Square Sig. (2-sided)					,191

Chi Square on difference on attitude towards history as teaching between two groups after course

		Attitude towards history as teaching after course				
		somewhat uninteresting	neither interesting or uninteresting	Quite interesting	Very interesting	Total
Experimental Group	Count	4	9	9	1	23
	% of group	17,4%	39,1%	39,1%	4,3%	100,0%
Control Group	Count	6	12	5	2	25
	% of group	24,0%	48,0%	20,0%	8,0%	100,0%
Pearson's Chi-Square Sig. (2-sided)						,527

Table 20: Shows the distribution of attitude to history before and after teaching with no significant differences.

Broadening the scope of learning outcome

It may seem somewhat reductionist and limited to focus on a weak factual test for accessing the learning outcome in this course. Although, I also draw on other sources the results above present the traditionally primary measurement for learning outcome in schools. Indeed I have in the previous chapters described other underlying themes that engaged the students significantly more than the teaching of historical facts. According to the students in the experimental groups factual historical information was not exclusively present in the course. It may, therefore, be completely unfair to the computer game course to merely measure its success on this axis.

Still, the factual test is maintained as important for assessing the teaching of history. Whether students like it or not the subject is taught to build knowledge of facts, events and methods within history. This is what the final exams prioritise. Still, it is interesting to shortly sum up some of the implications for learning outcome ripe in the discussions in the previous chapters. The students clearly continuously discussed the relevance of using computer games in the history course. Thereby, they also indirectly struggled with what history entails, why one should learn about it and different approaches to history. They didn't seem to recognize the significance and relevance of these discussions, and the course didn't encourage them sufficiently to explore the different understandings of history. The implicit assumptions in the course (somewhat naïvely) were that the students were not inclined to favour one history understanding over another. Therefore it was assumed that they would embrace the possibility to explore history as dynamic and changeable. Clearly, this only happened to a limited degree and somewhat haphazardly.

In hindsight, the struggle over the history field may have been the most relevant and long-term discussion you can introduce students to. It seems that many students can go through the educational system attending history with vague ideas about the scope, relevance and importance of history. This was indirectly reflected when one student commented that she learned history in order to get good grades, so she could get into university. This commodification and alienation of the educational experience is hardly new, but take on new importance with an increased societal interest in sustaining learning throughout life. There is a belief that we on own initiative should seek out new knowledge, which becomes hard to sustain if the direction is only given from a commodity perspective. The lack of intrinsic motivation can make it hard for history to penetrate into everyday life and in the long run history will not be very helpful if not meaningful in terms of something else than getting a high enough grade for the next level in the educational system.

Another theme that challenges the narrow learning outcome focus is the cross curricular potential implicit in the computer game. The gains for the subjects' geography, English and media studies are completely left out of the equation even though the students specifically commented on these potentials. Leaving out these areas will put computer games at a disadvantage compared to more traditional teaching methods. Although one may of course argue that history in general also supports these subjects, the point remains that when left unexamined we have no way of knowing their importance.

Conclusion: Same learning outcome but different ways to it

The findings from the quantitative part of the empirical study indicate that the learning outcome of students do not differ in relation to whether computer games are used or not. However, it seems that retention is better when using computer games and students are more intrinsically motivated despite criticism of the actual historical content of the course. This extends well from the qualitative findings, where we saw dissatisfaction with the computer game's history approach, but more interested students. It also makes good sense looking back to previous studies, both on traditional games and computer games for educational use.

Still, one should be careful with drawing any firm conclusions. Perhaps the current measurement of the learning outcome from computer games is too imprecise as the tools for measuring learning outcome from computer games in educational settings are still theoretically weak. We risk not really measuring the effectiveness of computer games, but rather the short-comings of our existing understanding of using computer games. Still, we have to start somewhere.

Part 4: Combining empirical findings with existing theory

This is the final part of the thesis bringing together theoretical work and empirical findings, resulting in a theory on educational use of computer games grounded in experiential learning.

Chapter X: A Theory on Educational Use of Computer Games

Colors fade, temples crumble, empires fall, but wise words endure

Thorndike

We have so far covered a lot of ground getting a fuller understanding of the elements necessary to understand the educational use of computer games. The intention has been to build a framework challenging the current dominance of edutainment. This chapter fits together the pieces by presenting a theory for educational use of computer games extending from experiential learning. The theory expands from the problems recognized in the first part of the dissertation by drawing on the theoretical foundation in part two and using the data from the main empirical study in part three as examples to support the theory.

The theory presented in the chapter describes an ideal for educational experiences with computer games, which includes both the strengths of computer games and the necessary instruction given by the teacher to qualify the game experiences. The chapter starts by looking at the role engagement plays for the appreciation and exploration of relevant educational elements in a computer game. This engagement is driven by students' perceived relevance of the game activity, and builds students' investment in an activity.

Historical elements in a computer game can with some difficulty be linked to other scientific concepts through instruction. The teacher should be very explicit in this linking and steering of the educational experience. Especially being alert to the problems with computer games' representation as this is a pitfall for many students. Students are easily distracted by representation not being in accordance with facts they already know, and therefore dismiss the educational relevance of the entire game. This leads them to stop appreciating and exploring the historical elements in the game. Teachers have an important role as promoters of the appreciation of historical elements, the exploration of these elements, and the linking of the exploration to other educational relevance sources.

The chapter concludes by characterizing educational use of computer games as follows: The student is playing and constructing knowledge through interaction with the game universe. Slowly building on top of existing knowledge from previous experiences arising from inside the game universe and other spheres of life facilitated by instruction. It is an experience-based hermeneutic exploration in a safe rich environment, potentially scaffolding the student while maintaining student autonomy and ensuring a high emotional investment in the activity.

Engagement in educational experiences with computer games

I have stressed earlier that it is essential for education to engage the student, hereby ensuring investment in the topic under investigation - the topic becomes relevant to the student. Engagement in computer games certainly seems to be higher than the engagement in most traditional school subjects. In computer games engagement is closely tied with relevance, when students see something as relevant they will engage with it and invest in a given topic.

We saw in chapter 5 that computer games provide a number of advantages in terms of building engagement compared to other media forms, which was supported in the main empirical study. Although these properties are not by themselves exclusive to computer games, the combined manifestation is quite powerful. The ability of computers to combine different semantic areas is well exploited in computer games and combined with strong audiovisual experiences, the overall manifestation is very engaging. Most game universes are modelled through 3D technology, providing detailed and rich universes that the user can interact with, leading to strong concrete experiences. A game universe can freely be designed so it allows the player to slowly explore the different layers from their perspective, while not risking major real-life repercussions. Computer games' pursuit of an open-ended game universe is also a strong feature to engage players, letting them make a difference. Despite the constraints from rules offering explicit purposes to the player, the playing of computer games is more open-ended than most other media. Overall, computer games provide strong and rich game universes that are interesting to engage with.

I have argued that computer games provide an interesting game universe, but the actual engagement in an educational setting is still unaccounted for. However, it is well-documented that computer games are seen as motivating and interesting by many students, apparent by their continuous success as a spare time activity (ESA, 2003), most studies reviewed in chapter 4, and the motivational test in my empirical study. This doesn't mean that computer games will necessarily maintain the engagement in a school setting and it doesn't necessarily imply a stronger learning experience, although providing an important impetus. Computer games are built so they challenge the player and push the students to the limit (Adams & Rollings, 2003). This challenge is direct and requires the student to make the right choices within the computer game and although many current computer games may not set-up the most educational choices the potential is there. In the empirical study some students would start by waging huge wars, others would explore the world, some would convert heretics and others would settle in a quiet part of the world developing their country. This leads to a sense of perceived choice and a feeling of autonomy that strengthens engagement as students can focus on what they find relevant. Additionally, the playing of the game happens in a safe environment, where you can make mistakes without repercussions. You can see the consequences of your actions and change your actions by reloading the game. The group pressure is also considerably less with the computer as the only observer – many students are not comfortable testing their assumptions in a class room context, where other students are listening. All this makes the computer game relevant to students if they can get beyond the initial scepticism of using computer games. However, engaging with a computer game may be more or less relevant from an educational perspective, depending on the educational quality made up of the curriculum goals, support for learning desire and ability to points forward in an educational direction (see chapter 5).

Educational quality in use of computer games for educational purposes

A good computer game provides relevance and engagement, resulting in investment from *players*, but not necessarily from *students*. Although you may be engaged as a player in a school setting you may not necessarily be an engaged playing student as seen in the empirical study, and the quality of the educational experience may consequently be lacking. Computer games should have a universe that aims at educational relevant goals while pointing in an educationally desirable direction. The engagement from computer games will for most students result in a stronger learning desire if the educational links are provided. However, few game universes have explicit educational quality.

This was an important problem in the main empirical study, where appreciation of historical elements, and hence the exploration and linking, was clouded by students not engaging with the computer game beyond play. The best students were capable of connecting the two modes - playing and studying, whereas the least successful students didn't master this connection. The somewhat successful students were capable of extending from either a student perspective or player perspective without finding exactly the balance that ensured that the concrete game experience connects with a student's existing experience-base while pointing in an educational direction. Such a balance is necessary, regardless of the general features computer games offer for building relevance and engagement. A computer game-like *Europa Universalis II* may for one student link to previous successful experiences of enjoyment with computer games, take place in a medieval setting and support the student's autonomy, but this is useless if the concrete experiences in the game cuts the student off from appreciating history as such. Topics can't be understood in a vacuum and although the computer game provides a rich audiovisual base of concrete experiences these need to be transformed through some form of instruction. This instruction potentially results in the building of scientific concepts rather than spontaneous concepts.

The transformation of the game experiences relates to a major problem, in previous research as well as my main empirical study, dealing with the clash identified between play and learning. The game experience becomes too strong and closed around itself instead of linking with other scientific concepts. Left to their own devices, students will gain concrete experiences and form spontaneous concepts that will mostly be useful in a game setting. However, they won't connect the game experience with the broader idea of understanding history. The appreciation, exploration and linking of game experiences require that the instructor is capable of seeing the concrete game experiences as pointing to a broader scientific concept and continuously attempts to extend the experience beyond the game context. Students will increasingly begin to look for these connections, once they experience this as fruitful and appreciated line of inquiry. However, the appreciation, exploration and linking of concrete experiences from playing a computer game with scientific concepts runs into problems. The play context supports the engagement computer games offer and provide a safe haven for exploring new experiences and concepts. However, the linking is hampered by the strength of the game as a frame for playing. A play frame clouds students' interest in seeing beyond the play frame and ultimately challenges the educational agenda of transforming experiences. Students are only interested in performing well in the game as a play experience and if the teacher cannot justify the instruction in relation to gameplay it seems irrelevant. In this way the initial use of computer games as a way to increase the relevance of a given topic may backfire if not carefully managed. To avoid the play frame from backfiring we should make sure that the computer game is built so knowledge of scientific concepts will improve gameplay. When the potential links from other sources and playing the game are present the teacher should be very explicit about them and should also attempt to link them to broader discussions outside of school and computer game. Furthermore, teachers should stress that there exists a difference between education and play, although not necessarily between learning and play. Certainly we will learn while playing, but education is a more controlled learning situation that will steer play in certain directions and make demands on the game experience.

From the above follows that one should be careful in assuming that appreciation, exploration and linking is an inevitable consequence of playing computer games. Indeed, the quality of the educational experience in computer games is often assumed rather than studied. As the overview in chapter 4 attests to many researchers' approach on computer games as theoretically having educational quality, but most studies will on closer examination find many problems – the educational quality will often be questionable. The limitations of assumed educational quality were encountered when previously analysing the empirical results. In the main empirical study we saw this on the lowest level of merely appreciating history elements in the computer games, and even more in the lack of exploring history elements beyond their game context. Even when students appreciated the historical elements and explored these, the linking to relevant historical concepts was hard. This is critical for giving the playing of the game a higher educational quality. Remembering the difference between scientific concepts and spontaneous concepts we would expect informal playing of computer games to at best result in spontaneous concepts. We will usually not reflect, generalize and systematize the concrete experiences into scientific concept, although we might make some kind of unconscious ordering in spontaneous concepts. Therefore the process from appreciation over exploration to linking is critical for using computer games in educational settings. One should be careful not to confuse one's own conceptual understanding of citizenship, geography, history or any other subject with the common student understanding. Educators, researchers and parents may be able to appreciate that certain concepts are mirrored in a computer game, but this doesn't mean that they arise automatically from the concrete experiences in the computer game. Indeed, Vygotsky (1986) stresses that this will not be the case in traditional learning and there is no indication that this should be different in computer games. Bearing in mind that the precondition for scientific concepts is some kind of instruction, the transformation of concrete experiences may happen in game culture through peers, parents, forums or tools. A computer game can be questioned, analysed and discussed with links to more general concepts and relevant issues in society. However, we saw in the empirical study that the strong peer-culture around computer games does not necessarily transfer to educational settings. Therefore, instruction becomes critical.

Instruction: From implicit to explicit

I do, of course, not contest that we can facilitate educational experiences with computer games, but we often expect too much from the computer games and the student's active knowledge construction. The main empirical study did certainly not show a seamless educational use of computer games. Therefore, instruction should aim at making explicit what is implicit. In the quote below the ideology question in the computer games *Freedom Fighters* with educational relevance is latent and not manifest - making it hard for most average students to dig out the ideology question:

> Freedom Fighters allows players to live out the ideologies surrounding the U.S.-Iraq war in reverse: Is the difference between a freedom fighter and a terrorist simply that the person using the terms believes, in one case, the cause is right and not in the other? In these games, such thoughtful questions are not abstractions, they are part and parcel of the fun and interaction of playing.

(Gee, 2004b: unpaginated)

The example with *Freedom Fighters* is interesting, because it is quite a different genre than *Europa Univeralis* II and has been the topic of some debate in research circles. The players of the action game *Freedom Fighters* may appreciate elements of terrorism, engage in an exploration of terrorism, and link this to a wider context, but the problem with the above claim is that it lacks substantiation. True, a student *may* engage in such activities, but we have not really examined it. Contrary, I would argue, extending from Vygotsky and my main empirical study, that such reflections require certain student skills and preferably instruction of some kind that may or may not be a part of game culture surrounding *Freedom Fighters*. Some students will benefit more from instruction than others, depending on the difference between actual and potential zone of development. This was also clearly the case in the empirical study of *Europa Universalis II* and is supported by previous research into educational use of computer games (Grundy, 1991; Leutner, 1993; Wiebe & Martin, 1994).

Especially if reflections are to have an impact outside the game universe we need quite explicitly to identify these links and nurse the students in that direction. This is not to say that students do not learn anything from playing computer games. They will learn to play the computer game that can be quite complex, continuous repetition can also provide them with factual information and different spontaneous concepts may also arise, although probably only to a limited extend usable beyond the game universe. Certainly students will learn from computer games, but the question is what, how and whether it is different compared to other forms of learning as previously discussed in chapter 2. I am for example convinced that more gamers than non-gamers will be able to identify a German soldier's uniform from the Second World War and know the year of some of the great battles. These are constantly mentioned in the stereotype fictional worlds in the computer game market, where students will constantly see quite realistic uniforms.

When thinking about making the educational qualities explicit in computer games one needs to recognize that computer games differ from other media. Primarily, computer games are about engaging and doing concrete things – not much different from any other physical activity like soccer. When playing soccer we will naturally draw on a number of important principles in the world, for example probability, force, movement, anatomy and social relations. All these elements are part of playing soccer, but during play we will not really appreciate or explore these elements, and certainly rarely link them beyond the soccer field. However, over time we transform our concrete experience to somewhat ordered spontaneous concepts. Although we may gain spontaneous concepts related to soccer and layered into the soccer context the learning will be narrow, random and fragmented.

An instructor may, however, afterwards try to expand these concrete experiences by generalising and ordering the experiences – digging out the important elements that can be transferred to other matches and contexts of life. For example, the concept of weak midfield provides an understanding of what happened in a game. Weak midfield relates to a number of different concrete experiences that explains why you keep losing the ball, never get any attacks and the opponents seem to occupy your half of the playing field. It is highly unlikely that any of these concepts would emerge among all the players without joint reflection in the community and the active inquiry of the coach as an old-timer in the community. Certainly, the instructor can order and generalize the concrete experiences by referring to existing knowledge that can qualify the recent experiences players had. The concept of weak midfield is certainly a returning topic in books on soccer tactics. It is not obvious how concrete experiences in soccer can be useful in a school setting as the soccer universe is quite detached from most school subjects. However, even in soccer an instructor could use the concrete experiences as examples of probability and force in physics or the hierarchy in society. It is important from an instruction perspective to recognize that some elements in soccer as well as in a computer game will typically be easier to appreciate, explore and link with other concepts, which was also clear in *Europa Universalis II*. In the main empirical study students tended to focus on the pop-ups which did not prove very useful, but at the end of the course general underlying rules were appreciated, explored and linked, albeit by few students.

The formal characteristics of computer games have earlier been described as a set of rules with semantic content making up a game universe (see chapter 5). This implies that our actions in computer games are guided by rules and our interpretation of the fictional world; to perform actions we manipulate rules to achieve a certain outcome. The set of rules is typically layered into the fictional world. However, a large part of the fictional world is not really activated and integrated in the game experience, you don't engage with a fictional world's setting. The setting is for example background history, cut-scenes or the semantic content in the game universe in *Freedom Fighters* with Soviet enrolment posters in the background.

The playing of the game does not really require an awareness of a large part of the setting. When you are playing a computer game the primary action is the manipulation of rules – these are the ones you learn to master and constantly engage with to win the game. It is only on a superficial level required to appreciate the setting and the conflict it enacts. When the setting is important for the game experience it will gain more attention, and potentially be part of the concrete experience, available for building concepts. The problems with relying on the setting for learning have been demonstrated in earlier studies (i.e. Malone & Lepper, 1987b).

The overall conflict in *Freedom Fighters* may be terrorists versus freedom fighters, but arguable it doesn't really play a role beyond creating the right setting and a progression in the cut-scenes. The primary focus is on learning the rules of playing and when the setting is not required to achieve this goal it becomes secondary. Should the rules in *Freedom Fighters* relate to what make up terrorists or freedom fighters, and not merely getting the next opponent killed, the case is another. This would change the focus and facilitate potentially stronger educational experiences on this topic. Also, the houses in *Freedom Fighters* can either be important for hiding and tactics or merely a neutral background. As a neutral background most players won't really notice or appreciate the significance of houses, whereas they will be appreciated and explored potentially linked with other areas, if they are important for actually playing the game. You will certainly only to a limited degree engage in larger discussions of the terrorism question from playing *Freedom Fighters*, which also happens to be evident if we scan game forums. Even when discussions surface in relation to *Freedom Fighters* students will lack the ability to go beyond the game, as you only have few concrete experiences to work from, and students will only have limited experience-base which they can connect the experiences. You do not have the concepts and experience-base to understand and qualify the discussion that would be considered necessary for educational experiences to emerge. Gee (2004b) may in the earlier quote see the potential for educationally loaded discussions from computer games; however, he misses the point. Computer games can indeed provide strong and rich concrete experience, but we need a context, where these can be transformed into something more – we need the coach from the soccer field. It is worth stressing again that this coach may be a teacher, parent, peer or partly even the computer game, but for now I will stay with an instructor perspective. The instructor makes players listen, focus and engage with the experiences.

The elements you focus on, appreciating, exploring and linking, differs in computer games. As described the rules often take precedence, but in some games this is to a lesser degree the case. The exact balance between rules and semantic content in a computer game differs depending on genre. A progression game (e.g. *Grim Fandango*) will rely more on the semantic content, whereas an emergence game (e.g. *Age of Empires*) is focused on the rules. This makes a difference when we discuss the educational quality – what is it students engage with. A difference that becomes clearer if we turn to traditional textbooks, which are usually closer to progression games. When you read a textbook some content will, of course, also be more prominent in the experience, but the interaction with the text is the same and there is not such an exclusive focus on the rules for reading. It is seldom the grammatical rules that become interesting when reading a textbook. But in a computer game it is actually the underlying rules (the grammatical rules) for the semantic content that are dominating and drawing most of the player's attention – playing a book could be described as finding ways to beat others by knowing the rules, like students competing on who finished the textbook first. Such book competitions are actually quite common in the first school years, where the semantic content is of little interest, whereas the underlying rules are paramount. In such competitions on reading the focus is seldom on the actual content of the book, but rather the mastery of the underlying rules that makes you the winner.

The instruction in the perspective outlined above can be described as the ability to help the student see the differences that make a difference. This is, however, only possible by referring back to concrete experiences, which give the concepts their substance – making them generalizable and orderable. The appreciation, exploration and linking are tools the student can use for seeing the important differences. The important point is that the concrete experiences used to build the concepts should not be confined to the domain of computer games. In summary, the educational experiences with computer games face the same challenge as any experiential learning activity: The transformation of the concrete experience to go beyond the immediate context and linking the experience to a broader conceptual understanding by drawing on students' existing experience base and engagement. Computer games can provide rich, safe experimentation through examples from any semantic area, securing student engagement leading to investment in the topic. Next, we will look at the inherent problem of representation in computer games that challenges the very appreciation of concrete game experiences as relevant beyond the game universe.

Problem of representation in computer games

The relevance and hence ultimately the engagement, of computer games described above can be hampered by a clash of expectations. The expectations that clash relate to perception of school, a subject and computer games. This problem is evident in the main empirical study related to the topic history. Many students are considerably more interested in history outside of school than in school. So apparently history changes when we engage with it in school and students have very firm expectations of what makes up the subject history.

When bringing computer games into the school setting demons and angels tag on and both influence the game experience. In my empirical study we saw a strong opposition and fight on whether teaching with computer games was acceptable. Although students liked computer games they didn't appreciate their educational value and didn't find *Europa Universalis II* to live up to their perception of history. The relevance of the computer game in the educational context was hard to see for students. Expectations of school as providing serious (or boring) learning were hard to reconcile with computer games. Furthermore, the history understanding entertained by students differed from the computer games' approach. Despite this, students actually seemed more motivated, interested and engaged. The above restraints were warranted on their own, but they were aggravated by the plasticity of the representations in computer games, which relates to students' active approach to computer games. The basic representational and plastic quality of computers is both a strength and weakness in relation to educational use of computer games. In the most basic sense a game representation may *miss important aspects* of a topic or *misrepresent aspects*. Some of the substance will always be missing in a representation and the threat of missing parts is enough to challenge the validity of the very representation itself. Furthermore, this can ultimately lead to students learning wrong things if they are not capable of seeing when a representation is skewed. This is true for any representation whether it is a computer game, a Hollywood movie, an interactive story or a television show. The challenge with computer games, inherited from computers, is that representations become even more unstable and untrustworthy than in other media due to student engagement in the game.

When using computer games for educational use we have at least two problems related to the representation. First of all, game designers do not know the background of their fictional worlds very well. This was less of a problem in *Europa Universalis II* compared to other commercial game titles, as *Europa Universalis II* was designed around a strong awareness and interest in history in the development team (Malmberg, 2002). Even when game designers know a topic well, a representation will always be an interpretation of the world. This leads to fictional worlds that are potentially ripe with problematic assumptions and assertions that students may pick up. Second, some students will be capable of picking up some of the problematic representations, which will make them sceptic of the entire educational experience. Third, the very threat of failure to represent a topic will cause uncertainty among students – can we trust this game to tell us what happened, when we are the puppet masters?

This is exactly what happened in the main empirical study on *Europa Universalis II* presented earlier, where the insecurity related to the degree of accurate representation in the historical computer games led students to question the value of the entire educational experience. They distrusted the representation of history that the computer game presented. Interestingly, distrust did not really grow out of a problematic game universe that didn't really have any historical problems the students could recognize. Students did point to some historical inadequacies that were actually not historically wrong as such, but were still at odds with students' knowledge which was mostly drawn from current times. Students would for example object to Denmark conquering the small German state Holstein at some point in history, although this is in line with most historical accounts. Scepticism seemed to run deeper than what a few factual mistakes in the game could accomplish. The problems related to the very interaction with the fictional world. Students were actually capable of appreciating that obviously this wasn't history as they could change the outcome. However, based on their historical 'superpowers', (changing the course of history) they began to distrust the entire game universe. Interestingly, such a critique was not aimed at the traditional textbooks, which is of course also a representation. It was in the actual *playing* of the representation the problems arose and the students' lack of ability for abstraction.

It is interesting to consider the above problem of representation from a different angle and remember what students are actually doing with the computer game representations compared to other representations. In reality, the student is setting new marks with every action in the game universe – constantly making new representations - seeking differences that make a difference. When we consider most computer applications like spreadsheets, browsers or archive systems, they are all setting up different universes. They are telling you what the map is, but they are also defining areas within the maps that you can influence. In principle the computer can set up any options for the user, but this is not really interesting as most computer applications are really focusing on a special semantic regime – a spreadsheet for calculations, a word processor for writing, an internet browser for seeking information and *Europa Universalis II* for making strategic decisions in a historical universe. The computer is basically setting up a small universe for us to manipulate, and this is different from the representations in books, movies or radio shows, where in reality there is no freedom to change the map, so to speak. Importantly this is different from the traditional teaching in schools, where there is a canon. Although the authority of teaching is under pressure the textbook and teacher are rarely challenged on their own turf.

This is different when we look at the playing of computer games, where the challenge of the representation and authority is central. The experimentation and exploration of the differences in a computer game are very much in line with the experiential approach to learning presented earlier, where you are constantly engaged with the topic you are learning. Here the process is one of having a concrete experience with a topic, reflecting on the topic and setting up concepts about it and actively experimenting with the fit between the topic and your concepts. Such active experimentation is typically hard with a textbook, where you do not really have any handles for experimenting – with computer games it is quite different.

If we are to believe Finnemann (1999), the computer medium, as discussed in chapter 5, should be capable of giving a richer representation by drawing on a variety of semantic regimes, which *Europa Universalis II* also did (i.e. linguistically, formally, pictorially and auditorily). However, the representation and the potential manipulations may increase the insecurity among students when entering a new semantic regime. A history textbook will have maps that don't change, and the history will remain in a fixed sequence until the next time you read it. This is certainly not the case in the most basic way for computer games, where the informational alphabet requires sequences to work and the user is usually actively constructing the application's progress. The computer may run without user input, although this is usually not the case. Although most computer games rely on the presence of a user to move forward many games also have an on-going progression more or less independent of the user – in *SimCity* your city will develop when you are not doing anything and similarly in most real-time strategy games[38]. The player makes a difference in the universe, and the game universe tends to revolve around the player, but the game has a course set which it follows without the player's input. Indeed, one typical criticism aimed at computer games is that the game centres on the player. This was also apparent in this empirical study with *Europa Universalis* where the historical processes were increasingly influenced by the player's actions. Playing England would lead to an England-centric historical development. As the students played, they moved away from the historical starting point and Europe was transformed based on the player's action and randomly influenced decisions by the computer game's AI. The students were quite capable of appreciating and seeing this as a problematic representation and knew not to see it as actual historical events – after all, other students could observe how other students in the class had different outcomes. So the problem didn't really lie in actual faulty learning, but rather in a lack of trust in the representations – in the very form of learning, which requires more active reflection, experimentation and thinking on the part of the students.

The unstable game universe requires quite a lot of work from the player/student. Students need to understand how representations are not necessarily the most important aspect of the computer game, but rather the underlying rules. These rules will let you explore how the representations you see before you are created – to get under the hood and explore the difference that make a difference – not simply by appreciating these, but challenging them in a constantly changing process. When students and teachers fail to appreciate the superficiality of the game representation in *Europa Universalis II* they run the risk of devaluating the entire educational game experience because you make the mistake that the representation is the truth. This happened when students playing Denmark in *Europa Universalis II* conquered Sweden and then rejected the game representation because they knew this wasn't historically correct. This does not entail that the concrete representations generated by the students' interaction with the computer are fruitless.

---

[38] This characteristic is included in a recent attempt to build a taxonomy for computer games (Aarseth, Sunnanå, & Smedstad, 2003).

However, it implies that these concrete representations are mostly important in the sense that they allow exploration of the underlying rules and are tools for referring to what you perceive as important differences. In *Europa Universalis II*, Denmark's victory over Sweden is not interesting as such, but the underlying rules that led to the victory are - your assessment and decisions that led to the results are. Still such a victory will reinforce a number of assumptions and assertions about Denmark and Sweden held by the student.

The student is required to have quite a high level of abstraction which is supported by the high achievers becoming the only ones in the empirical study occupying the high grounds of abstract thinking in relation to the computer game. The focus on the underlying dynamics of the representation is equivalent with the underlying forces that result in historical events, the subtraction rules that lead to a result or the grammar rules used to construct a sentence. You can say that in computer games the focus is on what makes $2 + 2 = 4$ rather that the result 4. One may also benefit from the actual representations in a computer game, but it will always be with the risk of students not really accepting these representations as they themselves can change them – students will rightfully question whether representations can tell them anything about history, geography, math or citizenship if the representations depend on their choices and randomly change. To really benefit from the concrete representations in themselves requires an initial understanding to validate the representations. Students may for example reinforce their understanding of Napoleon as a French general when playing France in the 18th century and their knowledge about the long history of hostilities with England.

The plasticity of representation in computer games doesn't completely reduce the educational relevance of the actual representations in a computer game, but it tends to require some prior knowledge of the topic the game relates to. This is interesting as many game designers explicitly avoid building games that require previous knowledge (Brake, 2002) and I think we may need to reconsider this if we are to build computer games that are successful in educational use. The question of game design also becomes relevant if we consider the most obvious way of representation to influence learning. We should remember that all the representations in a textbook, teacher talks, movies and computer games are based on the creators' interpretations of what differences make a difference – some things will be stressed over others – for example the Second World War, Pythagorean geometry, Darwin's evolutionary theory, the rise of Christianity, or the invention of the printing press. A computer game is capable of introducing certain representations and grant supremacy over others, which provides a way for students to appreciate the borders of a topic. Hardly any computer applications will grant the player complete freedom and the game universe's restrictions point to important information. In a word processor and browser, you work within confined limits, although you are able to run macros in word processor and produce plug-ins for the browser, these are not accessible to the ordinary user. Computer games similarly set limits for the player's actions based on the game designer's notions of what differences should make a difference – the designer may not have a very complete picture of the important elements of the Second World War and hence the representations and actual rules you can change as a user will be quite restricted. This is, however, also the attraction of the computer games – the confinements produce the challenge – levelling out the confinements equals cheating. The question is what confinements you set-up and whether these can point in an educationally relevant direction. To bridge the divide between an immediate game universe and an extension for introducing a deeper understanding we need to understand the role instruction plays.

A theory on educational use of computer games

The elements discussed above can be linked together to describe the most important elements in using computer games for educational purposes. The model below describes the final theory on educational use of computer games. It consists of an outer and an inner wheel. The outer wheel describes how Kolb's learning cycle can be expanded to more specifically address computer games, while the inner wheel is the basic learning process students go through in any experiential learning activity (Figure 20).

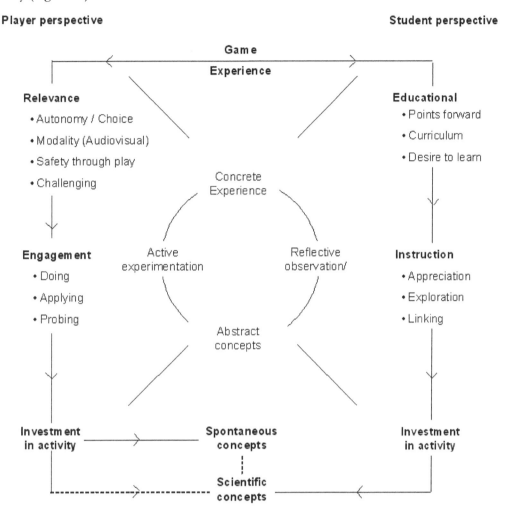

Figure 20: It shows how we can perceive the learning process for educational use of computer games extending from the concrete game experience.

The left part of the model describes the process from a player perspective. The student perspective is the right part of the model, which looks at how the game experiences are transformed beyond the game context. The starting point is the game experience, which the student has to see as relevant to engage with to build an investment in the universe leading to spontaneous concepts. Initially, the student has to see computer games as relevant to make way for an investment in the topic leading to some concepts representing the concrete experience. However, the formal learning (education) is necessary to take the computer game beyond the informal learning (playing), making the concrete experiences relevant in a broader context through the development of scientific concepts through appreciation and exploration of game experiences while linking these with other concepts. For this to work, the game experience has to point in an educational direction, implying that the game experience opens up for scientific concepts through instruction.

The relevance relating to computer games is increased by the autonomy, choice, audiovisuals, safe environment, playful approach and challenges that are part of game experiences. The perceived educational relevance is hampered by students' perception of school, games and the representation problem. It is, therefore, important that instruction early points to the educational relevance. The perceived relevance leads students to engage in computer games, which we have continuously seen throughout the dissertation. Relating the student side of the model with Kolb's learning cycle shows that computer games are especially helpful for providing the active experimentation that requires active engagement and investment of the students. In traditional teaching students can seem engaged without being so, when listening to the teacher. However, this is much harder with computer games where the game requires the student to interact to continue playing. However, as an activity computer games often provide little in terms of reflection and observation in a classical sense, which are critical for the educational quality from an experiential learning perspective. Most players will be quite engrossed in the game experience and not retract from the experience and reflect on it. This can happen in some computer games, but most reflection will then be closely linked to the game universe. For reflection and observation to work we need to introduce some form of instruction, which in schools is obviously guided by the teacher (the student perspective in the model). Instruction needs to point forward, include curriculum and a general desire to learn. Computer games are not making the instruction easier, on the contrary. The concrete game experience will be different for each student and the teacher cannot be entirely aware of the different student experiences. It, is therefore, hard to expand from the concrete experience. On the other hand, the rich amount of concrete experiences provide students with different starting points more relevant for them, which can spark discussions between students, and that can be used for sparking exploration and linking through instruction. The variety in concrete experiences also gives the teacher a chance to differentiate the teaching by drawing on different game experience to illustrate important concepts for different students. This requires that the teacher is well-versed in computer games, especially the one being used, otherwise important game experiences aren't recognized and used in the teaching. This will result in the game experience staying restricted to the game universe and no construction of scientific concepts that can generalize the concrete experiences.

Overall, my theory extends from an experiential learning approach, where the interaction with the game universe results in concrete experiences, which can be transformed through appreciation, exploration and linking. Computer games provide rich concrete experience that can be manipulated in the game universe providing more handles for the student opening up for an hermeneutic exploration from the students perspective. Students' experiences are maintained within a safe environment that is relevant and connects to each student's experience-base that is slowly built up by playing the game. Computer games are not a magic pill that can be used to automatically solve the hard problems in teaching and education. Computer games provide a rich experience base, strong relevance and richness letting students engage from their own perspective, but computer games also result in new problems for the quality of the educational experiences especially centring on the representational plasticity of computer games, the stereotype game universes and the strength of the play frame that has to be balanced with the educational agenda. The fruits of computer games can only be enjoyed if the teacher learns how to harvest the fruits.

Chapter XI: Final Thoughts

> As an educational scholar, I ascribe to the basic constructivist tenets. As an instructional designer, I despair that sometimes a more behaviorist approach seems so much easier to sell.
>
> Thomas Fox McManus (2004)

Educational use of computer games... One may ask is it worth it? Probably not in the short run, but in the long run I believe that computer games have something else to offer than other teaching styles: Namely, a dynamic and rich presentation of a given subject that the student has a chance to engage and challenge through interaction hereby building a strong investment in the subject. This investment must be guided by instruction from teachers, parents or peers to ensure the educational quality.

Often the underlying assumption is that computer games have a unique potential for revolutionizing education. Such an approach will paint the research area into a corner as has consistently happened with new media introduced over the last centuries. Although, computer games have some special qualities they are more than anything else an extension of other human practices. As a tool they are formed by culture and history and although they can inform human action with new potential these actions still remain guided by a cultural and historical grounding. However, we are constantly in a position to shape this tool by introducing it in new contexts and by developing the use of such a tool. We should learn from the history of educational computer games, but not be confined by it.

Throughout the dissertation I have gone through quite elaborate descriptions of the conditions surrounding educational use of computer games both in terms of practical problems such as the limited availability of relevant titles, the limitations of technical equipment and the few experiences with actually using computer games for educational purposes – we should pay attention to all of these areas. The structural conditions for actually using computer games in schools have been examined extensively in this dissertation and I have no intention of repeating my points. However, the structural conditions are crucial to keep in mind in order to avoid the fantasy that educational use of computer games solely relies on the maturation of the game medium and more research into the area. However, the problems did not stand alone, but were addressed through an empirical study and an overall theory on educational use of computer games.

The following are the most important findings from this dissertation:

- *Cultural position*: Computer games have a lot of baggage when they enter school, resulting in a both positive and negative influence on the educational use. Culturally, computer games are still often seen as entertaining, immature, boyish activities with violent and stereotype content, which leads to opposition from both teachers and students.

- *Market conditions*: The market for producing material, support and titles for using computer games in schools is practically non-existent. Publishers have failed to innovate, trapped in time somewhere in the 1980's.

- *School structure*: The evolution of the school hardly favours the use of computer games with classroom structure, short lessons, few cross-disciplinary courses, curriculum design, teaching practice, sparse computer equipment and no budget for software acquisitions.

- *Practical experiences*: We only have few experiences with using computer games for educational purposes and the barriers are substantial for most teachers on the classroom level. We need more actual experiences to see what happens when computer games are brought into the educational setting accompanied by sound didactic considerations.

- *Experiential learning with computer games*: Computer games provide concrete experiences building a strong sense of relevance and strong engagement leading students to invest in the learning activity. Instruction extends from the concrete experiences with computer games and the student's investment – instruction providing the necessary direction, order and reflection refining the experiences beyond the immediate student construction.

In conclusion, the structural limitations for educational use of computer games are still considerable on several levels. This should not discourage us from trying to further a deeper understanding of what it means to use computer games for educational purposes. It is important to remember that the educational system has always been 'blessed' with more critics than followers. However, among the few reformers is a recurring fantasy that new media will transform the educational system, providing an overall better educational experience for students. One recurring aspect is the individualization of the learning experience through different media and more dedicated time to each student. The idea of media empowerment has certainly not become less pronounced among educators with learning theories hailing different styles of learning.

In some sense, computer games along with the use of other popular culture expressions in schools are the final genuflection for this individualization and as such potentially an admission of failure for a wider socialization. The cultural expressions preferred by new media become the material that the older generations feed the younger generation, less interested in a richer socialization capable of building a bridge across generations. A wider discussion of these social implications is beyond this dissertation. I merely wish to address how computer games fit well within the current trend, where we are paying more attention to what is interesting, motivating and appropriate for the single individual rather than, what we as a society wish to convey to the next generation. It is, therefore, not surprising that the immediate attraction of using computer games lies more on the part of the student than on the part of the teacher. This is also an important element in the weak penetration of computer games in schools – it is basically more to the advantage of students than teachers. Hopefully, a genuflection for new generations will not be the sole reason for choosing to use computer games in the future.

Brief vocabulary and Game bibliography

Brief vocabulary

Action: This genre focuses on speed, physical drama with high demands on the player's reflexes and coordination skills.

Adventure: This genre focuses on puzzle solving within a narrative framework relying on the player's ability to think logical.

Commercial games: An overall term for computer games that are sold through traditional channels.

Drill-and-practice software: Software that primarily relies on training a number of very specific skills by letting the user repeat the activity endlessly.

Educational computer games: Computer games developed for educational use or titles often finding their way to educational settings both the fake, bad, ambitious and superb.

Educational games: Refers to traditional non-electronic game-like activities developed for educational use spanning board games, simulations, role-plays etc.

Educational software: The concept refers to all computer programs with an educational aim. Educational software is, therefore, a broader group than educational computer games and the applications are quite different in that they do not necessarily have game elements. When they have game elements, it is seldom an integrated part of the experience, but rather small separate activities. Educational computer games are often included under the heading educational software.

Edutainment: Edutainment is a sub-group of educational computer games that are heavily criticized. Typically edutainment titles are characterized by using quite conventional learning theories, providing a questionable game experience, simple gameplay and mostly produced with reference to a curriculum or some quite general overall skills like problem-solving.

Extrinsic motivation: Motivation that arises due to factors not directly related to an activity.

ICT: Is an abbreviation for Information and Communication Technologies.

Instructional films: Films produced for teaching a specific subject or topic in an educational setting.

Instructional technology: Instructional technology is an approach dedicated to the solving of instructional problems related to use of technology. In this dissertation it primarily refers to the application of strategies and techniques from behavioral and cognitive.

Intrinsic motivation: Motivation that arises as a natural part of a given activity.

Logo: A programming language designed by Seymour Papert to teach children math and science in line with the educational theory constructionism.

Narrative: A narrative is the organization of elements in a meaningful order that include the following elements: 1). A narrative has a world with characters and objects. 2). The world must change either as a consequences of user actions or events. 3). It must be possible for the user to 'speculate' around the events hereby creating a plot.

RTS: An abbreviation of real-time strategy games that refer to a combination of action a strategy typically involving resource management and the waging of war.

Serious Games: The concept serious games is used to describe the overarching perspective of games for something else than just entertainment. The term is coined by American Clark Abt back in 1968, and is the title of his influential book (Abt, 1968). Abt's book is an important hallmark for alternative uses of traditional games for educational purposes, and in this sense also leads the way for the later use of computer games for educational purposes. However, the modern use includes more than just educational use of games including advertainment, edutainment, political games, and news games.

Simulation: Games where realism is first priority. The player's ability to understand and remember complex principles and relations is paramount.

Strategy: Genre where the ability to make deal with dynamic priorities is key.

Game Bibliography

Developer, *Title*, Year. Publisher (platform)

Aegis International, *Ports of Call*, 1987. Aegis International (Amiga)

Amusement Vision, *Super Monkey Ball*, 2001. Sega (GameCube)

APh Tech. Consulting, *Electric Company Math Fun*, 1979. Mattel Electronics (Intellivision)

APh Technological Consulting, *Word fun*, 1980. Mattel Electronics (Intellivision)

Ascaron , *Patrician II*, 2000. Infogrames (Pc)

Atari, *Basic Math*, 1977. Atari (Atari 2600)

Big Huge Games, *Rise of Nations*, 2003. Microsoft Game Studios (Pc)

Black Pencil Ent., *Aids Prevention - Catch the Sperm*, 2004. Stop Aids (Pc)

Britannica, *Designasaurus 2*, 1990. Britannica (1990)

Brøderbund, Where in the World is Carmen San Diego, 1985. Brøderbund (Pc)

Chris Crawford, *Balance of Power*, 1985. Mindscape (Pc)

Chris Crawford, *Balance of the Planet*, 1990. Chris Crawford (Pc)

Chris Sawyer Productions, *Roller Coaster Tycoon*, 1999. Hasbro Interactive (Pc)

Click & Health, *Packy & Marlone*, 1997. Click & Health (SNES)

Click and Health, *Bronkie the Bronchiasaurus*, Click and Health, 1995 (SNES)

Cornerstone Industry, *Guard Force*, 2002. Army National Guard (Pc)

Cornerstone Industry. *Joint Force Employment*, 2000. Office of the Joint Chiefs (Pc)

Creative Wonders, *Sesame Street Toddlers Deluxe*,1997. The Learning Company

Davidson & Associates, *Math Blaster*, 1986. Davidson & Associates (Pc)

Deadline Game, *Blackout*, 1995. Deadline (Pc)

Deadline Games, *Globetrotter 2*, 2001. Vision Park (Pc)

DMA Design, *Lemmings*, 1991. Psygnosis (Pc)

Dynamix ,*The Incredible Machine*, 1993. Sierra (Pc)

Edmark, *Millie's Math House*, 1995. Riverdeep (Pc)

E-Gems, *Phoenix Quest*, 1994. E-Gems (Pc)

E-Gems, *Super Tangrams*, 1994. E-Gems (Pc)

Eisenstein, *Global Island*, 2002. Mellemfolkeligt Samvirke (Pc)

Electronic Arts, *Scooter's Magic Castle*, 1994. Electronic Arts (Pc)

Enlight Software, *Capitalism II*. 2001. Ubisoft Entertainment (Pc)

Enlight Software, *Virtual U*, 2003. Woodrow Wilson Foundation (Pc)

Ensemble Studios, *Age of Empires*, 1997.Microsoft Game Studios (Pc)

Ensemble Studios, *Age of Kings* 1999. Microsoft Game Studios (Pc)

Ensemble Studios, *Age of Mythology*, 2002. Microsoft Game Studios (Pc)

FDB, *Miljøstrup*, 1994. FDB (Pc)

FireFly Studios, *Stronghold*, 2002. Gathering of Developers (Pc)

Freeware, *Lemonade Stand*, 2001. Freeware (Pc)

Health Media Lab, *Hungry Red Planet*, 2002. Health Media Lab, Inc. (Pc)

Humongous Ent., *Freddi Fish 5: Creature of Coral*, 2001. Humongous Ent. (Pc)

Humongous Ent., *Pajama Sam*, 1996. Humongous Ent. (Pc)

Humongous Ent., *Putt Putt Saves the Zoo*, 1995. Humongous Ent. (Pc)

Id Software, *Doom*, 1993. id Software (Pc)

Ignited Minds, *America's Army*, 2002. U.S. Army (Pc)

Impressions, *Caesar*, 1993. Impressions (Pc)

Institute for Future Studies, *Brainbuilders*, 2002. Institute for Future Studies (Role-play)

IO Interactive, *Freedom Fighters*, 2003. Electronic Arts (Pc)

Kræfens Bekæmpelse, *Cell Fight*, 1997. Kræfens Bekæmpelse (Pc)

Kræftens Bekæmpelse, *Foodman*, 1994. Kræftens Bekæmpelse (Pc)

LCSI, *My Make Believe Castle*, 1996. LCSI (Pc)

Learning Company, *Rocky Boots*, 1982, Learning Company (Apple II)

Learning Company, *The Robot Odyssey*, Learning Company, 1984 (Apple II)

Learning Lab Denmark, *Tracks*, Forlag Malling Beck, 2004 (Role-play)

Lucas Learning, *DroidWorks*, 1998. Lucas Learning (Pc)

Maxis Software, *SimCity 2000*, 1993. Maxis Software (Pc)

Maxis Software, *SimCity 4*, 2003. Electronic Arts (Pc)

Maxis Software, *SimCity*, 1989. Infogrames (Amiga)

Maxis Software, *SimEarth*, 1990. SimEarth (Pc)

Maxis Software, *SimFarm*, 1993. Mindscape (Pc)

Maxis Software, *The Sims*, 2000. Electronic Arts (Pc)

MECC, *Oregon Trail*, 1985. MECC (Apple II)

MECC, *Super Munchers*, 1991, MECC (Pc)

MicroProse Software, *Civilization*, 1992. MicroProce Software (Pc)

MicroProse Software, *Railroad Tycoon*, 1990. MicroProse Software (Pc)

Nintendo, *Super Mario Brothers*, 1985, Nintendo (NES)

Nova Logic, *Delta Force 2*, 1999. Nova Logic (Pc)

Ozark Softscape, *Mule*, 1983. Electronic Arts (Pc)

Ozark Softscape, *Seven Cities of Gold*, 1984. Electronic Arts (Apple II)

Pandemic, *Full Spectrum Warrior*, U.S. Army, 2004

Paradox Entertainment, *Crusader King*, 2004. Pan Vision (Pc)

Paradox Entertainment, *Europa Universalis II*, 2001. Strategy First (Pc)

Paradox Entertainment, *Hearts of Iron*, 2002. Pan Vision (Pc)

Paradox Entertainment, *Victoria: an Empire under the Sun Game*, 2003. PAN Vision (Pc)

Pyro Studios, *Praetorians*, 2003. Eidos Interactive (Pc)

Quicksilver, *Full Spectrum Command*, THQ, 2004

Rand, *Monopologs*, 1956, U.S. Army (Mainframe)

ReLINE Software, *Oil Imperium*, 1989. Reline Software (Amiga)

Rockstar Games, *Grand Theft Auto 3*, 2002. Take-Two Interactive Software (Pc)

Sculptured Software, *Patton Versus Rommel*, 1987, Electronic Arts (Pc)

Sierra, *Castle of Dr. Brain*, 1991. Sierra (Pc)

Sierra, *Gabriel Knight*, 1993. Sierra (Pc)

Sierra, Leisure Suit Larry 1: In the Land of the Lounge Lizards, 1991. Sierra Online (Pc)

Sierra, *Mickey's Space Adventure*, 1984. Walt Disney Computer Software (Pc)

Sierra, Winnie the Pooh in Hundred Acres Wood, 1985. Sierra (Pc)

Sierra. *Troll's Tale*, 1984. Sierra (C64)

Smilebit, *The Typing of the Dead*, 2000. Sega (Dreamcast)

Spellbound Software, *Airline Tycoon*, 1998. Infogrames (Pc)

Sports Interactive, *Championship Manager*, 1992. Domark (Pc)

Strategic Simulations, *Panzer General*, 1996. Mindscape.

Taito, *Space Invaders*, 1978. Taito (Arcade)

TATI Mixedia, *Backpacker*, 1995. BMG Interactive (Pc)

The Creative Assembly, *Medieval: Total War*, 2002. Activision Publishing (Pc)

The Learning Company, *Dr Seuss Preschool*, 1998. Brøderbund

The Learning Company, *Logical Journey of the Zoombinis*, 1996. Brøderbund (Pc)

The Learning Company, *Math Missions Grades 3-5*, 2003. Scholastic (Pc)

The Software Toolworks, *Life & Death*, 1988. The Software Toolworks (Pc)

The Software Toolworks. *Mavis Beacon*, 1994. The Software Toolworks (Pc)

Thinking Tools, *SimHealth*, 1994. Maxis Software (Pc)

Tom Snyder Productions, *In Search of the Most Amazing Thing*, 1983. Spinnaker (Pc)

Tom Snyder Productions, *Snooper Troops*, 1982. Spinnaker (Apple II)

Tool Factory, *Chefren's Pyramid*, 2001. Alega Skolmateriel (Pc)

Transfiction Systems, *Hidden Agenda*, 1988. Transfiction Systems (Pc)

U.S. Army, *Marine Doom*, 1998. U.S. Army (Pc)

Unknown, *Traffic Jam*, 2002. Unknown (Pc)

US Air Force, *Top Management Decision Simulation*, 1957. US Air Force (N/a)

Valve, *Counter-Strike*, 2001. Sierra Online (Pc)

Westwood Studios *Red Alert*, 1996. Virgin Interactive Entertainment (Pc)

Literature

Abt, C. (1968). Games for Learning. In S. S. Boocock & E. O. Schild (Eds.), Simulation Games in Learning. London: Sage Publications.

Adams, E., & Rollings, A. (2003). Andrew Rollings and Ernest Adams on Game Design. Indianapolis: New Riders.

Adams, P., C. (1998). Teaching and Learning with SimCity 2000. Journal of Geography, 97(2), 47-55.

Aldrich, C. (2003). Simulations and the future of learning: Pfeiffer.

Andersen, P. Ø., & Kampmann, J. (1996). Børns legekultur. København: Munksgaard.

Asplund, J. (1997). Det sociala livets elementära former. Göteborg: Korpen.

Avendon, E. M., & Sutton-Smith, B. (1971). The Study of Games. New York: John Wiley & Sons, Inc.

Bateson, G. (1972). Steps to an Ecology of Mind. Chicago: University of Chicago Press.

Beavis, C. (1997). Computer Games, Culture and Curriculum. In I. Snyder & M. Joyce (Eds.), Page to Screen: Taking Literacy into the Electronic Era. New York: Routledge.

Beavis, C. (1999a). Literacy, English and Computer Games. Paper presented at the The Power Of Language, International Federation for the Teaching of English Seventh Conference, University of Warwick, UK,.

Beavis, C. (1999b). Magic or Mayhem? New Texts and New Literacies in Technological Times. Paper presented at the Annual conference, Australian Association for Research in Education and New Zealand Association for Research in Education, Melbourne.

Becker, K. (2001). Teaching with Games - The Minesweeper and Asteroids Experience. The Journal of Computing in Small Colleges, 17(2), 22-32.

Becta. (2001). Computer Games in Education Project. Retrieved 19. January, 2005, from http://www.becta.org.uk/research/research.cfm?section=1&id=519

Bergman, P. (2003). Digital games and learning: A research overview.Unpublished manuscript.

Betz, J. A. (1995). Computer Games: Increase Learning in an Interactive Multidisciplinary Environment. Journal of Educational Technology Systems, 24(2), 195-205.

BioWare. (2004). Sponsor_Nvidia. Retrieved 01. December, 2004, from http://www.bioware.com/2million/sponsors/sponsor_nvidia.html

Bloom, B. S., Engelhart, M. D., Furst, E. J., Hill, W. H., & Krathwohl, D. R. (1956). Taxonomy of educational objectives: The Classification of educational goals: Handbook I: Cognitive Domain. New York: David McKay Company.

Blossom, J., & Michaud, C. (1999). Postmortem: Lucas Learning's Star Wars DroidWorks. Gamasutra.

Boocock, S. S., & Schild, E. O. (1968). Simulation Games in Learning. London: Sage Publications.

Bowman, R. F. (1982). A Pac-Man theory of motivation. Tactical implications for classroom instruction. Educational Technology, 22(9), 14-17.

Brake, D. (2002). Interview - Sid Meier. Retrieved 12th November, 2004, from http://www.mindjack.com/interviews/sidmeier.html

Bransford, J. D., Brown, A. L., & Cocking, R. R. (1999). How People Learn: Brain, Mind, Experience, and School. Washington, DC: National Academy Press.

Bredemeier, M. E., & Greenblat, C. S. (1981). The educational effectiveness of simulation games: A synthesis of findings. Simulation & Games, 12(3), 307-331.

Broderbund. (2003). Retrieved 20th Jan. 2004, from http://www.broderbund.com/Product.asp?OID=4145761

Brody, H. (1993). Video Games that Teach? Technology Review, 96(8), 51-57.

Brown, S. J., Lieberman, D A, Gemeny, B A, Fan, Y C, Wilson, D M and Pasta, D J. (1997). Educational video game for juvenile diabetes: Results of a controlled trial. Medical Informatics, 22(1), 77-89.

Bruner, J. (1991). Acts of Meaning. Cambridge: Harvard University Press.

Bruner, J. (1996). Culture of Education. Cambridge: Harvard University Press.

Bruner, J., Jolly, A., & Sylva, K. (1976). Play: It's role in development and education. New York: Penguin Books.

Buckingham, D. (2003). Media Education: Literacy, learning, and contemporary culture. Cambridge: Polity Press.

Buckingham, D., Carr, D., Burn, A., & Schott, G. (Forthcoming). Videogames: text, narrative, play. Cambridge: Polity.

Buckingham, D., & Scanlon, M. (2002). Education, edutainment, and learning in the home. Cambridge: Open University Press.

Butler, R. J., Markulis, P. M., & Strang, D. R. (1988). Where are we? An Analysis of the Methods and Focus of the Research on Simulation Gaming. Simulation & Games, 19(1), 3-26.

Butler, T. (1988). Games and simulations: Creative Education Alternatives. TechTrends.

Calvert, S. L. (1999). Children's journeys through the information age. Boston: McGraw-Hill.

Campbell, D. T., & Stanley, J. C. (1969). Experimental and quasi-experimental designs for research. Chicago: Houghton Mifflin Company.

Cassel, J., & Jenkins, H. (1998). From Barbie to Mortal Kombat – Gender and Computer Games. Cambridge: The MIT Press.

Cavallari, J., Hedberg, J., & Harper, B. (1992). Adventure games in education: A review. Australian Journal of Educational Technology, 8(2), 172-184.

Children's Software. (1998). Stanford Children's Software Stanford Conversation Transscripts. Retrieved 14. december, 2004, from http://www.childrenssoftware.com/stanfordtranscripts

Clegg, A. A. (1991). Games and simulations in social studies education. In J. P. Shaver (Ed.), Handbook of research on social studies teaching and learning. New York: Macmillan.

Coleman, J. (1970). The Role of Modern Technology in Relation to Simulations and Games for Learning.Unpublished manuscript.

Coleman, J. S. (1967). Learning Through Games. In J. Bruner, A. Jolly & K. Sylva (Eds.), Play: Its Role in Development and Evolution. New York: Penguin Books.

Coleman, J. S., et al. (1973). The Hopkins' Games Program: Conclusions from Seven Years of Research. Educational Researcher(2), 3-7.

Coolican, H. (1994). Research methods and statistics in psychology. London: Hodder & Stoughton.

Corbeil, P. (1999). Learning From the Children: Practical and Theoretical Reflections on Playing and Learning. Simulation and Gaming, 30(2), 163-180.

Cotton, K. (1991). Computer-Assisted Instruction.: Northwest Regional Educational Laboratory.

Crawford, C. (1982). The Art of Computer Game Design: McGraw-Hill.

Crawford, C. (2003). Chris Crawford on Game Design. Boston: New Riders.

Csikszentmihalyi, M. (1992). Flow: The Classic work on how to achieve happiness. New York: Harper Perennial.

Cuban, L. (2001). Oversold and Overused: Computers in the classroom. Cambridge, MA: Harvard University Press.

Curtis, P. (1992). Mudding: Social Phenomena in Text-Based Virtual Realities. Paper presented at the Proceedings of Directions and Implications of Advanced Computing, Berkeley, California.

Danielsen, O., Olesen, B. R., & Sørensen, B. H. (2002). From Computer Based Educational Games to Actions in Everyday Life. In O. Danielsen, J. Nielsen & B. H. Sørensen (Eds.), Learning and Narrativity in Digital Media (pp. 67-81). Aarhus: Samfundslitteratur.

de Freitas, S. (2005). Learning through Play. Using educational games and simulations to support post-16 learners. London: London Learning and Skills Research Centre.

DeMaria, R., & Wilson, J. L. (2002). High score! : the illustrated history of electronic games. New York: McGraw-Hill/Osborne.

Dempsey, J. V., Rasmussen, K., & Lucassen, B. (1996). The Instructional Gaming Literature: Implications and 99 Sources. University of South Alabama.

Dewey, J. (1910). How We Think. New York: Prometheus Books.

Dewey, J. (1938). Experience & Education. New York: Simon & Schuster.

Din, F. S., & Caleo, J. (2000). Playing Computer Games versus Better Learning.Unpublished manuscript.

Dorn, D. S. (1989). Simulation Games: One More Tool On the Pedagogical Shelf. Teaching Sociology., 17(1), 1-18.

Dorval, M., & Pepin, M. (1986). Effect of Playing a Video Game on a Measure of Spatial Visualization. Perceptual Motor Skills, 62(1), 159-162.

Dowey, J. A. (1987). Computer games for dental health education in primary schools. Health Education Journal, 46(3).

Drotner, K. (2001). Medier for fremtiden – børn, unge og det nye medielandskab. Copenhagen: Høst og Søn.

Druckman, D. (1995). The Educational Effectiveness. In D. Crookall & K. Arai (Eds.), Simulation and gaming across disciplines and cultures. London: Sage Publications.

Duke, R. E. (1995). Opening speech: Welcome and Challenge. In D. Crookall & K. Arai (Eds.), Simulation and gaming across disciplines and cultures. London: Sage Publications.

Duke, R. E., & Seidner, C. J. (1975). Learning with simulations and games. London: Sage Publications.

Döpping, J. (1995). A social theory of distribution of knowledge as translation. Nordiske udkast, 23(2), 17-33.

Educational Software Classics. (1999). The Oregon Trail. Retrieved 3. June, 2005, from http://ldt.stanford.edu/ldt1999/Students/kemery/esc/otCompanyFrame.htm

Egenfeldt-Nielsen, S. (2001). Digitale udfordringer. Informationsteknologi i en skole under forandring. København: Gyldendal Uddannelse.

Egenfeldt-Nielsen, S. (2003a). Bagom Computerspil - et undervisningsmateriale. Copenhagen: Game-Research.

Egenfeldt-Nielsen, S. (2003b, 24. september). Computerspil på skoleskemaet. Berlingske Tidende.

Egenfeldt-Nielsen, S. (2003c). Exploration in computer games - a new starting point. Paper presented at the Digra - Level up conference 2003, Utrecht University.

Egenfeldt-Nielsen, S. (2003d). Keep the Monkey rolling: Eye-hand Coordination in Super Monkey Ball. Paper presented at the Digra - Level up conference 2003, Utrecht University.

Egenfeldt-Nielsen, S. (2003e). Thoughts on learning in games and designing educational computer games. Game-research.

Egenfeldt-Nielsen, S. (2004). Designing educational computer game experiences.Unpublished manuscript, Graz.

Egenfeldt-Nielsen, S., & Smith, J. H. (2000). Den digitale leg - om børn og computerspil. Copenhagen: Hans Reitzels Forlag.

Egenfeldt-Nielsen, S., & Smith, J. H. (2002). Online Gaming Habits. Game-research.

Egenfeldt-Nielsen, S., & Smith, J. H. (2004). Playing with fire: How do computer games influence players? Göteborg: Nordicom.

Elder, C. (1973). Problems in the Structure and Use of Educational Simulation. Sociology of Education, 46(3), 335-354.

EMU. (2004). Drabssag Melved, from http://drabssag.emu.dk/

ESA, T. (2003). Essential Facts About the Computer and Video Game Industry: The Interactive Digital Software Association.

Fabricatore, C. (2000). Learning and Videogames: An Unexploited Synergy.Unpublished manuscript.

Facer, K. (2003). Computer Games and Learning. A NESTA Futurelab Discussion Document.

Facer, K., Furlong, J., Furlong, R., & Sutherland, R. (2003). 'Edutainment' software: a site for cultures in conflict. In R. Sutherland, G. Claxton & A. Pollard (Eds.), Learning and Teaching Where Worldviews meet. London: Trentham Books.

Fagen, R. (1995). Animal Play, Games of Angels, Biology, and Brian. In A. D. Pellegrini (Ed.), The future of play theory : a multidisciplinary inquiry into the contributions of Brian Sutton-Smith. Albany: State University of New York Press.

Faria, A. I. (1990). Business simulation games after thirty years: Current usage levels. In J. W. Gentry (Ed.), Guide to business gaming and experiential learning. (pp. 36-47). East Brunswick: Nichols/GP.

Federal Communications Commission. (2003). Television Technology - A Short History., from http://www.fcc.gov/omd/history/tv/

Ferguson, N. (1997). Virtual History. London: Picador.

Finnemann, N. O. (1999). Modernity Modernised - The Cultural impact of Computerisation. In P. A. Mayer (Ed.), Computer Media and Communication: A reader. Oxford: Oxford University Press.

Flanagan, R. (2003). Gould's Book of Fish. London: Atlantic Books.

Fridberg, T. (1999). 7-15-åriges fritidsaktiviteter – Kultur- og fritidsundersøgelsen 1998. Copenhagen: Socialforskningsinstituttet.

Funk, J., & Buchman, D. (1995). Video Game Controversies. Paediatric annals, 24(2), 91-94.

Gagnon, D. (1985). Videogames and spatial skills: An exploratory study. Educational Communications and Technology Journal, 33(4), 263-275.

Gander, S. (2002). Does Learning Occur through gaming. Electronic Journal of Instructional Science and Technology, 3(2).

Gardner, H. (1983). Frames of mind: the theory of multiple intelligences. New York: Basic Books.

Garson, D. (Unknown). PA 765: Quantitative Research in Public Administration. Retrieved 27th October, 2004, from http://www2.chass.ncsu.edu/garson/pa765/standard.htm

Gee, J. P. (2003). What Video games have to teach us about learning and literacy. New York: PalGrave-McMillan.

Gee, J. P. (2004a). Learning about Learning from a Video Game: Rise of Nations.Unpublished manuscript.

Gee, J. P. (2004b, 24. March). Learning by Design: Games as Learning Machines. Gamasutra.

Gee, J. P., Lieberman, D., Raybourn, E., & Rajeski, D. (2004). How Can Games Shape Future Behaviors. Retrieved 21. October, 2004, from http://www.watercoolergames.org/archives/000263.shtml#howcan

Gentry, J. W. (1990). What is Experiential learning. New Jersey: Nichols.

Gleitman, H. (1995). Psychology - Fourth Edition. New York: Norton.

Goldstein, R., & Pratt, D. (2001). Michael's Computer game: A Case of Open Modelling. Paper presented at the The Twenty Fifth AnnualConference of the International Group for the Psychology of Mathematics, Utrecht: The Netherlands.

Good, T. L., & Brophy, J. E. (1990). Educational Psychology: A Realistic Approach. Fourth Edition. New York: Longman.

Grabe, M., & Dosmann, M. (1998). The potential of adventure games for the development of reading and study skills. Journal of Computer-Based Instruction,, 15(2), 72-77.

Gredler, M. (1992). Designing and Evaluating Games and Simulations: A Process Approach. London: Kogan Page Ltd.

Green, C. S., & Bavelier, D. (2003). Action Video game modifies visual selective attention. Nature(423), 534-537.

Greenblat, C. (1981). Teaching with Simulation Games: A review of Claims and Evidence. In R. E. Duke & C. Greenblat (Eds.), Principles of Practice of Gaming-Simulation. London: Sage Publications.

Greenblat, C., & Duke, R. E. (1981). Gaming-Simulation: Rationale Applications. London: Sage Publications.

Greenfield, P. (1984). Mind and Media. Cambridge: Harvard University Press.

Greenfield, P. M., Brannon, C., & Lohr, D. (1996). Two-Dimensional Representations of Movement Through Three-Dimensional Space: The Role of Video Game experience. In P. M. Greenfield & R. R. Cocking (Eds.), Interacting With Video (pp. 169-185). New Jersey: Ablex Publishing.

Griffith, J. L., Voloschin, P., Gibb, G. D., & Bailey, J. R. (1983). Differences in eye-hand motor coordination of video-game users and non-users. Perceptual Motor Skills, 57, 155-158.

Gros, B. (2003). The impact of digital games in education. First Monday, 8(7).

Grundy, S. (1991). A Computer Adventure as a Worthwhile Educational Experience. Interchange, 22(4), 41-55.

Guba, E. G., & Lincoln, Y. S. (1989). Fourth Generation Evaluation. Newbury Park: California: Sage Publications.

Hancock, C., & Osterweil, S. (1996). Zoombinis and the Art of Mathematical Play. Hands On!, 19(1).

Healy, J. M. (1999). FAILURE TO CONNECT: How Computers Affect Our Children's Minds. New York: Touchstone.

Heaney, L. F. (1989). Computer Adventure Games: Value and Interest to Teachers and Pupils. The International Journal of Educational Management, 3(4).

Herring, R. (1984). Educational Computer games. Analog Computing.

Hostetter, O. (2003). Video Games - The Necessity of Incorporating Video Games as part of Constructivist Learning. Retrieved 12-04-2004, 2004, from http://www.game-research.com/art_games_contructivist.asp

Hoyle, R. H., Harris, M. J., & Judd, C. M. (1991). Research Methods in Social Relations: Hartcourt Brace.

Hoyles, C., Noss, R., & Adamson, R. (2002). Rethinking the Microworld Idea. Journal of Educational Computing Research,, 27(1-2), 29-53.

Huizinga, J. (1986). Homo Ludens: A Study of the Play-element in Culture. Boston: Beacon Press.

Hunter, W. (2000). The Dot Eaters - Video Game History 101. Retrieved 23th of November, 2003, from http://www.emuunlim.com/doteaters/

Højholt, C., & Witt, G. (1996). Skolelivets socialpsykologi. Copenhagen: Unge Pædagoger.

Jensen, J. F. (1999). 'Interactivity' - Tracking a New Concept in Media and Communication Studies. In P. A. Mayer (Ed.), Computer Media and Communication: A reader. Oxford: Oxford University Press.

Jessen, C. (1995). Computeren i børnehaven - Rapport fra et forsøgsprojekt. Tidsskrift for Børne- og Ungdomskultur(35).

Jessen, C. (1998). Interpretive communities: The reception of computer games by children and the young. Retrieved 9. august, 2004, from http://www.carsten-jessen.dk/intercom.html

Jessen, C. (2001). Børn, leg og computerspil. Odense: Odense Universitetsforlag.

Jewitt, C. (2003). Re-thinking Assessment: multimodality, literacy and computer-mediated learning. Assessment in Education, 10(83-102).

Jillian, J. D., Upitis, R., Koch, C., & Young, J. (1999). The Story of Phoenix Quest: how girls respond to a prototype language and mathematics computer game. Gender and education, 11(2), 207-223.

Johansson, M., & Küller, R. (2002). Traffic Jam: Psychological assessment of a gaming simulation. Simulation & Gaming, 33(1), 67-88.

Jolicoeur, K., & Berger, D. E. (1998a). Implementing Educational Software and Evaluating Its Academic Effectiveness: Part I. Educational Technology, 28(10).

Jolicoeur, K., & Berger, D. E. (1998b). Implementing Educational Software and Evaluating Its Academic Effectiveness: Part II. Educational Technology, 25(10).

Jonassen, D. (2001). Learning from, in, and with Multimedia: An ecological Psychology Perspective. In S. Dijkstra, D. Jonassen & D. Sembill (Eds.), Multimedia Learning: Results and Perspectives. Frankfurt am Main: Peter Lang.

Jones, M. G. (1998). Creating engagement in computer-based learning environments. Paper presented at the ITForum.

Judd, C. M., Smith, E. R., & Kidder, L. H. (1991). Research methods in social relations. Fort Worth: Philadelphia: Hartcourt Brace.

Juul, J. (2003). Half-Real - Video games between real rules and fictional worlds. Unpublished PhD dissertation, IT University of Copenhagen, Copenhagen.

Kafai, Y. (1995). Minds in play: Computer game design as a context for children's learning. Hillsdale, NJ: Lawrence Erlbaum Associates.

Kafai, Y. (1996). Software by Kids for Kids. Communications of The ACM, 39(4).

Kafai, Y. B. (2001). The Educational Potential of Electronic Games: From Games-To-Teach to Games-To-Learn. Paper presented at the Playing by the Rules, Cultural Policy Center, University of Chicago.

Kafai, Y. B., & Resnick, M. (1996). Constructionism in practice: Designing, thinking, and learning in a digital world. Mawhaw, New Jersey: Lawrence Erlbaum Associates.

Kambouri, M., GarethMellar, HarveyPavlou, Victoria Thomas, Siobhan. (2003). Draft 3: Interim Report. London: Institute of Education.

Kaplan, R. M., & Saccuzzo, D. P. (1997). Psychological testing : principles, applications, and issues. Pacific Grove, CA: Brooks/Cole Publication.

Kashibuchi, M., Akira. (2001). The educational effectiveness of a simulation/game in sex education. Simulation & Gaming, 32(3), 331-343.

Kay, A. (1999). Computer Software. In P. A. Mayer (Ed.), Computer Media and Communication: A reader. Oxford: Oxford University Press.

Kelly, G. (1963). A Theory of Personality - the Psychology of Personal Constructs. New York: Norton.

Kirkpatrick, G. (2003). The Arrival of Computer Game Studies

Kirriemuir, J., & McFarlane, A. (2002). The use of computer games in the classroom. Coventry: Becta.

Kirriemuir, J., & McFarlane, A. (2003). Literature Review in Games and learning: Nesta Future Lab.

Klawe, M. M. (1998). When Does The Use Of Computer Games And Other Interactive Multimedia Software Help Students Learn Mathematics?Unpublished manuscript.

Klawe, M. M., & Phillips, E. (1995). A classroom study: Electronic games engage children as researchers. Paper presented at the CSCL 1995, Bloomington, Indiana.

Kliman, M. (1999). Choosing Mathematical Game Software for Girls and Boys. Retrieved 25042004, 2004, from http://www.terc.edu/mathequity/gw/html/ChoosingSoftwarepaper.html

Kline, S., Dyer-Witheford, N., & Greig, d. P. (2003). Digital Play. The Interaction of Technology, Culture and Marketing. Montreal: McGill-Queen's University Press.

Ko, S. (1999). Primary School Children's Inferential Problem Solving in a Computer Game Context., University of London, London.

Ko, S. (2002). An empirical analysis of children's thinking and learning in a computer game context. Educational-Psychology., 22(2), 219-233.

Kolb, A. Y., & Kolb, D. A. (2003). Learning styles and learning spaces: enhancing experiential learning in higher education. Academy of Management Learning and Education.

Kolb, D. A. (1984). Experiential learning : experience as the source of learning and development. Englewood Cliffs, N.J: Prentice-Hall.

Konzack, L. (2003). Edutainment : leg og lær med computermediet. Aalborg: Aalborg Universitetsforlag.

Krathwohl, D. R., Bloom, B., S, & Masia, B., B. (1964). Taxonomy of educational objectives: The Classification of educational goals: Handbook II: Affective Domain. New York: David McKay Company.

Lauppert, T. (2004). Lemonade Stand. Retrieved 3. June, 2005

Lave, J., & Wenger, E. (1991). Situated learning: Legitimate peripheral participation. Cambridge: Cambridge University Press.

Leddo, J. (1996). An intelligent tutoring game to teach scientific reasoning. Journal of Instruction Delivery Systems, 10(4), 22–25.

Lee, J. L. (1994). Effectiveness of the Use of Simulations in a Social Studies Classroom: ERIC.

Leeson, B. (Unknown). Origins of the Kriegsspiel. Kriegsspiel News. Retrieved 2504, 2004, from http://myweb.tiscali.co.uk/kriegsspiel/kriegsspiel/origins.htm#

Leutner, D. (1993). Guided Discovery Learning with Computer-Based Simulation Games: Effects of Adaptive and Non-Adaptive Instructional Support. Learning and Instruction, 3(2), 113-132.

Levin, J. (1981). Estimation techniques for arithmetic: Everyday math and mathematics instruction. Educational Studies in Mathematics, 12, 421-434.

Leyland, B. (1996). How can computer games offer deep learning and still be fun? Paper presented at the Ascilite, Adelaide , Australia.

Lieberman, D. A. (2001). Management of Chronic Pediatric Diseases with Interactive Health Games: Theory and Research Findings. Journal of Ambulatory Care Management, 24(1), 26-38.

Linderoth, J. (2002, 19-22 August 2002). Making sense of computer games: Learning with new artefacts. Paper presented at the Toys, Games and Media, London.

Littleton, K., & Light, P. (1999). Learning with Computers: Analysing productive interaction. London: Routledge.

Ljungstrøm, C. (1984). Differentiering og kvalificering: To væsensdimensioner i skole og uddannelsesforholdene. Udkast, 12(2).

Lockyer, L., Wright, R., Curtis, S., Curtis, O., & Hodgson, A. (2003). Energy Balance: Design and formative evaluation of a health education multimedia game. Paper presented at the EDMEDIA.

Loftus, G., & Loftus, E. (1983). Mind at Play: The Psychology of Video Games. New York: Basic Books.

Lopez, C. S. (2002). Le@rning in a Digitised Society. In O. Danielsen, B. R. Olesen & B. H. Sørensen (Eds.), Learning and Narrativity in Digital Media. Aarhus: Samfundslitteratur.

Lowery, B., & Knirk, F. (1983). Micro-computer Video Games and Spatial Visual Acquisition. Journal of Educational Technology Systems, 11(2), 155-166.

Macedonia, M. (2003). Games Soldiers Play. Retrieved 9. august, 2004, from http://www.spectrum.ieee.org/WEBONLY/publicfeature/mar02/mili.html

Magnussen, R., & Misfeldt, M. (2004, 6-8. December). Player Transformation of Educational Multiplayer Games. Paper presented at the Other Players, Copenhagen.

Makedon, A. (1984). Playful gaming. Journal of Simulation and Games, 15(1), 25-64.

Malmberg, F. (2002). Personal correspondence with Paradox Entertainment regarding Europa Universalis Game development. In S. Egenfeldt-Nielsen (Ed.) (pp. E-mail correspondence with developer). Stockholm.

Malone, T. W. (1980). What makes things fun to learn? Heuristics for designing instructional computer games. Paper presented at the Symposium on Small Systems archive., Palo Alto, California, United States.

Malone, T. W., & Lepper, M. (1987a). Intrinsic Motivation and Instructional Effectiveness in Computer-based Education. In Snow & Farr (Eds.), Aptitude learning, and instruction. London: Lawrence Erlbaum Associates Publishers.

Malone, T. W., & Lepper, M. (1987b). Making learning fun: A Taxonomy of Intrinsic Motivation for Learning. In Snow & Farr (Eds.), Aptitude learning, and instruction. London: Lawrence Erlbaum Associates Publishers.

Mamer, K. (2002). Ozark Softscape: Creators of MULE. Retrieved 2001, 2004, from http://www.geocities.com/conspiracyprime/e2_ozark.htm

Markgren, P. (2004). Europa Universalis/IT-Gymnasiet Västerås. In S. Egenfeldt-Nielsen (Ed.) (pp. E-mail correspondence with teacher). Västerås.

Mayer, R. (2001). Multimedia Learning. New York: Cambridge University Press.

Mayer, R. E., & Moreno, R. (1999). A Cognitive Theory of Multimedia Learning: Implications for Design Principles. In F. T. Durso, R. S. Nickerson, R. W. Schvaneveldt, S. T. D. Dumais, S. Lindsay & M. T. H. Chi (Eds.), Handbook of Applied Cognition. New York: John Wiley & Sons.

McCarty, C. T. (2001). Playing with Computer Games: An Exploration of Computer Game Simulations and Learning. Unpublished Dissertation submitted in part fulfilment of the requirements of the MA (ICT in Education) Degree., University of London, London.

McFarlane, A., Sparrowhawk, A., & Heald, Y. (2002). Report on the educational use of games. Teachers Evaluating Educational Multimedia. Cambridge.

McGrenere, J. L. (1996). Design of Educational Electronic Multi-player Games: A literature Review. Vancouver: Department of Computer Science.

McMullen, D. (1987). Drills vs. Games - Any Differences? A Pilot Study.: ERIC.

Mellemfolkeligt Samvirke. (2003). Global Island. Retrieved 18th February, 2005

Miller, C. (2000, 12012000). Designing for Kids: Infusions of Life, Kisses of Death. Gamasutra,.

Miller, C. (2002). Can Sesame Street bridge the Pacific Ocean? , Swarthmore College.

Miller, C., Lehman, J. F., & Koedinger, K. (1999). Goals and Learning in Microworlds. Cognitive Science, 23(3), 305-336.

Mitchell, A., & Savill-Smith, C. (2004). The use of computer and video games for learning: A review of the literature. London: Ultralab: Learning and Skills Development Agency.

Mortensen, P. O., & Svenstrup, C. (1998). Giv dem da bare en computer med hjem – Bro@ager - et udviklingsprojekt. København: Danmarks Lærerhøjskole.

Mouritsen, F. (2003). Childhood and Children's Culture: International Specialized Book Service Inc.

Multimedieforeningen. (2004). Spilundervisning. Retrieved 18th February, 2005

Murray, M., Mokros, J., & Rubin, A. (1998). Where's the Math in Computer Games? Hands On!, 21(2).

Newman, J. (2004). Videogames. Routledge Introductions to Media and Communications. London: Routledge.

Noble, A., Best, D., Sidwell, C., & Strang, J. (2000). Is an Arcade-style Computer game an Effective Medium for Providing Drug education to School children. Education for Health, 13(3), 404-406.

Okagaki, L., & French, P. (1996). Effects of Video Game playing on Measures of Spatial Performance: Gender Effects in Late Adolescence. In P. Greenfield & R. Cocking (Eds.), Interacting With Video. New Jersey: Ablex Publishing.

Okan, Z. (2003). Edutainment: is learning at risk? British Journal of Educational Technology, 34(3), 255-264.

Olive, J., & Lobato, J. (2001). The Learning of Rational Number Concepts Using Technology. In K. Heid, M. & G. W. Blume (Eds.), Research on Technology in the Learning and Teaching of Mathematics. Greenwich, CT: Information Age Publishing, Inc.

Oliver, M., & Pelletier, C. (2004). Activity theory and learning from digital games: implications for game design.Unpublished manuscript.

Pahl, R., H. (1991). Finally, a Good Way to Teach City Government! A Review of the Computer Simulation Game SimCity. Social-Studies, 82(4), 165-166.

Papert, S. (1980). Mindstorms: Children, Computers, and Powerful Ideas. New York: Basic Books.

Papert, S. (1996). The Connected Family: Bridging the Digital Generation Gap: Longstreet Press.

Pearce, C. (2003). Into the Labyrinth: Defining Games Research. Retrieved 2404, 2004

Pillay, H., Brownlee, J., & Wilss, L. (1999). Cognition and recreational computer games: Implications for educational technology. Journal of Research on Computer in Education, 32(1), 203-216.

Plotz, D. (2003). Iraq: The Computer Game: What "virtual world" games can teach the real world about reconstructing Iraq. Retrieved 9. august, 2004, from http://slate.msn.com/id/2084604

Prensky, M. (2001a). Digital Game-Based Learning. New York: McGraw-Hill.

Prensky, M. (2001b). What Kids Learn from Video Games: Five Learning Levels and their Implications for Public Policy. Paper presented at the Playing by the Rules, Cultural Policy Centre, University of Chicago.

Prensky, M. (2004). The Motivation of Gameplay. On the Horizon, 10(1).

Provenzo, E. F. (1992). What do video games teach? The Education Digest, 56-58.

Quinn, C. N. (1997). Engaging Learning. Paper presented at the Instructional Technology Forum.

Randel, J. M., Morris, B. A., Wetzel, C. D., & Whitehill, B. V. (1992). The Effectiveness of Games for Educational Purposes: A Review of Recent Research. Simulation & Gaming, 23(3), 261-276.

Remus, W. E. (1981). Experimental Design for Analyzing Data on Games - Or, Even the Best Statistical Methods Do Not Replace Good Experimental Control. Simulation & Games, 12(1), 3-14.

Rieber, L. P. (1996). Seriously considering play: Designing interactive learning environments based on the blending of microworlds, simulations, and games. Educational Technology Research & Development, 44(2), 43-58.

Roberts, N. (1976). Simulation Gaming: A Critical Review. Washington: US Department of Health & Welfare, National Institute of Education.

Robinett, W. (2004). Rocky boots. Retrieved 20th Jan. 2004, from http://www.warrenrobinett.com/rockysboots

Rollings, A., & Morris, D. (2000). Game Architecture and Design. Scottsdale: Coriolis.

Rosas, R. e. a. (2003). Beyond Nintendo: A design and assessment of educational video games for first and second grade students. Computers & Education, 40, 71-94.

Rousseau, J. J. (1993). Emile. London: J.M. Dent & Sons.

Ruben, B. D. (1999). Simulations, Games, and Experience-Based Learning: The Quest for a New Paradigm for Teaching and Learning. Simulation-and-Gaming, 30(4), 498-505.

Rubin, A., O'Neil, K., Murray, M., & Ashley, J. (1997). What Kind of Educational Computer Games Would Girls Like? Paper presented at the AERA.

Saegesser, F. (1981). Simulation-Gaming in the Classroom. Some Obstacles and Advantages. Simulation & Games, 12(3), 281-294.

Saegesser, F. (1984). The Introduction of Play in Schools: A Philosophical Analysis of the Problems. Simulation & Games, 15(1), 75-96.

Saettler, P. (1968). A history of instructional technology. New York: McGraw-Hill.

Salen, K., & Zimmerman, E. (2003). Rules of Play - Game Design Fundamentals. Cambridge: The MIT Press.

Schank, R. C. (1999). Dynamic Memory Revisited. Cambridge: Cambridge University Press.

Scott, D. (1999). The Effect of Video Games on the Mental Rotation Abilities of Men and Women.Unpublished manuscript.

Sedighian, K., & Sedighian, A. S. (1996). Can Educational Computer Games Help Educators Learn About the Psychology of Learning Mathematics in Children? Paper presented at the 18th Annual Meeting of the International Group for the Psychology of Mathematics Education, Florida.

Sedighian, K., & Sedighian, A. S. (1997). Aesthetic Response: Children's Reactions to Color and Graphics in Educational Software. Paper presented at the ED-MEDIA 97: World Conference on Educational Multimedia and Hypermedia, Calgary, Canada.

Seidner, C., J. (1975). Teaching with Simulations and Games. In R. E. Duke & C. J. Seidner (Eds.), Learning with simulations and games. London: Sage Publications.

Sluganski, R. (2001-2004). State of Adventure Gaming. Retrieved 18. October, 2004, from http://www.justadventure.com/Articles.shtm#SOAG

Social Impact games. (2004). Retrieved 28. January 2004., from http://www.socialimpactgames.com/modules.php?op=modload&name=News&file=index&catid=9&topic=&allstories=1

Softbase. (2004). SoftBase Top 100 Educational Games. Retrieved January 20, 2004., from http://softbase.150m.com/top73.html

Soloway, E., & Bielaczyc, K. (1995). Interactive Learning Environments: Where They've Come From & Where They're Going. Paper presented at the Chi '95.

Squire, K. (2003a). The Birth of Civilizations, from http://www.thinktv.org/education/ntti/ntti/lesson03/squire.html

Squire, K. (2003b). The Global Age: World History from 1450-1770., from http://www.thinktv.org/education/ntti/ntti/lesson03/squire.html

Squire, K. (2003c). Video games in education. International Journal of Intelligent Simulations and Gaming, 2(1).

Squire, K. (2004). Replaying history. Unpublished Dissertation submitted in part fulfilment of the requirements of the Doctor of Philosophy (Instructional technology). Indiana University., Indiana.

Stearns, P. N. (2000). Student Identities and World History Teaching. The History Teacher, 33(2), 185-191.

Stern, G. (1998, 24. April 1998). Life after Twitch: An Interview with Margo Nanny. Gamasutra.

Strein, W., & Kachman, W. (1984). Effects of computer games on young children's cooperative behavior: An exploratory study. Journal of Research and Development in Education, 19(1), 40-43.

Subrahmanyam, K., & Greenfield, P. (1996). Effect of Video Game Practice. In P. Greenfield & R. Cocking (Eds.), Interacting With Video. New Jersey: Ablex Publishing.

Sutton-Smith, B. (1997). The Ambiguity of Play. Cambridge: Harvard University Press.

Sutton-Smith, B., & Kelly-Byrne, D. (1984). The idealization of play. In P. K. Smith (Ed.), Play in Animals and Humans. Oxford: Basil Blackwell Inc.

Sørensen, B. H. (2000). Multimedieaktører - Børns multimedieproduktion i skolen. In B. H. Sørensen & S. Olesen (Eds.), Børn i en digital kultur - forskningsperspektiver. Copenhagen: Gads Forlag.

Sørensen, E. (1997). Kan man lære noget af fiktion? Unpublished Dissertation submitted in part fulfilment of the requirements of the MA (Psychology) Degree., Copenhagen University, Copenhagen.

Sørensen, E. (2001). Performing Spaces with 3D virtual Environments in an After-School Activity". Retrieved 19. October, 2004, from http://www.psy.ku.dk/estrid/INDHOLD/sorensen.pdf

Tapscott, D. (1998). Growing up digital. New York: McGraw-Hill.

Taylor, J. (2003). Home Interactive Entertainment Market Update 2002-2003.: Arcadia Investment Corp.

The ESA. (2003). Industry Sales and Economic Data: Consumer Spending Poll. Retrieved 20th Jan 2004, from http://www.theesa.com/industrysales.html

Thiagarajan, S. (1998). The Myths and Realities of Simulations in Performance Technology. Educational Technology, 38(5), 35-41.

Thomas, R., Cahill, J., & Santilli, L. (1997). Using an interactive computer game to increase skill and self-efficacy regarding safer sex negotiation: field test results,. Health Education & Behavior: the Official Publication of the Society for Public Health Education, 24(1), 71-86.

Turnin, M. C., Couvaras, O., Jouret, B., Tauber, M. T., Bolzonella, C., Fabre, D., et al. (2000). Learning good eating habits playing computer games at school: A 2000 children evaluation. Diabetes Research and Clinical Practice, 50(1001), 239-239.

Uddannelsesstyrelsen. (1999). Undervisningsvejledning for gymnasiet: Historie med samfundskundskab. Copenhagen: Undervisningsministeriet.

Van Sickle, R. (1986). A Quantitative Review of Research on Instructional Simulation Gaming: A Twenty-Year Perspective. Theory Research in Social Education, 14(3), 245-264.

Vandeventer, S. (1997). Expert Behaviour among outstanding Videogame-playing Children. Unpublished Dissertation submitted in part fulfilment of the requirements of the Doctor of Philosophy (Curriculum and Instruction). University of South Florida., Florida.

Veen, W. (1995). Factors affecting the use of computers in the classroom: four case studies. In D. Watson & D. Tinsley (Eds.), Integrating Information Technology into Education. London: Chapman & Hall.

Verbinski, G. (Writer) (2003). Pirates of the Caribbean: Behind the scene. In J. Bruckheimer (Producer). USA: Buena Vista Pictures.

Veta. (2004). VETA website. Retrieved 18. October, 2004, from http://www.veta.com/

Vogel, H. (2001). Playing the Game: The Economics of the Computer Game Industry. Retrieved 0703, 2004

Vygotsky, L. (1986). Thought and Language. Cambridge, Massachusetts: MIT Press.

Walker de Felix, J., & Johnson, R. T. (1993). Learning from video games. Computers in the Schools, 9(2-3), 199-133.

Walther, B. K. (2004, 23. march). Computerspil er dannelse. Politiken.

Wellington, W. J., & Faria, A. J. (1996). Team Cohesion, Player Attitude, and Performance Expectations in Simulations. Simulation & Gaming, 27(1), 23-40.

Wenger, E. (1999). Communities of Practice: Learning, Meaning, and Identity. Cambridge: Cambridge University Press.

Wentworth, D. R., & Lewis, D. R. (1973). A review of research on instructional games and simulations in social studies education. Social Education, 37, 432-440.

Wertsch, J., V. (1991). Voices of the mind: A sociocultural approach to mediated action. Cambridge, MA: Harvard University Press.

Wertsch, J., V. (1998). Mind as action. New York: Oxford University Press.

White, B. Y. (1984). Designing computer games to help physics students understand Newton's laws of motion. Cognition and Instruction, 1(1), 69-108.

Whitebread, D. (1997). Developing children's problem-solving: the educational uses of adventure games. In A. McFarlane (Ed.), Information technology and Authentic Learning. London: Routledge.

Wiebe, J. H., & Martin, N. J. (1994). The impact of a computer-based adventure game on achievement and attitudes in geography. Journal of Computing in Childhood Education, 5(1), 61-71.

Willis, J., Hovey, L., & Hovey, K. G. (1987). Computer simulations: A source book to learning in an electronic environment. New York: Garland Publishing, Inc.

Wolf, M. J. P. (2002). The Medium of the Video Game: University of Texas Press.

Wolfe, J., & Crookall, D. (1998). Developing a Scientific Knowledge of Simulation/Gaming. Simulation & Gaming, 29(1), 7-19.

Woods, S. (2002). Fair Game? Possibilities for the Design and Implementation of Face-to-Face Social System Simulation Games in a Computer-Mediated Environment. Unpublished Submitted in part fulfilment of the requirements of the Bachelor (Design). Curtin University of Technology.

Woods, S. (2004). Loading the Dice: The Challenge of Serious Videogames. Game Studies, 4(1).

Aarseth, E. (1997). Cybertext: Perspectives on ergodic literature. London: Johns Hopkins University Press.

Aarseth, E., Sunnanå, L., & Smedstad, S. M. (2003). A multi-dimensional typology of games. Paper presented at the Level Up - Digital Games Research Conference, Utrecht.

Lightning Source UK Ltd.
Milton Keynes UK
UKOW07f1116280416

273144UK00004B/25/P